WANDERING WORDS

Frontispiece.

FROM THE LAND OF THE RISING SUN.

WANDERING WORDS

BY

SIR EDWIN ARNOLD

WITH

*ILLUSTRATIONS FROM DRAWINGS BY BEN BOOTHBY
AND FROM PHOTOGRAPHS*

Essay Index Reprint Series

BOOKS FOR LIBRARIES PRESS
FREEPORT, NEW YORK

First Published 1894
Reprinted 1972

Library of Congress Cataloging in Publication Data

Arnold, Sir Edwin, 1832-1904.
    Wandering words.

    (Essay index reprint series)
    Reprint of the 1894 ed.
    CONTENTS: An earthly paradise.--Watching the stars.
--An adventure on the Nile. [etc.]
    1. Voyages and travels. I. Title.
G469.A75 1972   910.4   75-39660
ISBN 0-8369-2739-7

PRINTED IN THE UNITED STATES OF AMERICA
BY
NEW WORLD BOOK MANUFACTURING CO., INC.
HALLANDALE, FLORIDA 33009

TO

MY COLLEAGUE FOR SO MANY YEARS

AND

EVER KIND FRIEND

J. M. LE SAGE, Esq.

I DEDICATE

THESE

"𝕸𝖆𝖓𝖉𝖊𝖗𝖎𝖓𝖌 𝖂𝖔𝖗𝖉𝖘"

CONTENTS

LIST OF ILLUSTRATIONS

FULL-PAGE ILLUSTRATIONS

LIST OF ILLUSTRATIONS

ILLUSTRATIONS IN TEXT

HONOLULU.

P. I.

BEN BOOTHBY.

WANDERING WORDS

I

AN EARTHLY PARADISE

KANAKA GIRL.

IT is good to be able to date a letter from Paradise! Would you like to know the exact locality? You must sail south of west for 2100 miles from San Francisco, or south of east 3440 miles from Yokohama, and then you will arrive at the beautiful Hawaiian Islands, where we are anchored at present in the steamship *Belgic*, of the Occidental and Oriental Line, Captain W. H. Walker commanding, bound by way of Honolulu to Yokohama. We are come down to this archipelago out of the usual direct course to Japan, having 600 Chinese coolies to deliver, as labourers, upon the sugar plan-

A

tations of Oahu and Hawaii. They were taken on to
San Francisco last month by the steamship *Rio de
Janeiro*, because small-pox had broken out among
them before arriving here, and now, having been
duly purged in an American quarantine, the unlucky Celestials must be brought all the way back
again, and we shall disembark them to-night and
to-morrow. It was an unpleasant cargo to carry—
these much-wandering Mongolians—since at any
moment the disease might again declare itself
amidst them, in which case we should have been
obliged to take the 600 on to Yokohama, perhaps to
Hong-Kong. But the *Belgic* has kept a clean bill of
health from the moment of starting, and we and they
are to-day safely arrived under the green and golden
hills of Oahu, the northernmost of the Sandwich
group. Even from the sea the view is charming and
full of promise of these delightful islands ; none the
less so if, as in my own case, the voyager has recently
traversed by rail 3800 miles of mainly unlovely scenery
between New York and San Francisco, coming by
those dreary, drab wildernesses of Texas, Arizona,
and New Mexico, and has then steamed for a week
without anything to look at except rolling seas
and driving clouds. Of course, therefore, we have
passed every available hour of our detention here
ashore, and seen enough to wonder why people
dwell in the changeful latitudes of London and
New York, when they might breathe the heavenly
air of these ocean paradises, and live in the perpetual Garden of Eden which Nature has laid out

for her happiest children in these hollows and uplands.

There is always a curious difference between one's previous idea of any place and the visual realisation of it. I myself had imagined the Hawaiian cluster to be composed of densely-wooded islets and isles, with dark foliage spread all over the plains and climbing to rounded hills. But I see a broken land much more open and varied than in my anticipation ; the lowlands rather bare of trees and vegetation, the uplands ascending by slopes tinted with the tender green of coming crops, to a volcanic Sierra, very rugged, naked, and majestic in outline, seamed and fissured with innumerable glens, each nursing a gradually diminishing riband of verdant embroidery. At one extremity of the long crescent in which Honolulu nestles amid her groves of cocoa-nut palms and bananas, rises precipitously the yellow and red steep of Diamond Head, and on the other soars away into far distance a lofty line of peaks, lifted from the bottom of the sea by some ancient and stupendous telluric spasm. The golden Sierra fades afar into a ridge of rose and violet against the horizon, where the sapphire of the Pacific blends with the turquoise of the sky. The north-east trade-wind, which was blowing in a lively way outside, is quite shut off from our anchorage by those lofty mountains, rising to 4000 feet of elevation and upwards, so that the good ship *Belgic* rides quietly outside the reef to a single cable. The channel is narrow by which the quiet inner harbour is reached, and we did not enter; but there is plenty of water there, as is evidenced by the U.S.S. *Charleston*, an ironclad of the second class, which is moored within, under the very plumes of the cocoanut groves. Where the coral reef girdles the island beach there occurs a sudden and sharply-marked change from the indigo-coloured waves of the outer deep sea, ruffled with sparkling wavelets, to the sleeping water of the lagoon, motionless, and reflecting the trees and houses in its narrow, unbroken belt of vivid grass-green. The rampart of coral which thus surrounds this side of Oahu lies about six feet under the surface, yet at that depth it amply suffices to break the roll of the ocean ; and even the sharks—of which many are cruising about—seldom or never cross the barrier. Exposed to air, the coral hardens into a good building rock, of which many of the Honolulu edifices are constructed ; but under water it is soft, and can be broken up easily, so that we observe a steam-dredger busy upon the entrance-channel, deepening it by simply scraping, in order to admit vessels of every burden.

Honolulu from the sea looks a smaller town than she really is, being so much buried in groves and gardens ; nor indeed at biggest does she number more than 22,000 citizens, the entire island containing no more than 31,194 inhabitants, and the whole group about 89,000. Of these about 35,000 are natives, 15,000 Chinese, 13,000 Japanese, and 8600

Portuguese; the American residents totalling 1928, and the English 1344. There are, besides, over 1000 Germans scattered about the group, and 600 other foreigners, more or less, including seventy Frenchmen—a mixed population, amid which the indigenous Kanaka race, that well deserved to be perpetuated, is, alas! sadly and steadily decreasing.

That this Paradise of the Pacific is not without its drawback, the voyager will be grievously reminded as he approaches Diamond Head, and comes round into the anchorage of Honolulu. Broad on the port side of the ship, about thirty miles from the little city, Molokai rises fair and fertile from the ocean— the Island of Lepers. Here, as all know too well, banished from the beautiful isles to the west and south, are imprisoned for the term of their natural lives more than a thousand victims of leprosy, that curse of the Hawaiian archipelago; and here Father Damien's example of fearless humanity and divine compassion is being followed by more than one devoted priest and woman. Molokai itself is beautiful enough to be a fitting "Purgatorio" to the "Paradiso" beyond.

You round Diamond Head, as I have said, and, in the bright Pacific morning, with the fresh strong breath of the trade-wind bringing you health and appetite, drop anchor before the town. Then a wild passion will seize you to land; and if this has become so strong after only a week's run across from 'Frisco, how imperious it must have been with those ships' companies of Captain James Cook, of immortal memory, when the *Endeavour* and *Resolu-tion* first touched at the Sandwich Islands, and gave this enchanting scenery to their own eyes and to the knowledge of the world? For us there are questions of quarantine and of bills of health, which—being at last happily settled—leave passengers free to land. We jump into a native boat, rowed by two lusty Hawaiians, and pull quickly to the shore, passing through the channel of the coral reef, and noting how the water instantly shifts within it from dark blue to light green. The U.S. ships of war *San Francisco* and *Pensacola* are lying inside, together with several large Californian merchantmen, and one or two of the schooners which ply regularly between the islands.

The waterside wharves are without pretension; and the little town in its business portion looks commonplace and untropical. It disappoints, indeed, at first, for the shops and offices are just like those of a third-rate American city, with the usual tram-cars running along the streets, and the inevitable telegraph poles bordering the side-walks. But the islanders at once attract your attention; the men, well-built, brown as coffee-berries, many walking or riding with " leïs " (flower garlands) wreathed round their straw hats, the women with nice oval faces, very often pretty, always intelligent, animated, and gentle, dressed in that long, loose, coloured night-gown, without a waist, which the early missionaries invented for their too lightly-clad converts. Those excellent men were but poor *modistes*, and it is to be regretted they did not hit upon something more becoming. Yet the Kanaka damsels and matrons manage to wear such absurd garments with all the grace of which the attire is capable; and it is a pretty sight to see one of them, in this clothes-bag of a disguise, leap lightly into the saddle, astride, neatly jerking the lower part of her garb between her knees, as she settles into her seat, thus making the loose sac cover her lower limbs to the ankle with perfect fitness and decorum. The king has lately died, and many of these robes are, therefore, still black; but the Kanakas love bright colours, and you will encounter girls dressed like humming-birds or tiger-moths as regards gay tints. We call at the office of a gentleman well known and respected in the islands—a great sugar-planter, employing more than 5000 hands—and in an instant, upon his cordial greeting, the gates of the place seem all to fly open. Mr. W. G. Irwin, our very kind and genial host, puts lips to the telephone—which is an universal institution here, used in every abode,—and begins by calling forth, from his high duties of state, the Prime Minister, the Hon. Samuel Parker, as if it were the most natural thing in the world, in these graceful and lazy latitudes, that a Cabinet should suspend its sittings to make good cheer for passing unknown friends and visitors. His Excellency soon turns up, a handsome native gentleman of good stature, a dark, highly intelligent countenance, and soft brown eyes, directly descended—as his manly carriage might betoken—from the chieftains

of the island whom Captain Cook met 114 years
ago. He plunges genially into the task of making
a festive and instructive programme for us, which is
even to include the honour of presentation to her
Majesty Queen Liliuokalani. Afterwards, drives,
excursions into the country, a dinner with "poï"
and other native dishes, and in the evening the
"Hula" dance, and indigenous songs and music. It
seems a positive delight to the Hawaiians, high and
low, to welcome their guests and to do the honours
of their lovely archipelago.

Our first visit is to the abode of "The Hon. Sam,"
as everybody seems to style the Premier. You soon
get clear of the commonplace little business streets
and horrible tram-cars, and emerge into the Honolulu
of your dreams ; Honolulu proper, with charming,
low-fronted houses, fringing long embowered lanes,
dark and cool with overhanging foliage and gay with
countless blossoms. There is no winter, of course,
in these happy isles, and thus, albeit we are arrived
here in the early part of March, the groves are all
green and the garden-fences everywhere brilliant
with red hibiscus, the splendid lilac loveliness of
the Bougainvilliers, pomegranate, orange, and ohia
blossoms.

Fragrances, combined of heliotrope, the Indian
champak, and many another sweet-scented flower,
fill the soft air. The ample shaded gardens are
stately with all sorts of tropical and sub-tropical
trees, including palms of many varieties, the cocoa-

nut being most predominant. I observe the koa,
a kind of acacia, the iron-tree, the hala—known in
India as the keora, having the sweetest of all
perfumes—umbrella-trees, bread-fruit trees, guavas,
bananas, papaws, and a hundred others familiar to
memory, together with many which are new. I
noticed everywhere an old bird friend, the Indian
myna, hopping about the roads—the lively creature,
it seems, has been imported; and I meet at once
the sagacious sparrow, that true cosmopolitan, who
has taken up his abode in these fair islands. The
apartment where Mrs. Parker receives us is, like
those of all good houses here, spacious, and open
by venetian blinds and verandahs to any soft airs
wandering around. This Hawaiian lady—the first
whose acquaintance we are privileged to make—
wears mourning for the late king, and is easy and
charming in her manners, with an unaffected
cordiality and goodwill which seem, we find afterwards, to be universal. She honours me by preparing and presenting a lovely bouquet of flowers
from the garden, in which the yellow roses are of
special splendour and perfection.

Next we drive, with excellent American horses,
along the line of the sea-beach, and through a public
park, prettily laid out, to Mr. Irwin's rural residence
at Waikiki, where again you behold the Honolulu
of your dreams. On the way rice-fields—with the
young plants in their tenderest green tint—alter-
nate with copses of ironwood trees, acacias, and
palms, and great breadths of banana-plantation, while

always, on your right hand, thunders softly the
far-off surf, shut from the beach by that girdle of
gleaming emerald, the still water inside the coral
reef. Every house along the beautiful highway running round to Diamond Head has this glorious sea-
frontage of the golden sand, the green lagoon, the
coral barrier, and the gleaming open ocean ; and for
bathing, fishing, and boating delights, nothing anywhere could surpass it. We see the canoes of the
natives come shooting in, like sea-arrows, from the
main, on the white neck of a breaker ; the paddles
flashing, the men—wild with the pleasure of their
strength and skill—singing at the top of their well-
modulated voices, and no more fearful of the milky
roll of a vast Pacific breaker than if it were one of
their own little white ponies. They are all accomplished swimmers, and do not seem at all afraid of
the sharks, even if capsized outside the coral barrier.
It is as good and manly a sight as I have ever seen
upon the water, to watch these brown Kanakas drive
their frail craft into the mid-fury of the big wave,
and then come shorewards leaping with it, high in
the air, amidst a storm of spray and broken blue
water, safe and peaceful into the sleeping green
sanctuary of the lagoon.

At 4.30 P.M. we were to have audience of
Queen Liliuokalani. Her Majesty succeeded to the
Hawaiian throne rather more than a year ago, on
the death of her royal brother, King Kalakaua ;
but in the first happiness of her reign had the
misfortune to lose her consort, His Royal Highness

John Owen Dominis. This deceased Prince was
of foreign extraction, and, leaving no issue, the present Heir-Apparent to the throne is the Princess
Victoria-Kawekia-Kailani-Lunalilo-Kalaninui-Ahi-
lapalapa, daughter of Princess Liki-liki and of his
Excellency A. S. Cleghorn. I know it all reads
like the libretto of a fairy-play, where lovely Queens
and Princesses marry Jack and Tom, who land from
the other side of the globe in full possession of the
magic ring; and I should not have felt greatly
surprised if we had been met in the Queen's garden
by the customary *corps de ballet*, dressed in feathers
and flowers, with somebody as Captain Cook to
dance a hornpipe. But it is all real, serious, and
solid enough, with a very natural, gracious, and
noble Queen in Liliuokalani, and a Court, modest
but respected, which combines much dignity with
unaffected simplicity. I was a little laughed at by
my American companions for feeling somewhat shy
of entering the presence of her Majesty in my pea-
jacket and shipboard attire. But deshabille is the
custom of the islands, and the " Hon. Sam," First
Minister of the Crown, was himself wearing a
shooting-jacket and straw hat; while the father of
the Heir-Apparent, also accompanying us, shone
resplendent in a red tie and white waistcoat. In
fact, the audience was rather by way of a friendly and
informal afternoon call, such as the kindly, simple
fashions of the island permit, than of any ceremony;
although it must not be understood that the Hawaiian
Court does not at times observe the most elaborate

ceremonials, and maintain a very strict etiquette indeed.

As for her Majesty, she is "every inch a queen," and bears with noble grace and lofty gentleness the lonely honours of her rank. When we passed from the anteroom of her palace, guarded by a Hawaiian soldier in white uniform, and filled with objects of ancient island royalty and portraits of island potentates departed, we found in a pretty inner apartment, seated, and attended upon by two ladies-in-waiting, the good, intelligent, sweet-faced, and kind-hearted Liliuokalani. The Queen rose, with all the simplicity of a lady welcoming friends, to receive us, and shook hands cordially with each of our party, as each was presented, addressing also a word or two of greeting to him. Dressed in complete mourning, she wore a black robe of silk crape, banded loosely below the bosom after the native fashion, and she carried a black lace-edged handkerchief, but displayed no ornaments, except a magnificent diamond ring. Her countenance— distinctly handsome, and of the most decided Kanaka type—has the colour of coffee, and is sur-mounted by thick black hair, growing luxuriantly, touched here and there with silvery flecks. At first sight the Queen wins anybody's heart, and commands his true respect and loyalty. Her voice has the soft musical intonation heard in the speech of all her countrywomen, and I have seldom listened to English more perfect or more graceful than that spoken by her Majesty. She did me the honour to place me in a chair at her side and to enter upon an animated conversation. A blue lotus-blossom expanded in a silver cup upon the table gave occasion for us to talk of the flowers, trees, and fruits of the archipelago, and of ancient flower-fashions there. This led to mention of the first discovery of the group, only 114 years ago, and the Queen became singularly interested when I ventured to tell her how, when a boy, I had ofttimes seen, lying moored as a coal-hulk, amongst the other coal-hulks in the River Thames, the good and famous ship *Endeavour*, which, with her sister vessel the *Resolution*, made such wonderful discoveries under the command of that noble navigator, Captain James Cook, and was the first to cast anchor at the Hawaiian group. Afterwards her Majesty was pleased to describe to us her visit to England at the time of Queen Victoria's Jubilee, renewing the splendid memories of which her heart and mind were full. She recounted to me, with charming enthusiasm, how she sat near our Queen in Westminster Abbey, and what the Queen said to her, and how kind and great-hearted the English Sovereign was, and about the German Crown Prince, how soldierly and grand he looked, and our late departed Prince, the Duke of Clarence, how courteous and amiable he showed himself to her. It was delightful to recline in the milk-warm air, with the broad fans of the bananas waving at the window, and thus listen to the low, pleasant tones of this dark Island Queen, so gentle in her

bereavement, so stately and truly royal in her
womanly simplicity. I should judge her to be
about fifty years of age, but her rich black hair is
only just streaked with grey, and her deep soft
brown eyes are as bright and limpid as those of
any Kanaka maiden. I shall always preserve the
flowers which she gave me, and the memory of her
gracious and kindly "Aloha" at parting.

From the Queen's house we went to the Iolani
Palace, a large and well-looking, if not exactly an
imposing structure, where we saw the royal apartment of state, especially the throne-room. This
last is a spacious and handsome chamber, having
around it portraits of all the Kings and Queens of
Hawaii, from old Kamehameha the First, in his cloak
of red and yellow "oo" feathers, who reigned from
1782 to 1819, down to that of the gracious lady whose
presence we had just quitted. Between the royal
portraits were suspended under glass the various decorations received by the late King Kalakaua, among
which I noticed the "Chrysanthemum" of Japan.
On either side of the throne—a large arm-chair,
upholstered in crimson and gold—stood the Hawaiian emblems of sovereignty, tall staves sur-
mounted with tufts of "oo" feathers, and gilt; from
which the "Honourable Sam" politely detached and
presented to us "leïs" or scented garlands, made of
some dried flower-seed. By this time the dinner-
hour had arrived, and we sat down with quite a
large party, comprising more than one Minister of
State and several of the most prominent gentlemen

of Honolulu. There were two things on the *menu* which merit attention—the golden plovers, a most delicate and toothsome island-bird, and the chief native staple of the islands, " poï "—which I tasted for the first time. Made of the starchy extract of the " taro," it is a sort of sour gruel, served in large wooden bowls, without salt or seasoning. It is etiquette to eat it with the forefinger, which is dipped into the sticky mass, and emerges charged with a long festoon of " poï." By a quick motion, easily learned, you twist this round the finger-point and suck it off, dipping the wet digit again and again in the bowl. There is no real indelicacy in this habit, because the viscid stuff sticks to what touches it, and thus you cannot come in contact with any of your neighbour's portion, beyond the "dollop" on your own finger-end. All through dinner-time and afterwards we had a choir of native "boys" singing to us native songs, with accompaniments on the "tarapatch," a kind of small guitar. Some of the songs were very sweet and tender, particularly one which we made them repeat again and again, beginning, "Ninni-mai, apeelee" —which, being interpreted, is "Come to me close, close until you touch me." The Kanakas also sang us the music of the "Hoola" dance, and performed some of its figures, which were of a decidedly Polynesian character, and not quite such as could be taught in a polite dancing academy of New York or London. The musicians finally came off to the ship with us in our steam-launch, and continued their native chants of love and farewell until the anchor was weighed, when they departed with the "Honourable Sam" and all our other kind and warm-hearted friends for the shore, singing "Aloha loë" as long as we could hear, and taking with them our grateful thoughts.

March 8th, 1892.

II

WATCHING THE STARS

INTERIOR OF THE LICK OBSERVATORY.   *P.* 19.

THE LICK OBSERVATORY.

II

WATCHING THE STARS

THERE was no national institution in all the United
States which I more desired to visit than the famous
Observatory on the top of Mount Hamilton, in California. The great Republic abounds with noble
monuments of the public spirit and generosity of
her citizens. In almost every town and city of the
sixty or seventy where I have lately delivered my
poetical readings, I saw with admiration schools,
colleges, libraries, hospitals, lecture-halls, music-
halls, lyceums, gardens, parks and picture galleries,

given to the people by rich men who had made their money among them. No country in the world shows such examples of civic generosity, and the foreigner —if an Englishman in America ought ever to bear that name—grows positively dazzled with the splendid succession of those bountiful endowments.

But the Lick Observatory appeals in a special manner to his imagination. He thinks of it as a gift to the world at large—a magnificent dowry bestowed on the science of astronomy under circumstances of advantage hardly to be equalled elsewhere. The more he knows, no doubt, of that science, the less exaggerated expectations he will have of what "the biggest glass in the world" can accomplish compared with smaller instruments. But all the same he will want ardently to see it, to look through it at certain special objects in the heavens, to hear the official astronomers talk who have the great "optick" in their charge, as well as by a personal pilgrimage to do homage to the memory of the California miner, James Lick, who has his tomb on that sky-piercing height under the huge telescope which his well-spent wealth planted on the Pacific Hill. Accordingly, on arriving in San Francisco, at the close of my engagements I put aside more than one delightful social attraction, in order to secure ample time for the visit which I had promised myself to this most remarkable and interesting spot.

Modern astronomy owes, it must be confessed, a heavy debt to the vanity—or may we say the self-respect?—of man. The general mind, perhaps, hardly realises, even at this day, what a tremendous blow was dealt at human self-conceit and against all the Ptolemaic religions founded to suit it, by the discoveries of Copernicus and Galileo. Well might the priests of the old orthodoxies stand aghast at the latter, and even go so dreadfully far as to burn the gentle and wise Giordano Bruno! At a stroke the Florentine astronomer's ejaculation "E pur se muove!" swept away all the theology of Dante and his sacerdotal doctors, made the cosmology of the "Divine Comedy" impossible and grotesque, and dethroned the race and this planet which it inhabits from its imagined pre-eminence to an obscure and insignificant position.

Old-fashioned Christianity had taught that our world was the centre of things round which the sun revolved; for the sake of which the stars were hung up like Japanese lanterns in the firmament; and in direct relations to which all the forces of infinite space were established. The " scheme of salvation," as then understood, fitted in well enough with such an egotistic view, as also the austere Dante's basin-shaped Hell and conical Purgatory with the concentric circles of Paradise upon its top. But as soon as Copernicus and Galileo exploded the theory, and proved that we are almost the "last of the least," dwelling on one of the smallest bodies in space, invisible to all but a small number of our closer neighbours, religions had to suppress such men, or else, as will hereafter need to be done, to expand their own doctrines and contract their own previous preten-

sions. At present they have only partially performed all this. The boldest and truest, even, have
not yet come into step with " star-eyed Science."
Those ancient, mediæval, and so-called orthodox
absurdities of a local "hell" and "heaven," with
the fables of Joshua's miracle and of Hezekiah's
reprieve, linger still, like our popular expressions
of " sunrise " and " sunset " and the belief in the
Mosaic cosmogony. Christianity itself has not yet
sufficiently assimilated Copernican and Darwinian
doctrines. When it does, it will earnestly thank
Science for showing how much more glorious it is
to be " least in the kingdom of heaven " than greatest
in that petty sub-kingdom of nature which the priests
constructed ; and of how much nobler promise we
should consider it to be descendants of a mollusc
and afterward of an ape, with all the heights of
creation to ascend to, than creatures suddenly made
out of clay to occupy a garden. But astronomy,
which has so rudely thrust man down from the
pinnacle of his bygone ignorant arrogance, certainly
owes him the reparation of such a scientific solace,
and will, year by year, bring him more and more
of this by perpetually extending his knowledge
of the vastness and splendour and wonder of the
visible universe, of which to be a portion, even
the most humble, is to be incomparably higher and
grander than to be feebly and fixedly alone in that
old absurd cosmogony, and to have the stars for
candles.

Astronomy, I indeed think, is the chief present

hope of humanity, the best teacher of real and practical religion, which will redeem men from the folly of materialism by showing matter as infinite and as spiritual as spirit itself. To effect her high and destined work she needs, first, good equipments, like those on Mount Hamilton, for the prosecution of research; and, next, interpreters of insight and genius to convey with simplicity, but without scientific degradation, to the popular understanding, the immense and elevating generalisations, the stupendous conclusions of the professional star-gazers, who can seldom themselves do full literary justice to the terrestrial and human purport of the mighty facts which their skill elicits and establishes.

With these ideas in mind I was very glad to find at last an opportunity of visiting the Lick Observatory. To reach it, you take train from San Francisco, and travel fifty miles almost due south of the City of the Golden Gate, as far as to the depot of San José. From this pretty half Spanish town Mount Hamilton lies distant, " as the crow flies," not farther than thirteen miles ; but to reach Observatory Peak, where the colossal telescope is erected, and where the founder of the institution sleeps, implies a journey by coach over twenty-six miles of winding road, so steep is the range and so hard of access. The actual elevation of the summit on which the buildings stand is 4029 feet. It is one of the main eminences of that inner coast Sierra, called Monte Diablo, lying between the bays of San Francisco and of Monterey, and rising due eastward of San José.

Just as I was wondering which would be the best method of proceeding, a bright-eyed boy, some fifteen years of age, with a delightful manner of address and intelligence sparkling in his brown eyes, addressed me by name, having somehow satisfied himself as to my identity; and then announcing himself as the son of Professor Holden, Director of the Observatory, informed me that he was commissioned to take me in charge and to deliver me safely on the mountain, where his father had invited me to pass the night as his guest. A better guide it would have been impossible to have found. Glad of his sudden holiday from the San José school, and full to the brim with information about the mountain, my new friend did not allow a single moment of the journey to be dull or without profit.

A pair of sturdy California horses were soon harnessed to an open carriage, and off we went together through the great aloes and forest-trees of the city, and along the straight and well-kept road which leads to the foothills, passing farmhouses and well-kept fields, vineyards and orchards, in a country of splendid fertility. We talked natural history, sport and travel. He told me how he had trapped forty-two foxes last year upon the hills and two coyotes: he had killed, among many others, a rattlesnake with twelve rings in its tail; made me for the first time familiar with the California robin, the "wood runner," the black buzzard, the painted jay, and the ground squirrels, of which there were hundreds to be seen, and showed me the nest of a golden eagle in the fork of a tall fir-tree, from which he had taken two eggs, so that by the time we had reached Smith's Creek, within eight miles of the top, we had become fast friends.

Up to this point, where we shared some lunch, the winding road had absorbed and entranced me by its beauty. Like a snake it coils in and out of lovely thickets and coppices of golden oak, pine and wild bay trees dressed and festooned with the Spanish moss. At every turn we gained fresh views of the green valleys, shut within the folds of the range—" canyons," as they are here called—some of them full of grazing herds, others devoted to vineyards, grain, crops, and orchards of peach and almond just breaking into tender rosy blossom. At Smith's Creek there occurs a flat, with houses and an inn; and a bridge here also crosses the " canyon," which brings you into the wilder and more stony regions of the upper heights, above which you see the iron dome of the Observatory now plainly towering. There are still, nevertheless, seven or eight miles of steep winding road to traverse, along the edge of a perpetual precipice; but the driver was skilful, the horses inured to the dangerous journey, and the road all the way most excellently made. Moreover, a message through the telephone, which runs all the way to the Observatory, had hospitably cheered us.

"I have got Sir Edwin!" my young friend blew triumphantly through the mouthpiece at Smith's Creek.

"Bring him along!" was the satisfactory reply, and with a fresh pair of horses we started again.

I noticed that a common English garden bloom, the escholtzia, grew everywhere as a weed on the rocks —people say that the Golden Gate gets its name from the Californian coast being bedecked with this bright flower when the first discoverers entered there. On these higher levels grow also freely the manzanita and the madrone, from the tough brown stems of which drinking cups and walking sticks are turned.

Plainer and plainer now looms the big dome on the upward gaze; more sterile the crags become and more "qualmy" the precipices as we wind higher and higher. We pass "Jack's Slide," an awful slope, where a Mexican teamster rolled over the edge with his waggon and mules, and brought up, alive but sorely bruised, five hundred feet below, between two big pine trees. We meet the "stage" coming down with four horses, for Saturday is the public day, when the sovereign people have the right to ascend in any numbers they please and gaze through the gigantic glass. It is early in the season, however, and there are few or no visitors to-day at the summit. We shall have the heavens to ourselves, and all the wonders of the proud temple of science this happy evening, which is as clear as purple crystal in the east, and in the west just beginning to prepare for the splendour of a gorgeous sunset.

Safely landed on the top, under the vast cupola

of the telescope, I am most cordially greeted by
Professor Holden, and know in a moment that I
shall like him as well as I already like his delightful boy. Truly the site of the Lick Observatory has
been well chosen! It occupies the loftiest point of
a long serrated chain, the various peaks of which
have been appropriately named after the most renowned ancient and modern astronomers. Near at
hand, for example, are " Kepler," " Copernicus,"
" Tycho Brahe," "Newton," " Huygens," "Herschel,"
and even " Ptolemy." The view all around is, of
course, magnificently extended. To the eastward
you look over a wilderness of rolling hills and em-
bosomed valleys to where, one hundred miles away,
the snow-capped line of the Sierra shuts the vast
prospect in. Nearer to the eye, on the westward,
spreads the immense Pacific main, but its shore-
waters are veiled from the gaze by a row of foothills,
which serve, nevertheless, an admirable purpose for
the astronomers, since they intercept and catch the
sea mists, and keep them from obscuring the upper
sky. Even now, near to evening, a white shroud of
clouds spreads all over the San José valley, completely
closing out the spacious city and all the works of
men there below.

To a great extent that twinkling of the stars
which troubles the observer, and which is caused by
the refraction of rarified lower air, has been avoided
at Mount Hamilton by the happy selection which
has interposed all this wide valley of San José between the ocean and the Observatory. Towards the

south and south-west your gaze travels over green
canyons and grey rocky peaks, to the broad lowlands of Salinas, San Benito, and Monterey, and the
lofty range of Pavilan. Lassen Peak, one hundred
miles south of Mount Shasta, may sometimes be
distinguished in the far north, but the giant mount
itself is four hundred miles distant, and of course
invisible at all times.

Turning reluctantly from that majestic landscape,
one notes next the fine group of buildings erected
on the solitary summit. The vast iron dome, within
which the great equatorial telescope works, is the
first thing to fasten attention. The lower part of
this structure is of red bricks, and a considerable
economy was effected herein by the discovery close
at hand of a bed of clay, from which the bricks
for the Observatory and adjacent buildings were
all made. This saved the institution no less than
$46,000, which would have been otherwise expended
in purchasing the bricks below and hauling them up
the steep twenty-seven miles of mountain roadway.
That road itself—splendidly engineered, as has been
said—was cut and finished by the Government of the
State at a cost of $10,000, and links the isolated
shrine of science with the busy world below by a
long white wandering ribbon, which you see appearing and disappearing for many and many a league
under your feet.

A range of official buildings connects the great
Observatory with a lesser dome, containing a powerful but much smaller telescope than the equatorial;

while near at hand rise the very commodious re-
sidences of the director and his staff of assisting
professors. Grouped around are the offices of the
establishment, the cottages for the working-men,
and the rooms for the photographing, carpentering,
engineering, and all the various service of the mighty
glass, while at a distance, under " Kepler," you observe the water-tanks where the rainfall is stored,
and on the crest of that same peak a supplementary
observatory. Water is naturally precious here, since
sometimes long spells of dry weather occur, and a
notice over every tap in Professor Holden's house
bids the guest not to waste the element.

Would it be imagined that one of the principal
nuisances of the place is the rattlesnake ? For my
own part, I had no idea that that noxious reptile could
live at an elevation of over four thousand feet upon
mountain crags so arid ; but in the week before my
visit they had killed three of these serpents within
the great dome itself, and the director told me,
sweeping his hand around a neighbouring canyon,
" There are probably at this moment hundreds of
rattlesnakes in that one hollow." They live upon
squirrels, which abound everywhere, or small birds
and their eggs, and come up to the tanks and
Observatory buildings chiefly in quest of water. It
was by the edge of a water-trough on the roadside
that my young friend Edward Holden had killed
three of the dangerous creatures.

I was told upon this topic something very curious
about the " road runner," the bird already men-

tioned, which is also called the "chapparal cock." The rattlesnake is the deadly enemy of its species, always hunting about in the thickets for eggs and young birds, since the "road runner" builds its nest on the ground. When, therefore, the "chapparal cocks" find a "rattler" basking in the sun, they gather, I was assured, leaves of the prickly cactus and lay them in a circle all round the serpent, which cannot draw its belly over the sharp needles of these leaves. Thus imprisoned, the reptile is set upon by the birds and pecked or spurred to death.

But now we enter the great dome and stand under its cover beside the gigantic telescope given to America and to Science by James Lick, the Californian miner. The third clause of James Lick's second deed of trust (September 21, 1875), authorised the Board of Lick Trustees "to expend the sum of seven hundred thousand dollars ($700,000) for the purpose of purchasing land and constructing and putting up on such land as may be designated by the party of the first part a powerful telescope, superior to and more powerful than any telescope yet made."

Among the documents "engrossed on parchment, placed between two fine tanned skins backed with silk, shut again between two leaden plates, soldered securely in a tin box, and finally deposited within the coffin itself" of James Lick, which was laid in the foundation pier of the great equatorial telescope on the 9th day of January 1887, is one recording that "this refracting telescope is the largest which has ever been constructed, and the astronomers who have tested it declare that its performance surpasses all other telescopes." The diameter of the great glass is 36 inches and its focal length 56 feet 2 inches, the weight of it amounting to several tons. Yet, as soon as Professor Campbell, the very accomplished lieutenant of Mr. Holden, has released the machinery, I am able with one hand to move the enormous weapon of science in either direction, revolving the whole structure of the cupola, and directing its broad slit— through which the huge object-glass looks forth like a Cyclopean eye—toward any quarter of the heavens. An extremely ingenious arrangement of wheels working upon oil chambers furnishes this indispensable mobility, and the spacious floor itself of the dome, circular in shape, can be also raised or lowered by turning a little hand-wheel. Against the eye-piece of the monstrous instrument is established a staircase, upon which you mount to a sliding seat, so as to be able always to keep a just position ; and, for fine movements of latitude and longitude, small wheels, conveniently placed for the observer's control, permit him to sway the huge "optick" up or down, this side or that side, with the utmost ease and accuracy. The ironwork of this great cupola was furnished by Mr. Scott's firm at San Francisco —now engaged in constructing ironclad men-of-war for the United States Government—and appears to be of an excellent craft.

With my hand upon the colossal tube, lightly managing it, as if it were an opera-glass, and my gaze wandering round the splendidly equipped interior, full of all needful astronomical resources and built to stand a thousand storms, I think with admiration of its dead founder, and ask to see his tomb. It is placed immediately beneath the big telescope, which ascends and descends directly over the sarcophagus wherein repose the mortal relics of this remarkable man; a marble chest, bearing for inscription, "Here lies the body of James Lick."

From what I gather, he amassed his fortune chiefly by lucky mining speculations, and was led to dedicate a large portion of it to this noble purpose rather by vague, dreamy, transcendental ideas than upon strictly scientific grounds. He had come across some "spiritualistic" books, full of wild theories about life upon the moon and the planets, and the possibility of some day or somehow communicating with them, or at least of demonstrating the existence of "other races in other worlds." The bigger the glass the better the chance of this, he thought; and so the vast instrument was ordered of Alvan Clarke, and the trust formed. He would be disappointed, probably, if he could gaze through his own wonderful tube, and see how little it can do with stars and suns and far-off depths of space beyond the powers of a six-inch reflector, but it remains none the less a magnificent implement of astronomy, which has already accomplished marvellous work, and will effect more; while, to resolve double or triple stars, to define nebulæ and study the lunar surface and the markings of planets and satellites, its capacity is far beyond all that science ever before possessed.

It was still broad daylight, however, and the time would not come until after darkness to enjoy the privilege of searching the heavens with that splendid memorial of the California miner. We wandered, therefore, from section to section of the buildings, examining apparatus, looking at vastly interesting photographs of the moon, of various planets, of nebulæ, and galaxies, and double stars, and at the dappled spectra of different celestial bodies.

Under the smaller cupola was fixed a heliostat, and Professor Campbell, quickly adjusting the reflector to the sinking sun, and holding a white card against the eye-piece, showed me a limb of the sun over which a spot was slowly moving. As he dexterously shifted the card this way and that, you could see the curious *faculæ* on the solar disc delicately reproduced, like the marks upon watered yellow satin, albeit these faint shadings were probably far-off aspects of fiery whirlpools and geysers, inconceivably enormous, unimaginably intense, in the blazing, seething, roaring garment of incandescent hydrogen worn by our central orb. Professor Holden made a remark here which lingers in my memory. I had been speaking of the curious suggestion of Lord Kelvin, to the effect that the first germ of life might have been conveyed to our planet upon a meteorite or small asteroid.

"I cannot think him in earnest," said my kind

C

and highly gifted host. " As a hypothetical idea it is perhaps defensible, but look at that spot on the sun ! Ever since it appeared a short while ago, and while it has moved across the disc—a little freckle in seeming, but in reality a huge and terrible abyss in the photosphere, with awful forces at work around and within it—my magnetic needles have been perturbed by it. We are so close to the sources of life and light that everything is possible without any such far-fetched means. The whole universe is linked in mutual neighbourhood and mutual influence by the universal forces and laws. If life is anywhere, it is likely to be everywhere."

We dined four thousand feet above the sea mists enveloping San José, as satisfactorily as if in the plain ; and drank the pious memory of James Lick in excellent " Crestabianca " of the Napa vineyards. I am of the opinion that California will some day supply the world with wine, if her vineyards can add to the purity which now happily distinguishes their products, education and character. As matters stand, the white Rieslings, Sauternes, and Crestas of the State are better than what France and Germany supply at twice the price ; and the Zinfandel clarets and Schramberger Burgundies want only less youth and less of the soil to be as admirable as they are cheap. But " this is another story," as Mr. Rudyard Kipling has taught us to say.

After dinner the longed-for darkness had fallen upon the mountain ; the last of the very few public visitors had departed ; a glorious night of perfect brilliancy and clearness drew its spangled curtain over the peak, and I repaired with my accomplished entertainers to the great cupola to pass some happy and privileged hours alone with the mighty Lick telescope, and with two among the skilful and devoted "Magi" who manage it, Professors Holden and Campbell.

Never shall I forget that memorable night! It was not that the huge weapon of science revealed so much that was new to me, but to hear the rich and deep astral wisdom of those learned astronomers, with the great glass under our touch to illustrate each subject, proved indeed an enjoyment. Like a 110-ton gun to look at—but, ah! how different in purpose and service—the colossal instrument reclined under our hands, peering broadly through the black embrasure of that slit in the cupola, obedient to the wheels and levers which moved it, as I have written, as though it had been a lady's lorgnette.

We had been talking much of La Place's famous nebula theory (widely accepted, though largely modified and expanded since his day), and Mr. Campbell deftly swung the huge telescope upon the nebula in Orion and bade me climb into the observing chair. That marvellous object of the heavens was full and clear in sight, defined with exquisite precision as it could be in no other place and with no other instrument. I saw, in the well-known region of "Beta Orionis," the vast separate system of that world of glory clearly outlined ; a fleecy,

irregular, mysterious, windy shape, its edges whirled
and curled like those of a storm-cloud, with stars and
star clusters standing forth against the milky white
background of the nebula, as if diamonds were
lying upon silver cloth. The central star, which
to the naked eye or to a telescope of low power
looks single and of no great brilliancy, resolved
itself, under the potent command of the Lick glass,
into a splendid trapezium of four glittering orbs
arranged very much like those of the Southern
Cross. At the lower right-hand border of the beautiful cosmic mist there opens a black abyss of
darkness, which has the appearance of an inky
cloud about to swallow up the silvery filagree of
the nebula, but this the great glass fills up with un-
suspected stars when the photographing apparatus
is fitted to it.

I had seen at Harvard College Observatory, under
the gifted hands of Mr. Pickering, that fascinating
operation by which all the black spaces of the sky
are made in turn to yield up their secret of hidden
suns and systems to the sensitised collodion film at
the eye-piece of the telescope ; and similar opera-
tions, with a view to map out the visible universe,
are constantly in progress at Mount Hamilton. It
was necessary from time to time to raise the sliding
seat on the ladder in order to keep the glorious
prospect of Orion's nebula in the field, but the lateral
motion was easily governed by the wheel moving the
dome. I understood Professor Holden's view to be
that we were beholding, in that almost immeasurably

remote silvery haze, an entirely separated system of worlds and clusters, apart from all others, as our own system is, but inconceivably grander, larger, and more populous with suns and planets and their stellar allies.

Next we lightly turned the mighty astral weapon of Mr. James Lick to Sirius, and held the splendid star fast in its field—a white diamond of the darkness, incredibly clear, burning and brilliant. Yet those almost blinding rays by which it flashed its glory to our eyes had left its surface many years ago, and what we saw was but the light of Sirius emitted in about 1874, so that, for all our feeble wits can tell, the star may be extinguished long after we still continue to seem to behold it. I remarked to myself that, skilful as the labour of Alvan Clarke has been in preparing the three-foot lens, it is not, and indeed could not be, entirely achromatic. A faint tag of pale blue haunts the image of each star, and paints a pencilled azure ray emerging from its edge, so that there is therefore a supplementary lens, also of yard width, kept in the cupola, which can be fitted for photographic purposes. Of course, when I speak of the "image" and of the "edge" of a star seen in the field of vision of the great telescope, it must be understood that the Lick glass itself cannot show any disc even of the nearest or the brightest fixed star. These immensely remote suns—the closest of which is so distant that its rays occupy four years in reaching our earth—reveal themselves to the colossal instrument on

Mount Hamilton, as to all others, merely as a point of light.

But step by step astronomy wrests fresh secrets from the starry abysses, and far away as all those shining, mysterious worlds are which passed that night before my eyes, fastened to James Lick's magic lens, it is possible now—as everybody knows who knows anything at all about the matter—to settle the questions both of the matter composing them and also of the special rate of speed at which they are advancing toward this earth or receding from it. It is the wonderful spectroscope, in the hands of Dr. Huggins and others, which has not only largely revealed of late the physical constitution of stars, comets, and nebulæ, but added to bygone methods a totally new one of comparing proper motions in the heavenly bodies. Probably no star is really a "fixed star," and Shakespeare, with his usual miraculous omniscience, was right in making one of his characters say—

> There's not a single orb which thou beholdest,
> But in his motion like an angel sings.

Relatively they move so slowly, that in ten thousand years it is unlikely any visible alteration would be detected in such constellations as the Great Bear or Orion. Positively, they move with immense rapidity, and when this is in a direction toward or from the earth, the spectroscope can measure their rate of advance or retreat quite accurately. Sir Robert Ball has explained this very lucidly in a recent article,

and the explanation is so good an example of what
I have styled " popularising the methods and facts
of astronomy without degrading them," that I will
venture to quote a passage from it. He writes :—

The logic of the new method is simple enough. Our eyes are
so constituted that when a certain number of ethereal vibrations
per second are received by the nerves of the retina, the brain interprets the effect to mean that a ray of, let us say, red light has
entered the eye. A certain larger number of vibrations per second
is similarly understood by the brain to imply the presence of blue
light on the retina. Each particular hue of the spectrum—the
red, orange, yellow, green, blue, indigo, violet—is associated with
a corresponding number of vibrations per second. It will thus be
seen that the interpretation we put on any ray of light depends
solely, as far as its hue is concerned, on the number of vibrations
per second produced on the retina. Increase that number of vibrations in any way, then the hue shifts towards one nearer the blue
end of the spectrum ; decrease the number of vibrations per second,
and the hue shifts along the spectrum in the opposite direction.

From these considerations it is apparent that the hue of a light,
as interpreted by the eye, will undergo modification if the source
from which the light radiates is moving toward us or moving from
us. Let us suppose the existence of a star emitting light of a pure
green colour corresponding to a tint near the middle of the spectrum.
This star pours forth each second a certain number of vibrations
appropriate to its particular colour, and if the star be at rest relatively to the eye, then, we assume, the vibrations will be received
on the retina at the same intervals as those with which the star
emits them. Consequently, we shall perceive the star to be green.
But now suppose that the star is hurrying toward us ; it follows
that the number of vibrations received in a second by the eye will
undergo an increase. For the relative movement is the same as if
the earth were rushing toward the star. In this case we advance,
as it were, to meet the waves, and consequently receive them at
less intervals than if we were to wait for their arrival. Many
illustrations can be given of the simple principle here involved.
Suppose that a number of soldiers are walking past in single file,

and that while the observer stands still twenty soldiers a minute pass him. But now let him walk in the opposite direction to the soldiers, then, if his speed be as great as theirs, he will pass forty soldiers a minute instead of twenty. If his speed were half that of the soldiers, then he would pass thirty a minute, so that in fact the speed with which the observer is moving could be determined if he counts the number of soldiers that he passes per minute and makes a simple calculation. On the other hand, suppose that the observer walks in the same direction as the soldiers, if he maintains the same pace that they do, then it is plain that no soldiers at all pass him while he walks. If he moves at half their rate, then ten soldiers will pass him each minute. From these considerations it will be sufficiently apparent that if the earth and the star are approaching each other, more waves of light per second will be received on the retina than if their positions are relatively stationary. But the interpretation which the brain will put on this accession to the number of waves per second is that the hue of light is altered to some shade nearer the blue end of the spectrum. In fact, if we could conceive the velocity with which the bodies approached to be sufficiently augmented, the colour of the star would seem to change from green to blue, from blue to indigo, from indigo to violet; while, if the pace were still further increased, it is absolutely certain that the waves would be poured upon the retina with such rapidity that no nerves there present would be competent to deal with them, and the star would actually disappear from vision. It may, however, be remarked that the velocity required to produce such a condition as we have supposed is altogether in excess of any known velocities in the celestial movements. The actual changes in hue that the movements we meet with are competent to effect are much smaller than in the case given as an illustration.

On the other hand, we may consider the original green star and the earth to be moving apart from each other. The effect of this is that the number of waves poured into the eye is lessened, and accordingly the brain interprets this to imply that the hue of the star has shifted from the green to the red end of the spectrum. If the speed with which the bodies increase their distance be sufficiently large, the green may transform into a yellow, the yellow into an orange, the orange into a red; while a still greater velocity is, at all events, conceivable which would cause the undulations to be received with such slowness that the nature of the light could no longer be interpreted by any nerves which the eye contains, and from the mere fact of its rapid motion away from us the star would become invisible. Here again we must add the remark that the actual velocities animating the heavenly bodies are not large enough to allow of the extreme results now indicated.

It is a fortunate circumstance that the lines in the spectrum afford a precise means of measuring the extent of the shift due to motion. If the movement of the star be toward us, then the whole system of lines is shifted toward the blue end, whereas it moves toward the red end when the star is hastening from us. The amount of the shift is a measure of the speed of the movement. This is the consideration which brings the process within the compass of practical astronomy. In the skilful hands of Vogel and Keeler, it is possible in favourable cases to obtain determinations of the velocities of objects in the line of sight with a degree of precision which leaves no greater margin for doubt than about five per cent of the total amount.

The Lick Observatory is very strong in spectroscopy. This fascinating study is there confided to most skilful hands, and I believe the astronomical world will be likely soon to hear some very remarkable developments in this branch from the Californian mountain, in connection with some discoveries in spectroscopic manipulation, strangely simple, yet most productive, hit upon lately by the staff. The " demon star " Algol, in the constellation of Perseus, has recently yielded up its secular secret to Vogel, armed with the spectroscope. It is known now that Algol advances toward us for thirty-four hours and retreats from us for the same period, and that this is the explanation of its strange variability of light, which is as if a heavenly lamp was alternately flashed and shaded. It is also proved that

Algol revolves round a dark companion which occasionally shuts off a portion of its luminosity. When we bear in mind the prodigious distances of the celestial ocean, these feats of astronomy magnificently exalt the dignity and demonstrate the power of man's intellect. It has been computed that the sun, which looms so large for us, would be to an observer on the nearest fixed star no plainer to behold than to our own eyes an eagle soaring at an altitude three times as great as the distance from Japan to New York! How little we are—and how large!

We turned the massive telescope from region to region of that

blue Pacific of Infinity.

At each new star-scape I heard, with an advantage and delight never to be forgotten, the elucidations, views, and conclusions of the learned and courteous gentlemen who took so much kindly interest in my "intelligent ignorance." Quite a long and lively discussion arose when the huge reflector was levelled at the new and astonishing star lately appearing in Auriga, which has blazed up so quickly and flickered into dimness again. They were watching and carefully measuring its variations of lustre at Lick, comparing it night after night with Polaris, by exposures ranging from two to one hundred seconds. It was Professor Holden's opinion that we were gazing there, amid the jewelled labyrinths of the Charioteer, at a world in fiery ruin, flaring to its utter destruction, its elements melting with heat unspeakable, its live things, if it possessed any, scorched to a white

annihilation. My erudite and kindly friend was inclined to be pessimistic at the spectacle.

"See! it is to this that all stars and systems—let
alone planets and asteroids—must come at last. Can
you find much ground for optimism in the sight?"

I was obstinate in my usual fixed faith—that destruction is reconstruction and all endings are only
new beginnings. "Let the great Mother," I said,
"cast her condemned or discharged materials into
the crucible of change and work them up again to
fresh miracles of beauty and evolution. Flame, and
fury of liquefaction, and elements bubbling in the
furnace of stellar collision, are only terrible to us because we think of them from notions of a burned
finger and the boiling-point of Fahrenheit. To
angelic intelligence the process may be gentle and
pleasant to witness as the weaving of white satin.
We talk of angels as ascending and descending
in interplanetary space, where nevertheless the
temperature must be three hundred degrees below
zero! Do they therefore wear overcoats and
blankets? I am not disconcerted by your heavenly
fireworks."

Whereupon Astronomy smiled indulgently at
Poetry.

From the great cupola we should have repaired
to the smaller one, to see the spectra of stars being
taken, and to measure the speed of a flying orb or
two. But outside the door stood a lighted lantern,
and that was a sign, not to be disregarded, that one
of the professional staff was busy within, taking

stellar photographs. Like an African chief, who leaves his slippers and his spear outside the hut where he has sought the society of his mistress, one of the "Magi" of Lick was closeted there with Urania, and even Mr. Holden did not dare to enter. Deep is truly the debt of America first, and next, of all the civilised world, to these accomplished and devoted men, who on the summit of that lonely mountain work patiently through the clear suitable nights, noting and recording whatever is moving in the heavens, sleepless and faithful, sufficiently rewarded when

> Some new planet swims into their ken.

They come to love their lofty work with a silent enthusiasm which the visitor will be quick to note. Lifted on high above the world and its petty pursuits, immersed in these noble and far-reaching studies, they contract a positive distaste for the commonplaces of existence, and are as happy as kings upon their rocky throne. The director told me that when any of his professors took leave of absence, they almost always returned long before the expiration of their term, unable to keep away from their peaceful and exalted temple of science. He himself had not left his learned eyrie for two months before accompanying me in my downward ride to San José. And sleeping that night in the deep tranquillity of the mountain crest, four thousand feet above railways and public readings, politics and publishers, I, too, felt that " it was good to be here," and half wished that I, too, might have a little tabernacle builded to dwell therein with the wise men of Lick.

Would that there were words to describe the landscape which opened its loveliness in the morning before the blinking eyes of those high-minded nocturnal watchers and my own not less sleepy vision. Far and near, the undulating wilderness of peaks and canyons rolled at our feet. The light of dawn caught the snow on the Sierra and edged it with rosy colour, while the intervening deep hollows were all dark blue. Over the San José valley lay an unbroken sea of cloud, a vast silver shroud, covering up everything except a lofty foothill here and there. Black and idle the great telescope leaned forth in its iron embrasure, waiting again for the darkness, and the blinds were down in the bed-chambers of its nightly servitors.

Truly James Lick sleeps gloriously under the base of his big glass! Four thousand feet nearer heaven than any of his dead fellow-citizens, he is buried more grandly than any king or queen, and has a finer monument than their pyramids furnish to Cheops and Cephrenes. Nothing I had seen in the United States of America impressed me more than the institution founded by the California miner; and I descended the mountain, in the company of Professor Holden and his son, too full of admiration and meditation to pay much attention to the precipices alongside of which we recklessly rattled down, or to the exquisite prospects of hill and valley which make Monte Diabolo so varied and so fair.

III

AN ADVENTURE ON THE NILE

PYRAMIDS AT EVENING.

P. 49.

III

AN ADVENTURE ON THE NILE

I<small>T</small> is useful, as an educational experience, to have been so near to death as to see it face to face. This steadies the nerves for any subsequent incidents of life, and especially for that last and inevitable incident, when the end—which is also, of course, the fresh beginning—does really arrive. Once, in the course of holiday wanderings, it happened to me to come as near to finishing suddenly with the business of earthly existence as a man could well come, and yet finally escape alive; so that, since the story has some picturesque surroundings, it shall be narrated here.

We had arranged to sail up the Nile in a daha-beeah as far as the first cataract, perhaps even to the second. It is now about seven years ago since we set forth on that memorable journey, the party consisting of Lady Arnold, my second son Julian, and my only daughter, together with the writer of this. The climate of Cairo is delightful in winter, and it was no loss of time, but a most agreeable novelty— to at least three out of that happy four—to linger in the Egyptian capital while the necessary negotiations and arrangements were being made for our river trip. We lodged at the pleasant Hotel du Nil in

D

the "Muski," where the daily life of Cairo flows
up and down the gay bazaar; and, though the city
has become wofully altered since I remember the
Esbekieh covered with Arab coffee-houses, and
showing none of the new Frenchified buildings now
defacing the Maidan, still Cairo, especially in her
native quarters, is always interesting. A turn to
the right or left hand in any one of the narrow, cool,
silent lanes, will always take you at a plunge, as
it were, into the scenery of the "Arabian Nights,"
where you shall meet one after the other Alnaschar,
and Mesrour the Eunuch and the one-eyed Calendar,
perhaps even a veiled princess going to her bath.
Wandering on foot or by donkey in the "silver
street;" or up the alley, called by dragomans "the
smelly bazaar," where attar of roses, myrrh, gum
labanum and civet make the warm atmosphere delicious; or among the booths, where they sell shawls
and pipes, tobacco and embroidery; all this amused
sufficiently the ladies, while I transacted our river-
side affairs. It was late in the season to select a
dahabeeah. The best were already all engaged,
and I had to be content with the *Bedouin*, a craft
of five cabins, with a *jenin*, or garden, and an upper
deck; an old but not a bad boat, which had been
up and down the ancient river so often that no one
could have dreamed we were destined to charter
her for the last of her voyages.

A dahabeeah is a large, flat-bottomed vessel of
wide beam, with a mainmast and a short mizen,
upon the former of which is hoisted the great

lateen sail, with its long and towering yard of
lashed bamboos. These Nile boats look extremely
graceful, and even imposing, skimming the stream
with their vast white or striped wings outspread,
the point of the braced yard forking high up into
the sky, and always terminated by a pretty filigree-
work pennon, with a bit of gay coloured silk bear-

DAHABEEAH ON THE NILE.

ing the name of the ship. Our ill-fated, but not
unhandsome, craft had an ample waist for the
sailors, and a cook's galley midships, with two
cabins on either side of the passage going aft, as
well as another commodious stateroom in the extreme stern. The roof of these cabins formed an
upper deck, protected by an awning and approached

by a flight of steps, where it was very nice to
walk or sit, as the *Bedouin* glided before the wind,
or was lazily towed against the current by a party
of the sailors.

She was well provided with all needful furniture,
and our dragoman, who bore the name of Khalil, given
anciently to Abraham, and meaning " The Friend of
God "—an inherited appellation wholly undeserved—
set to work to provision her for the trip.   Besides all
sorts of tinned and canned goods and groceries, there
were coops full of turkeys and chickens to put on
board, along with the bread for the Arab crew, which
bread they chopped into small pieces, and spread
for two whole days upon the upper deck to dry in
the sun.   Sheep and eggs and fruit could be procured
as we sailed along.   Guns, clothes, rugs, books and
drawing materials were not forgotten, the latter particularly, for Lady Arnold was an accomplished artist,
and the pure atmosphere and brilliant hues of Nile
landscapes make everybody wish to preserve some
more or less faithful memoranda of them.   We
agreed to take the captain and the crew already
attached to the ship, upon the guarantee of recom-
mendatory letters from previous employers ; and hired
in the city a skilful Syrian cook, very clever at
curries, with a bright, serviceable young body-servant
named Ali, as well as a pretty Egyptian boy called
Mustapha.   The captain, or Reïs, was a charming old
navigator, whom we soon grew to like and to call
affectionately " Aunt Mary," for his gentle ways.

The crew consisted of about seventeen hands,

docile and friendly Egyptians, full of quiet mischief, and fairly ready to do the hard work of the voyage, which is occasionally very hard indeed, since the men have to jump overboard every now and then to push the vessel off sandbanks, to watch and trim and furl the huge lateen sail, and for hours together to toil along the bank with the tow-rope braced round their shoulders, dragging the ponderous and lazy craft along at about a mile and a half or two miles per hour. A very serious and elaborate document has to be signed before embarking, between the hirer and the captain, specifying the sums to be paid and the dates of payment, with certain pledges of "backsheesh" or presents in money if all goes well and satisfactorily. As will be seen, the *Bedouin* was fated never to return. The decree of the god Hâpi was written that she should leave her bones in the bed of his Nile, among all the countless wrecks of ancient and modern craft—Ptolemœan galleys and Nubian "buglas"—which must fill the hidden slime of the "Father of Waters." But of this dark edict of the river deity we happily knew nothing, and never was any party more joyous or full of anticipated pleasure than ours when we went finally on board and settled down for a start, the red ensign of England fluttering at the mainmast, and the bright little name-pennon at the point of the lateen yard.

Sailing the Nile thus, day after day, is surely the very "cream of the cream" of travelling, with a good dahabeeah, a well-fitted company of holiday-makers and a rightly chosen crew. Our ship, though old, was stanch and comfortable; our party perfect in harmony and numbers, and the hands won daily more and more our patience and attachment, as we learned to put up with their absurd little foibles and to make the most of their simple virtues. They would "say the thing which is not" with the most reckless inaccuracy and the wildest imaginativeness, and would invent the most humorously false and flagitious excuses to linger at a pleasant spot, and so cause our social arrangements to fit in with their own, for they had friends at every station. But as we were in no sort of hurry, their stratagems suited our idle programme well, and very quickly we all got on together quite perfectly. They would do anything and everything at last for the Sitt and the Sittina, and since my Turkish decorations gave me the status of a pacha, they were full of the necessary respect for the " effendi."

Three or four among their number gained our especial favour: a strong, good-tempered Arab named " Salim "— whom we almost instantly rechristened "The Buffalo;" a tall, graceful Nubian lad, called " Moya ; " a one-eyed Egyptian sailor, known as Hassan, who wore a red loin-cloth and was dubbed " Scarlet Fever ; " the boy Mustapha, and Ali, the cabin servant. There came, moreover, a black kitten on board, nicknamed " Sheitan," or the Devil, to which the sailors objected as being unlucky, but this feeling was rashly overruled. As for the weather, that indispensable factor in a happy water trip,

there was no need to be anxious about it. The
Egyptian winter is splendid for steady brilliancy
of sky and pleasantness of temperature, a little too
much cooled, perhaps, each morning when the north
wind blows. But that breeze lulls as the sun draws
westward; and evening after evening the sunsets
on the Nile are beyond all description lovely and
inexhaustible in combination of tender and beautiful tints. Night after night the ancient god Ra
sank to his couch in robes of more glorious magni-
ficence than we had before seen, so that the hour
of his declination and departure was a regular
rendezvous on the upper deck for us all; and while
Lady Arnold would seek to fix some of the divine
blendings of gold and crimson, amber and purple,
turquoise green and silvery grey painting the west,
the Reïs was on his knees and nose saying his
evening prayer toward Mecca, and half the crew
would be cooking the last meal, while the other
half tramped the broken bank with the tow-rope
over their brown shoulders, singing some song of
the Nile, not always too decent if faithfully translated.

The simplicity of manners to which one has to
be accustomed in Nile travelling is, in truth, a little
startling at first. Our men, like all the other sailors
of the river, would at any moment strip stark naked
to plunge in the river or to handle the tow-rope,
and the best way for those who objected, or who en-
deavoured in vain to make them wear drawers, was
to regard their brown skin as a real dress, of which

indeed it gives the idea. The improprieties of Arab talk were, however, veiled to most ears, and the river-songs at night or when hauling on the warps are mostly as innocent as they are melodious.

It is the golden dream of travelling, I say, to glide along day after day upon that antique water channel between the two strips of brilliant fertility which mark the range of the yearly inundation creating and recreating Egypt. Justly has the old chronicler Herodotus said that " Egypt is the gift of the Nile." Exactly so much of the desert valley lying between the yellow sunburned hills as the wave of the life-giving stream can touch, by flood or artificial irrigation, is transformed as if by magic from a waste to a paradise. One does not realise what water is to the earth until many a stroll has been taken along those emerald strips of barley and millet fields, and those long, waving groves of palm-trees, which embroider the Nile all the way from Cairo to the second cataract, and, indeed, much higher. In a thousand spots you may stand in Middle and Upper Egypt with one foot deep in rich, verdant growing crops, and the other buried in barren sands. The line is as sharp between the fertility and the sterility as between the water and the bank ; in truth, the mid-river itself is accompanied throughout its course by these two sister streams of eternal fecundity, and Egypt is that ever-gleaming ribbon of blue with green edges, now widening, now diminishing, which meanders, always bright and glad, in the heart of the hot desert, from Korosko to the Delta.

It is a supreme pleasure, I repeat, to make your way day after day up the grand old river in a well-found Nile boat, with pleasant company and a good, willing, friendly crew. In the early morning, before the sun has cleared the hills which shut us from the Red Sea, the dahabeeah spreads the great white wing of her "trinkeet" if there be any serviceable breeze, and gracefully resumes her daily task of stemming the perpetual downward current of the river. The scene is then charming. The fair Egyptian dawn has broken, pearly and roseate. The stream is alive with water-birds—cranes, pelicans, wild geese and ibis—whose happy cries fill the air. Numerous native boats, of the strangest build and rig, with tattered but picturesque sails, go up and down laden with heaped-up grain or chopped fodder or sheaves of sugar-cane and maize. Their swarthy crews, in white or blue gowns and red "tarbooshes," make water-pictures which you long to preserve ; while upon the bank an endless procession passes all day of equally artistic figures—peasant people, merchants, Arabs, Turkish officials, soldiers and boatmen, all seen in sharp silhouette against the clear azure of the western sky.

The river, never running far in one and the same direction, constantly shifts the point of view, and so makes a succession of delightful combinations out of the otherwise changeless features of the Nile landscape—the yellow desert hills, the strips of sand waste at their feet, the broad or narrow belts of culti-vation, the raised banks, and the shining channel.

At every few miles a minaret, jutting its delicate
white needle into the air above the palm-groves, or
a fleet of little cargo-boats fastened to the shore,
betoken a village, which will look like a rubbish
heap alive with human insects, so humble in architecture are the huts of mud with their flat roofs of
maize and dhoura straw, and so all alike the inhabitants, in white and blue, swarming about them.

You have left behind at Gizeh the last of the
great group of pyramids, but now and again the
hills on the eastern side show ranges of square
black holes hewn in the limestone or granite, which
are entrances to ancient tombs ; and wherever these
are numerous or famous you will probably land to
examine some of them. Then will you perceive—in
climbing from the palm-grove to the breast of the
yellow crag—what a fast faith those ancient Egyptians of the Pharaohs had in the immortal life of
the soul. Otherwise they would not have cut away
the solid rock so patiently into smooth, roomy, imperishable chambers, to deposit therein two or three
bodies at most, against such time as the respective
souls belonging to them, their fated wanderings
completed, should come back to look for and to
resume the earthly tenement. Joyous and confident
paintings on the tomb wall, as fresh in this dry, pure
air as though drawn and coloured a week, and not
three thousand years ago, symbolise the happy
future of the justified dead. The tombs are now
all rifled, and the patient mummies are gone—some
to museums, some to be manure for farmers or pig-

THE PYRAMIDS OF GIZEH.

ments for artists, since there is quite a large trade
done to-day in Nile mummy dust for fertilising,
and for a special brown tint much employed by oil
painters. Yet the significance of those antique,
rock-hewn graves is the same. It was the land of
resolute belief, the land of an assured and universal conviction that man's real existence is eternal,
of which every one of these elaborately excavated
sepulchres is a monument, noble and pathetic. As
I myself have written to the mummy of an Egyptian
lady, whose burial-chest we opened, to find only her
dust and her slippers—

> You were born in the Egypt that did not doubt;
>   You were never sad with our new-fashioned sorrows;
> You were sure, when your playtimes on earth ran out,
>   Of playtimes to come, as we of our morrows.
>   Oh! wise little maid of the Delta! . . . .

The pyramids themselves are mighty witnesses of
the same firm belief, being, as they were, gigantic
caskets, with astronomical and geodetical meanings,
constructed to preserve the dead body of the king,
until His Majesty's soul had need of it for a new
earthly existence.

What with such occasional landings to explore
tombs, to shoot hares and palm-doves, and to get
necessary exercise; and what with the strong current and the slow pace of these broad-beamed, flat-
bottomed Nile boats, it is not very much progress
that you will make in any one day. From twenty-
five to forty-five miles may be taken as the rate, and
this absence of hurry and this daily sedate advance

suit well the genius of the land and the atmosphere of peace and philosophy which surrounds the dahabeeah. Never for a moment is the properly constituted mind bored upon that marvellous and delightful river. You can read or sketch or write, sitting on the upper deck under the striped awning, with the pretty water-wagtails of the Nile running about between your feet, and the solemn Reïs ascending now and again to say his prayers toward Mecca, at noon, or at the " Azan," which is our " four-o'clock tea." The crew alone would be a perpetually interesting study to a close observer; ours certainly proved so, especially when they found out that we liked them to dance and be happy in their own way. If, as often happens, there is no wind, overboard go half-a-dozen of the brown " hands," rolling up their blue coats to their armpits, and the tow-rope is rigged and hauled for hours and hours. Should a lively puff of breeze arise, helter-skelter they rush for the boat, leap and scramble on board, hoist the huge lateen sail, and away the little ship buzzes once more, churning the Nile into cream below her square bows. But you must never allow the main sheet to be made fast. A trusted sailor must constantly squat on the deck holding that in his hands, with half a hitch only round the cleat, and at the moment when the helmsman cries " *Khalis!* " ("Loosen!") he must let the sheet run. Otherwise the dahabeeah will surely capsize. I was very particular and careful, indeed, upon this point, being an old yachtsman, and it was not from any neglect as to the main sheet that our catastrophe, soon to be related, befell.

In the delicious afternoon, as the sun sinks nearer the western horizon, casting long shadows from the palm stems, the river grows more and more entrancing. The north wind, which ofttimes blows hard, and even cold, in the forenoon, is lulled. The chief work of the " *shadoufs* "—the water-wheels—is done, and their shrill creaking no longer so much grieves the sensitive ear. The buffaloes, released from the slow toil of turning the pole, go homeward with the goats and chickens. Long lines of wild geese, flamingoes, pelicans, and vast flocks of blue pigeons streak or cloud the sky, now gradually assuming toward its western border a delicate tint of turquoise green— nay, more decidedly green than that—a veritable *ciel de Nil* colour, upon which the gathering cloud- lets of the early evening lie in soft masses of silver and gold and violet. The cook begins to be busy with his charcoal fires, and the Arab crew gets ready the mooring ropes and pins. Down drops the last faint breeze, and some of them must plunge over- board again to drag the dahabeeah to her berth for the night, under the palms of the village. As we pull and pole the sluggish vessel to her resting- place, the ever-crumbling bank of the river tumbles in large fat masses of black soil, with loud splash, into that current which is always eating up the Egypt that it has created.

The ship is laid alongside the shore, pegs are driven into the bank and ropes made fast to them,

stem and stern ; a plank is cast from the deck to the
land, and your floating home is as quiet as a church,
under the mud ledge.   From the town or the village
now come down coffee-coloured loafers to chat and
question, together with women in long dark blue
gowns, veiled and barefooted, bearing vessels of
milk, grain, fruits, and tobacco leaves.   The sky
has lost the sun and has become a curtain of soft
heavenly glory, through which the first stars twinkle.
Opposite the sunset the east is lighted with the
lively and wonderful colours of the " afterglow."
The old captain is finishing his evening prayer upon
his little carpet by our side.   The " gaffer," the official
watchman, with long staff and head-cloth, approaches
solemnly and sits on the bank to take charge of the
safety of the ship.   Dinner and the divinely placid
Egyptian night ensue ; and, while the Arab crew
dance and beat their drums in the light of the paper
lanterns, and you smoke the long narghileh and sip
the perfectly prepared coffee, your wish is that the
ancient and majestic stream would run for ever and
for ever from the southward in the same tranquil
manner, and that you could go on stemming it for
ever and for ever in the same daily and delightful
peace and ease.

   We had sailed and tracked the Nile thus for
twenty-one days, each day adding to the agreeable
experiences and growing contentments of the voyage,
and increasing our friendship with the crew, particularly those heretofore named, and the dear old
Reïs.   Lady Arnold had been very kind to that

venerable Arab, giving him tea and pills when out
of sorts; and Reïs Achmet had come to regard her
with deep loyalty, though they could exchange no
words of conversation. My son Julian, an enthusiastic sportsman, had shot much game for the men,
and my daughter had made special and devoted
adherents of Ali, the boy, as well as of Mustapha, and
of a sick Egyptian to whom we had given a passage.
The black cat had been transferred to a passing grain
boat troubled with rats, and all seemed fair and
favourable. But now we were doomed to realise the
truth of that Arabic word, *yasoul*—*i.e.,* "it will come
to an end;" and very nearly indeed, as will be seen,
did we also, and all the nineteen Egyptians attending
us, come to an end along with those too happy days.

It was an object, that luckless January morning,
to start early and make the whole run to Girgeh, a
considerable town, where we were to take in new supplies, and where we had arranged to reward the good
service of the crew with a sheep for a feast and a
"*fantasia*" of dancing and fireworks. Accordingly,
though a rather too fresh wind was blowing, I rose
early, and, after consulting the captain, gave word to
start. My wife and son and daughter were still in
their cabins, and we had thus far only sailed about
half a league. Coming under some high red cliffs of
sandstone on the eastern shore, named Jebel-esh-
Sheikh, I was on the upper deck watching to see
that Selim did not make fast for one moment the
sheet, the Reïs was giving directions for the course,
and his next in command was steering, when, on a

sudden, a fury of wind fell from the desert ledge high overhead upon the lofty lateen sail, sweeping at the same time across the breadth of the river, which it lashed into white tumult. The little ship heeled over, and I rushed down from the upper deck to help let fly everything and get the sail reefed. As she righted and rocked over the other way my wife came hurriedly and half dressed out of the cabins, from which my son and daughter had not yet emerged, and called to me in alarm. I was saying something conventional to reassure her, when another blast laid the dahabeeah violently down, and my cook, apparently just risen from sleep, toppled and fell overboard. Obeying an instinct to render him help, I flung myself across the gunwale of the *Bedouin* to clutch and save him, but missed his hand, and was throwing the bight of a rope toward his sinking form, while I could feel my wife seizing my coat from behind to keep me from going overboard, when the ship seemed suddenly to rear up and plunge, and the next moment we were all hurled pellmell into the river, the hull rolling right over and the big sail lying flat upon the water. Gear, poultry coops, oars, cordage, sailors, water jars, everything and everybody, with one or two exceptions, were violently flung forth from the dahabeeah into the turbulent river waves, in such a helpless and sudden confusion and horror of calamity that it gives me a thrill, even now, to write of that wild moment.

My part in the miserable instant was to see my wife sinking at my side, to fling one arm round her

waist and seize her wrist, while striking out for the
wreck with the other. A coop of drowning poultry
under my left elbow enabled me to support her and
bring her to the hull, upon which several of the
sailors had already scrambled up from the water; and
these men, in obedience to my call, drew Lady
Arnold upon the keel. I could not lift myself up
there, being too exhausted, but clung to the ship,
and hearing my son, an excellent swimmer, in the
river near me calling to his sister, I exclaimed de-
spairingly, "She is dying under the dahabeeah!"
But as soon as I found strength to raise myself out
of the water upon the side of the Bedouin, there
was my daughter sitting in her night-dress, having
escaped by coolness and good fortune through her
cabin window. This sight greatly inspired me, especially as I also saw my son Julian just then dragging
the old Arab captain out of the river. In effect,
all but the drowned cook had by this time crawled
back upon the vessel's bilge, and there was a chance
to save at least the ladies before she should fill and
founder. I shouted to the men, therefore, to cease
their ridiculous lamentations and useless curses, and
to listen to orders.

Never did I behold such a limp, miserable, hopeless
lot as my smart Egyptians had become. They wept,
they tore their clothes, they threw their turbans into
the waves. They were most of them abjectly useless
and nerveless. "*Attini felucca, ya Reïs,*" I cried
("Give me the little boat"), for we had a dingey
towing astern, which had not capsized and was now

E

our only hope. " *Felucca mafeesh*," the old gentleman plaintively cried, pointing to the thick manilla
rope holding the skiff, the knot of which was far
under water, so that to get the little boat we must
cut that thick cord. " *Sikkin, sikkin !*"—" A knife,
a knife ! " I called out impatiently, but nobody produced one until Julian drew from his pocket Lady
Arnold's little one-bladed penknife, truly a poor
affair for such a crisis. I tried ; Salim tried ; my son
tried to sever the manilla with that tiny blade, while
the wretched log of a ship was steadily settling down
with us in mid-stream. At last, seeing that the others
would break the blade, I regained it, and, strand by
strand, I painfully cut that rope through ; and then,
after sternly checking an egotistical desire of some of
my Arabs to take the first seats on the skiff—by knock-
ing them overboard again—the two ladies, three of
my best sailors, the boy Mustapha, and the sick
Arab to whom we were giving a passage, with Ali,
were all put in, and glad I was to thrust them safely
off from the ship, tossing into the boat some of the
floating oars. Of course they all cried to us—myself
and my son—to come; but that was inadmissible. Had
we gone, the others would have justly wished to escape
also, and the felucca must then have been swamped.

Rejoiced indeed we were to see them draw clear
from the wreck and pull out of the broken water,
while the hapless *Bedouin*, relieved of the weight of
eight persons, now floated a little higher in the water,
on her side, and might possibly continue to float until
we touched one or other shore. To cut a sad tale

short, she did continue to drift down-stream with us
for some two miles, finally touching land at a sand
point, where we all sprang off and tried to hold her
with a rope round a palm-tree stump. But the rope
broke; the hull, now almost full of water, whirled
madly away, and sank out of sight in a deep bend
of the Nile, about a quarter of a mile lower.

I had got my poor Egyptians well in hand long
before this time, aided by the eloquent scorn which
the Reïs expressed for their conduct, and by the
good example set them by my son, who had behaved
throughout, of course, like a true English lad, admir-
ably. They were touchingly grateful to be still alive,
especially the bad swimmers, and bitterly ashamed
of such childish despair as they had exhibited. But,
truly, the fix was ugly enough at its worst, and
although the strongest swimmers might perhaps have
got to shore, the majority of us must have perished
if the felucca had not been freed and the wreck
lightened sufficiently to float a little longer, as it did.
I was grateful for having boated every day at Oxford,
and glad that Julian had studied swimming more
than conic sections at Marlborough.

By-and-bye Selim and "the Buffalo" brought the
boat over to us, and Julian and I rejoined the unhappy ladies, who supposed themselves to have
lost sight of us for ever. The Reïs was to march
his men up the left bank to Girgeh. We landed
on the right bank to find our forlorn castaways
sitting under a red rock drying what garments
they possessed. We were in an uninhabited spot

—a naked, unvisited desert, six miles from the
nearest village — with only one pair of slippers
among the party. But it was sweet to be still
living, and the laborious march across the sands
proved even a joyous one. The hot Nile sun soon
dried our clothes, and with limping feet we reached
an Arab hamlet, where the women put warm, dry
native dresses on Lady Arnold and Miss Arnold,
while the old Sheikh lent his own pipe to myself and
my son, and caused provision of parched pulse and
melted butter to be served to us. The fellaheen whom
I had caught on the road, and despatched up and down
the river-banks with messages of our luckless plight,
soon found American and English friends at Girgeh,
and after a long day in the Egyptian huts a boat came
down and fetched us to the friendly shelter of the
dahabeeahs at that town. Boundless was the kindness we received ; lavish the help proffered in the
shape of garments, dresses, shoes, &c., and truly
dire was our need, for of that well-stored *Bedouin*
and the £300 or £400 in ready cash on board her,
only about seventy piastres remained in my saturated pockets when I turned them out that night.

We all found hospitable asylum, and my son, indeed, afterwards completed his voyage to the second
cataracts, wearing the clothes of the late Lord Henry
Lennox and of a Boston friend. I returned to
Cairo in the shoes of a kind Dutch gentleman and
in an Arab dress, my wife and my daughter also
wearing borrowed plumes. That night the lady
doctors on board the dahabeeah *Rachel* were for

some time puzzled by a broad black mark on my
wife's wrist. Suddenly she remembered that it
was where I had gripped her in the water at that
abominable and hopeless moment when we were
all flung into the Nile, like gooseberries from a
basket. I held her more tightly than I knew.

One little incident I must append to the dismal
recital, because it reflects well upon Arab politeness,
and I am so sorry to have had to record the ill-
behaviour of our theretofore nice Egyptian crew.
At the instant when the *Bedouin* was reeling to her
fate, the old Reïs, "Aunt Mary," approached Lady
Arnold, and respectfully raising her hand to his lips,
kissed it, and then drew his "kefieh" over his eyes,
to die. It was his supreme and grateful farewell!
Not even in the moment of death would this true
Arab gentleman fail in courtesy, especially since, in
his idea, the kind "Sitti" was going, as an un-
believer—not to Paradise, like himself—but "elsewhere." It was the touch of Oriental grace and
honour which redeemed for me the ugly business,
and I am glad to finish my Nile story with that
pretty action of the captain of the *Bedouin*.

I sent a Greek diver afterward to the wreck, but
I suppose he soon found my bag of sovereigns and
went off with it, for he reported that the ghost of
my cook and other dreadful "Afreets" haunted the
spot, and that he could and would search no more.
The *Bedouin* has long ago disappeared in the
muddy bed of the Nile, but her fate is still a legend
of the Nile. For myself, I do not wish to experience

another moment like that when the sail of the dahabeeah lay flat on the water like the wing of a wounded pelican, and the Nile seemed to lift up and drag away my limbs like shreds of river-grass. But it was indignation and swift meditation of resource which occupied my mind. I am persuaded a man has no time to be frightened in such emergencies. I felt no fear and had leisure to feel none, but I was furiously angry, and the anger was useful in controlling my helpless Egyptians, and saving a score or so of human lives.

EVENING ON THE NILE.

IV

IN THE HOLY LAND

JERUSALEM FROM THE MOUNT OF OLIVES.

IN THE HOLY LAND

AMONG all the experiences of travel, none, I think, more deeply impresses the mind or lingers longer in its memories than a journey through Palestine. First of all, the country itself is, in its character and natural aspects, extremely interesting. *Esh Shams*—as the Syrians themselves call it—"the land of the sun," sits well for climate, history, and influence, on the eastern edge of the great Midland Sea, the centre of so many empires; which, seen from Carmel or any spot along the coasts thereabout, is almost always of a heavenly blue colour, changing at sunset to that deep purple tint which Homer called the "wine-dark wave." Next, while various regions of travel present here and there points of ethnological or religious attraction, in Palestine every site, every rock, every hill, every valley and stream is full of associations of the most extraordinary and absorbing kind, inextricably blended with the concerns of humanity. Sail down the shores of Asia Minor from Smyrna, where Polycarp was burned by edict of the Emperor Marcus Aurelius; past the seats of the "Seven Churches" to the little Isle of Patmos, steep and rugged and gloomy, where St. John found a fit

dreaming place for writing his Apocalypse; to
Mersina, which was Tarsus, the birthplace of St.
Paul, and to Alexandretta, which is close to the
River Granicus, where Alexander the Great broke
up the Persian Empire; past the mouth of the
"silver Cydnus," on whose channel Cleopatra met
Antony, and past the Bahr-el-Kelb, where the
rocks bear the inscriptions of Sennacherib; on to
Beirout, under the majestic Lebanon—the Lebanon
of King Hiram of Tyre and of Solomon. All
that long way the wanderer's thoughts grow
more and more full of the records of those
events which helped or hindered the spread of
Christianity, and so become ripe for disembarking
with him in Palestine and traversing "the paths that
Christ hath trod." From Beirout to Jerusalem and
Bethlehem and Hebron, all through that narrow
but hallowed land, every step taken in its interior
becomes an emotion, a revelation, an illumination.
At every stage you are vividly led to comprehend,
as was never possible before, the details and surroundings of the simple but sublime Oriental story
which has conquered and remoulded the civilised
world. Here, on the slopes of Lebanon, as you
slowly climb them by the Damascus road, grow
the "locusts" of St. John, the caroub tree, with
its pods of sweet beans, though, indeed, he may
well have eaten, as I have done, the insect itself,
fried in butter. In "Hollow Syria" you shall see
the "Cedars of Lebanon," and that wonderful chaos
of ruined beauty and splendour, "Tadmor of the

Wilderness," coming upon the Temple by paths where every bush and flower is a picture fitted to Holy Writ. Thence you ride down to the white and outspread city of Damascus, immensely ancient, and so fair with its environing apricot gardens and green watercourses, that the Prophet Mohammed is said to have turned his eyes away from it at first sight in order "that he might not forget Paradise." Here you shall be shown the "street that is called Straight," where St. Paul was healed of his blindness; the spot on the road where he encountered the heavenly vision; and the gate from which he was let down in a basket.

I remember breakfasting there with some Bedawee Arabs, whose coffee was the finest that could be tasted, and manners the most polished that could be beheld, though they were a cut-throat set of gentry, and had come to pay a tribe fine to the Governor for a plundered caravan in the Hauran. On the same day I entered the little village of the lepers, close by, and sat long with the sad victims of that mysterious Scriptural malady, asking many questions about it of the sufferers, to the horror of my dragoman, who would not accompany me into the unclean place, but, nevertheless, to my own considerable profit and information. I do not think that leprosy is to any general degree communicable by contact. It is very prevalent in Syria, as in many countries of Asia, but more, it always seemed to me, by personal constitution or actual inheritance than by contagion or infection.

The hapless lepers reminded us of the Great
Healer, whose name is stamped everywhere upon
the land, and, indeed, as you pass southward from
Damascus and come to the sources of the Jordan
at Banias, in the country of the tribe of Dan, it
is, at each new day's journey, as though the very
pages of the Evangelists turned one by one before
your eyes, with comments made by the hand of
nature and the voice of the desolate country itself.
All through one morning's ride you will be rounding
the green breast of Tabor, and threading the oak
groves of that great and famous mountain which
looks down the whole long vista of the valley of
the Jordan, and can be seen from end to end of
the little territory of Palestine. For very small,
mesquin, petty, parochial, the Holy Land is. The
least of the big American States would swallow it
up entirely. It is inferior, I suppose, in area to
Vermont or Rhode Island, and therefore so intensely condensed in historical associations that
they indeed succeed each other too rapidly for
full realisation. Hardly have you ridden out of
the country of the Judges, and finished thinking of
Deborah and Barak and Sisera, before Carmel rises
out of the sea at your right hand, and you are
absorbed in recalling Elijah and Elisha and the
prophets of Baal, while to the left, beyond Jordan,
lies Bashan, and the " Country of the Giants," suggesting fresh lines of reminiscence.

Only half a day's ride farther—by hills that seem
to stand up proclaiming the great deeds and words

of the Son of Mary; by streams that trickle down
to Jordan or Kishon, murmuring His teachings; by
groves of oak and oleander and palms, where the
winds whisper His parables and miracles—you come
to where the hill of Safed (the Sepphoris of Pontius
Pilate) rises above the basin of the Lake of Tiberias.
Climbing this, you suddenly behold

> His lake, the Sea of Chinnereth,
> The waves He loved, the waves which kissed His feet
> So many blessed days.

What waters in all the world can inspire
thoughts and reflections more absorbing or profound than that sheet of sleeping silver thus
beheld between the desert hills of Gadara and
the plains of Bethsaida and Gennesaret? Many
and many a well-known inland sea, renowned for
its beauty or its scenes of history, have I visited in
all parts of the world, from Lakes Superior and
Michigan to the meres of Bulgaria and Greece, and
the inland waters of Scandinavia and Japan; nor can
a candid traveller fail to call the Lake of Galilee well
nigh the least imposing and attractive of them all
as regards outward scenery and surroundings. The
range which bounds it on the east is bare, arid, and
sadly coloured. The highlands to the westward are
rugged and stripped of soil and foliage by the storms
of many centuries; while southward toward Tiberias
the sheet of lifeless and ill-shaped water is seen
narrowing off under unlovely shores, to let Jordan
pass forth again, for the completion of its gloomy

course into the Dead Sea. Yet that diminutive, unprepossessing, and non-picturesque expanse of Syrian hill-drainage counts in the annals of mankind for more than all the lakes, and even oceans. Swifter and stronger than the flood of the impetuous Jordan, which breaks southwards through the dry nebbuk bushes from its extremity, and not destined, like that, to be lost in the oblivion of a "Sea of Lot," a stream of divine and mighty influence has poured over Christendom from this little Syrian mere, and by the words spoken on those shores has transformed the face of the world. As you sit on Safed amid chattering Jews and Arabs ignorant or heedless of the immortal recollections of the scene, it appears to you, and very truly appears, that no other locality in the world can crowd together such commanding, such overwhelming associations. If you know where to look for them, in the wide, hot, sterile champaign lying at your feet, grey with desolate, uncultivated rocks, yellow with desert sand, and only relieved here and there by green ribbons and partial patches of verdure where a watercourse divides or a swamp moistens the thirsty plain ; provided you have a good map and a good memory, what a prospect ! Near at hand below you is Tell Hum, "His City," Capernaum. Opposite the ruins of that memorable site, beyond the lake, steam in the sun the crags of Gadara, the region of the possessed swine ; of the demoniacs ; of the man in the tombs, who was "exceeding fierce." That small, verdant oasis of reeds, tamaracks, and

oleanders, with a few scattered palms, jutting into
the lake, is Bethsaida, the "house of fish," and
beyond it, where the ancient Roman road cuts deep
into the limestone rock, at yon cluster of huts lurks
El Mejdel, the village of Mary Magdalene. Think
only for a moment what the world owes to that one
parched, obscure, sand-buried Syrian hamlet, where
Mary of Mejdel was born, who came to be Christ's
nearest and most faithful of friends, and who heard
from His lips—alone among women, alone of all the
world—her own name spoken at the door of the
empty sepulchre by One who uttered it from the
farther side of the gateway of death, "Conqueror for
us of the unconquerable."

Beyond Bethsaida and El Mejdel, upon the western
border of the lake, opens the plain of Gennesaret,
where a spring of water renders cultivation possible ;
and then, southward still, among peaks and points,
amid which every rock has a record of surpassing
interest, you pass under the "Horns of Hattin,"
by the "Valley of the Doves," over the foot of the
"Mount of the Sermon." Yes, there above your
path on this green headland, where the crocus, the
anemone, and the amaryllis are alone left to tell of
it and to celebrate it, He pronounced those wonderful words which are the eternal code of Christian
ethics, the immortal pandects of man's highest
morality. There, amid those thorn bushes, armed
with the savage tricuspid spikes which were to
make His crown, and among the juniper clumps
creeping dark along the grass, and the deep green,

glossy nebbuk thickets, lit here and there with a
rosy gleam of oleander blossoms, He gave the whole
world that simple prayer to pray which makes us
the family of one Father, and which binds us all to
forgive trespasses as we ask to be forgiven.   There,
with His sacred lips, speaking the mild and holy
wisdom of heaven, He abolished those old, hard
laws of Mosaic hatred, revenge, and retaliation, and
substituted for them that guiding rule of life—
" golden " as the sunlight upon the lake, and just as
plain to see and follow—which is the earthly side
of " all the law and all the prophets," and which,
with love and fear of God, fulfils the whole duty of
existence.   There, amid those lilies and cyclamens,
He tenderly praised the matchless beauty of the
flowers, and lightly smiled at the want of faith
which fears lest the children of men be not so dear
to the Universe as the " grass of the field."   What
fane in all the world can be visited, what famous
site of ancient or modern annals, what sumptuous
cathedral, spacious palace, stately capital, or splendid
and powerful seat of lordship and wealth, where mind
and heart must become so enthralled and meditative
as here ; where the very camels seem to go wistfully,
swinging you up to the Mount of the Sermon, and you
draw the nose-string of your long-necked beast and
reverently dismount, that you may not presume to
ride where Christ the Lord has walked and taught,
and opened to all mankind the "light of the world ? "

A little way farther, among those rough but
wonderful pathways of Galilee, you shall come,

full of all these irresistible and potent recollections, to Cana, to the hamlet of the Miracle of the
Marriage, where a stream of thin crystal still trickles,
from which those drinking pots were doubtless
charged,

> Whose modest water saw the Lord and blushed.

Cana-El-Jelil is a well-authenticated spot lying
among the uplands of Nazareth, with a handful of
mean huts clustered near the rivulet, and a strip of
sloping ground painted gay with crocus and cycla-
men in the Syrian spring. From its border I remember plucking one of the purple blossoms, which I
afterward presented to a beautiful American lady on
her wedding-day with the accompaniment of these
verses—

> Only a flower ! but then it grew
>   On the green mountains which enring
> Cana-El-Jelil, looking to
>   The village and the little spring.
> The love that did those bridals bless
>   Soft upon yours this morning shine !
> Make happier all your happiness,
>   And turn its water into wine !

From Cana to Nazareth is only a step, and, indeed,
all the Holy Land is so small in its proportions, as
has been said, so condensed in its localities, so
minute and geographically insignificant in its areas
and distances, that it seems a mere handful of soil,
so to speak—the last corner in the world man
would have chosen to become the most memorable
and most important ! Yet every furlong of ground

F

hereabouts is richer with great reminiscences than hundreds of leagues elsewhere. You journey forward after leaving Cana, from the "hill of the Beatitudes" and the "rock of the feeding of the five thousand" to a sort of amphitheatre in these Galilean uplands, and there, suddenly—all white and small and silent, with its Church of the Annunciation, its monastery of Latin monks and its Fountain of the Virgin, where evening after evening Mary the Mother and her divine Son drew well-water together —is Nazareth. Old Quaresimus calls it "a rose set sweet within the green leaves of its encircling hills;" but that is pious flattery. It is a poor, small, whitewashed collection of mean, flat-topped houses, with tiny domes, and one steep, dirty, ill-kept street; yet is it nevertheless a spiritual metropolis of the earth, as you must feel when you stand inside the Church of the Annunciation and read the golden letters on the rock in the cave, "Hic Verbum Caro Factus Est"—"Here the Word was made flesh." There can hardly be a passage of travel so long or surely remembered as when, evening after evening, you walk down from the hill where the old city stood, to the Well, and know that you are treading in the daily steps of the "Carpenter's Son." When I was at Nazareth I purchased the seven acres of wild rock and ruins on that hill—the exact and certain spot where our Lord "opened the Book and read"—hoping to found a small hospital there; and at first my humble enterprise prospered. But the Greek and Latin monks quarrelled about it;

NAZARETH.

P. 82.

difficulties intervened, the sailing ship which carried the beds, fittings, and inscription-stone went down at sea. The project had to be abandoned. Latterly, however, it has been revived, with new hopes and efforts ; and just before leaving England last year, I agreed to make over the Sultan's firman, which I still held, to those who are again endeavouring to establish the "Katharine Arnold Hospital."

Then, onward from Nazareth, with Mount Carmel still towering on the right and standing grandly up from the sea, this intensely absorbing and un-equalled journey leads the traveller down the rugged slope from "His native city" into the plain of Es-draelon, over the brook Kishon, with such remarkable places as Nain, Shunem, Chesulloth, Megiddo occur-ring by the wayside, to King Ahab's country, to Jezreel and Gerizim and the regions of Samaria. There lives in my recollection a memorable ride I took hereabouts from the walls of Nablous, at the special request of Dean Stanley, my old tutor at Oxford, to visit and sketch the alleged tomb of Joshua. We got into temporary difficulties with the Moslems at that out-of-the-way spot for breaking off a twig of a tree growing by the tomb, which, they averred, was of miraculous character, moving itself once a year away from the structure in order to allow the walls to be newly whitewashed. A line of telegraph posts runs now-a-days between Mount Ebal and Mount Gerizim, under the gates of Nablous, and actually skirts the broken and scattered masonry of Jacob's Well, where our Lord talked with the woman of

Samaria.   All the way from Nazareth to Jerusalem
you follow—and must follow—the path trodden by
His feet whenever He went up to the Holy City,
the first sight of which from the hill Scopus, when
you have treaded the "Valley of the Robbers" and
the desolate stone country of the Prophet Samuel, is
more impressive, I think, than that of any other city
on the earth.

All along the road the sorrow-stricken and de-
serted land is so poor and depopulated, but its
name and fame so rich! There are not twenty
miles of good road where you can canter your Arab
horse from Damascus to the Mount of Olives; and
if it rains too hard to pitch tents, you must put
up every night in the squalid, bare huts of the
miserable peasantry, where the only furniture will
be a roll of bedding, a few brass and clay vessels, a
Koran in a silk bag, and a bottle of antimony, with
a pointed stick in it to blacken the under lids of
the women's eyes.   There is no exit for the smoke
of the fire lighted on the floor, except the low door;
and the cattle share the only apartment with the
family and their guests.   One side of a street in
Chicago would buy the fee-simple of all Palestine!
Yet at Nazareth, at Bethlehem, and on that first
view of the City of the Cross and the Passion, lying
under the fair slopes of Olivet, all fatigues, all hard-
ships fade from the wanderer's mind, and the bare,
hungry, neglected, ill-governed land seems proud
and rich, powerful and queenly, simply by possessing those sites and furnishing those scenes.

In Jerusalem itself you sleep, as it were, on the very lap of religious history, and breathe an air charged with imperishable, sacred recollections. Too probably it will be charged with a good deal of fever besides, from such places as the Pool of Hezekiah, by which your hotel will in all likelihood stand, and from other unsanitary but deeply interesting spots. For most pilgrims the interest of Palestine centres and culminates within the walls of Jerusalem, and truly wonderful it is to mark the deep fervour of adoration provoked among those crowds of poor and pious votaries from all nations, which gather in and around the Church of the Holy Sepulchre. There the irony of history is shown by the two strange and significant facts that, spite of the Crusades, the soldiers of the Sultan of Turkey guard its gates, and that not a Jew is ever permitted to enter them. Of course the precise localities pointed out in this edifice and near at hand are almost always fictitious. Nobody knows for certain a single spot connected with the trial and crucifixion of Christ, and probably great surface changes have effaced the features of most of them. But enough in and around the city has been spared to fill and feed the imagination. The Mount of Olives, Bethany, the Garden of Gethsemane, Kedron, the site of the Temple, the Pools of Bethesda and of Siloam, the road to Jericho and that to Bethlehem and Hebron, such are surely enough to satisfy, to saturate rather, the reasonable sojourner. For me, during

those never-to-be-forgotten days of residence in
Palestine, it was the city and the country itself, its
daily life, the scenes in its valleys, towns, and villages, its air and trees and creatures and landscapes,
which taught me most, and most occupied and enthralled me.

Meantime all this discursive and irrepressible retrospect springs from a question asked of me, whether I recollected any special incident of travel in
the Holy Land. I do, indeed, remember a curious
night passed there, full of solemn and far-reaching
thoughts, mingled with the most incongruous scenes
and pursuits. It was a night spent on the plain
of Jericho in shooting wild boar amid the company
of the Arabs of Er-Riha—that is to say, the "village
of the strong odour"—which place is, by the way,
very justly named. My sister and I had ridden
over the arid hills from Jerusalem to the Ghôr,
as the deep depression is called wherein lies the
Dead Sea. We took an escort of Turkish soldiers,
for the district was dangerous, and especially so
about that particular locality on our way where
"the man fell among thieves." From the brow of
the western range, where they locate the "Mount
of Temptation," you look into the deep, hot hollow
of the "Sea of Lot" (Bahr-Lut), and all over the
lower portion of the Jordan's course. The impetuous river, hastening to die, rushes through the
thickets of thorn and reed beds into the great,
still caldron of the brimming lake, and makes a
long line of whitish water where it enters the

thick and foul basin. Then it perishes, like everything else around. There is no exit for the lost
stream, which is sucked up by the hot sun as
fast as it enters, leaving in the scorched and
yellow hollow only that evil, sticky, poisonous,
but beautifully blue and placid sheet of stagnant
slime. The Dead Sea's borders nourish nothing
of either animal or vegetable life, but are fringed
with gaunt, dry, white trunks and branches of trees,
carried down by the Jordan, seared and salted by
the asphalt of the "Lake of Death."

If you bathe in it, as I did, you cannot sink,
albeit you may very likely float feet upward and head
beneath the sickly wave, unless you are a practised swimmer. The water—if such hell-broth may
claim that wholesome appellation—tastes like petroleum, lamp-oil and colocynth blended together.
When you emerge, it is to find your body crusted
all over with a salt deposit, which it is well to wash
off immediately by a good dip and swim in some
quiet part of the Jordan. In the full stream, however,
of that swift river no swimmer could live. I asked
one of my soldiers for what amount he would
ride across the swollen current, and he replied,
"Effendi! not for all the dollars of the Pacha of
Jerusalem!"

The surrounding scenery is not without a wild
and desolate beauty. Beyond the Sea of Death
the mountains of Moab present that fine, serrated
ridge called by Lamartine "*Une ligne droite tracée
par une main tremblante*," and in the changing

influences of sunrise and sunset show alternately
rose-pink, purple, blue and blood-red. The vast
plain of the Ghôr stretches from range to range,
apparently rich in vegetation and strangely pretty.
Nevertheless most of the foliage is of the dry glossy
nebbuk, the bush of barrenness, mingled with the
Dead Sea apple, a kind of thorn on the hideous
and acrid fruit of which the Arabs say the damned
in hell daily feed. Still there are springs and trick-
ling streams here and there, which render a sparse,
fitful cultivation possible ; and such occasional crops,
together with the natural roots and berries, bring
the wild pig to the spot, in quest of whom we were
to sally forth as soon as the moon rose, about 9 P.M.

I shall not easily forget that odd, savage, sleepless
night, between solemn hills that shut out Jerusalem
on the west and the dark rampart of the Moabitish
mountains on the east. I had become popular with
the Arabs by reason of having rebuked my Bashi-
Bazouks for tearing down the thorn fence of their
village to make a fire. I had compelled my armed
escort of rascals to pluck a camel-load of thorns and
repair the damage, and the desert people, unused
to justice, were anxious to show me good sport
with "the accursed beast." We sallied forth in
single file silently under the bright moonlight, and
brought up in an open space with the Arabs in
company and eight or ten mangy, prick-eared dogs,
which did not appear very likely to tackle such
boars as I had known in India. I carried a double
gun loaded with buckshot and my cook's green

handled knife in my belt. My dragoman had his sabre only, and the Arabs their matchlocks and spears. We squatted a long time on the sand, every dog receiving instantly a tremendous blow with a cudgel if he fought his fellows or barked, for it was to be essentially a still hunt.

"What do we wait for?" I presently asked, and the answer given was, "We are waiting for El-Nimr." This I supposed would prove some doughty hunter, styled "the Tiger" for his personal qualities, but it turned out to be a famous dog infallible at scenting and fighting pigs, which dog presently came up in the society of a master as ugly as himself. A one-eared, scarred, battered, cock-eyed mongrel cur it was, but El-Nimr knew his business thoroughly, and being by-and-bye ordered to seek for game, disappeared in the thick bushes, we silently following.

The method of the strange chase turned out to be this:—Everybody, including the dogs, had to attend patiently and respectfully upon "the Tiger," who again and again emerged from the cover, mute and wistful, without any results; but after two miles of wandering we heard a low yelp from him at a distance, and immediately all the other dogs sprang silently into the thicket, going off, *ventre à terre*, toward the sound. Soon El-Nimr raised a short, sharp howl of certainty, and my dragoman exclaimed, "Now we shall get wild pork!" The rest of the scratch pack joined hereupon in a hoarse uproar, making the wandering jackals yell and fly, and we

all ran hard in the direction of the clamour, to find
the centre of it a dense clump of prickly thorns and
nebbuk, where apparently a pig had taken refuge.
Animated by our approach, "the Tiger" went boldly
into the darkness, and soon forth into the moonlight
jumped the unhappy hog, which fell to an easy
double shot at close quarters from my gun. However, as nearly every Arab also blazed off his matchlock, and madly danced in the way of his fellows, I
saw there would be manslaughter as well as "wild
pork" if we continued such a loose, illegitimate
pastime, and therefore gave the word to go back
to camp, especially as we had already obtained a
pair of tusks and enough forbidden meat for all
the Christians in our camp. Needless to say, the
Arabs and Turks would not touch the unclean
creature, which nevertheless affords no bad food
when young.

On our way back to the encampment, El-Nimr had
three or four other *alertes*, one of which was due
to a roving jackal and the other to a wandering
Bedouin, probably bent on no honest errand, whom
we saved with difficulty from the dogs which had
encircled him. But the chief attraction of that
singular nocturnal chase was the scene itself. The
deadly pallid sheet of the Sea of Lot stretching away
to Petra and Egypt; the hills so full of history and
religion, this side and that; the dark patches of
bitter thorn glittering in the moonlight, with here
and there a whispering palm-tree standing high
among them, suggesting Zacchaeus and the days of

the journey to Jericho, with close at hand " Betha-
bara, beyond Jordan," and the very pool of the
ancient river quite near us, where our Lord Himself
underwent baptism. What a locality for a hunting
party ! We were too rugged and irregular a lot in
aspect to apply to us that verse—

> Oh, why so bold,
> In steel and gold,
> On the paths that Christ has trod ?

But it did seem ridiculous and well-nigh irreverent
to be chasing wild hogs over such a sporting ground.

Riding back next day to Jerusalem, we stayed to
lunch at the khan, built near the traditional spot
where the parable of the Good Samaritan had its
happening. There is a beautiful blue hyacinth with
small, dark blossoms which grows in early spring
along this dry, steep road, albeit it was too soon
in the year for the real lily of the Sermon of the
Mount, the scarlet martagon, which—

> Decks herself, still,
> Mindful of His high words, in red and gold,
> To meet the step of summer.

At the little spring near the khan an Arab of
good address and breeding sat down with us, and,
after salutations and a little talk, calmly offered to
buy my sister for his wife at the price of all his long
string of camels. The offer was meant kindly and
respectfully, but the lady, on being acquainted with
her conquest, abruptly declined it, whereupon the
young Sheikh gravely removed the silk and gold

rope from his haick and laid that small offering at the feet of the English "Sittina" who had charmed him. No, indeed! What with the wild pork and Arabs, and my would-be Bedawee brother-in-law, I shall never forget the time I passed at Jericho.

V

INDIAN PRINCES AT HOME

BEN BOOTHBY.

THE TANK, ULWAR PALACE.

P. 95.

V

INDIAN PRINCES AT HOME

THIS world we live in is becoming sadly monotonous as it shrinks year by year to smaller and
smaller apparent dimensions, under the rapid movement provided by transcontinental trains and swift
ocean steamships. Along with the ceaseless rush
of "civilisation" go also inevitably the ubiquitous
evening dress suit, the latest fashion plate from
Paris, the tall silk hat, and the other ugly things
which are so convenient because they are so universal. Costumes and ethnological variety are meantime vanishing before the face of such invasions
from the surface of the globe, and your fellow-
passenger in the Pullman palace car, or in the saloon
of the Cunarder, may be of any European or North
or South American country on the map, for anything
that can now-a-days be gathered from his attire.

The manners of all peoples are getting levelled
down to one dull, dead plane by the same agency,
and differences of language alone preserve a certain
lingering distinction. The graceful mantilla is being
silently abolished from Spain, and the pretty faldetta
from Italy, while even in Japan the city folk have
taken to red socks and wideawakes, and the ladies
think themselves out of the mode on public occasions

if they do not substitute the artificial "confections"
of Paris, London, and New York for the lovely and
always becoming kimono and obi.　Posterity more
and more is threatened with residence upon a dismal
orb, where everybody will wear one common style of
garment, will talk, think, and live in the same way,
so as to be at last as rigidly and dolefully like each
other as peas in a sack, or ants toiling and moiling
upon a log.

In Asia and Africa almost alone does the Old
World preserve something of its bygone rich and
refreshing variety of existence.　The custom, indeed,
of even dressing at all, except, perhaps, in brass
wire and beads, has yet to invade the greater part of
the "Dark Continent," where there accordingly pre-
vails a perfectly delightful dissimilarity of taste and
habit in the coiffure, in the loin aprons, and in fantastic methods of treating the ears, the nose, the lips,
and the limbs.

India is also a land where the increasing dreary
sameness of modern times and habits does not and
can not penetrate, or else is lost sight of in the vastness and picturesqueness of those antique Hindoo
societies.　As in the untouched portions of Japan,
you find all over the Indian peninsula that the
decrees of the great goddess of fashion are unknown
or powerless.　The people wear the beautiful and
seemly garments which their ancestors wore two
thousand years ago, unaltered in seam, or selvage,
or shape, but allowing an endless range of individual choice for tints, materials, richness of adorn-

ment, and charm of general effect. There men and
women, unlike ourselves, seem to clothe their bodies
as the flowers do, for innate joy of hue and grace of
good-fellowship and animation. A mob of Europeans or of Americans differs from a crowd of Asiatics
as a stubble of wheat, or a prairie grey and grim
with sage brush, differs from a bed of tulips or a
brightly-waving field of poppies and buttercups.
Looking, indeed, at the sombre garb and despondent
aspect of our crowded modern cities, one often sighs,
even in Anglo-Saxon communities, for a return to the
"peach-coloured satin coat with lace ruffles," of
which in good Queen Anne's time Oliver Goldsmith
was so prettily vain. To see popular gatherings alive
and brilliant with happy colours, and to find the
lost repose and delightfulness of daily life extant,
and visible, and placidly prized, one must wander
to-day among Indian cities and enter the precincts
of the temples of their gods and the courts of the
Hindoo princes. Let us, then, "come into the sun"
for a space, and realise a little the peaceful, glowing,
varied, and picturesque daily life in and around the
royal homes of India.

How an Indian city itself, and its everyday sights
and sounds under the continual and exhilarating
sunlight, would astonish some of this overdriven
American public! No tram-rails cut up the streets,
no importunate clang of the electric bell, no rush and
pelt and rattle of hack and cab and express waggon
or overloaded omnibus upon rugged paving-stones
jar the nerves. The very busiest street in Delhi,

G

Jeypore, Agra, or Poona is a perfect garden of repose
for its calm and quiet compared to the uproar and
diurnal fever of a byway in any third-rate American
town.   The unpaved sand or loam of the broad or
narrow passage between the shops and houses gives
back no echo to the footfall of the men, cattle, and
vehicles that traverse it.   They might be moving
flower-beds for their colour and their silence of soft
motion.   The men are all diversified with clean, becoming robes of white or grey, and with brilliant turbans surmounting their neat, cool attire—turbans of
purple, lilac, sky-blue, rose-red, green and amber—and
the women draw over their smooth black brows and
shapely shoulders *saris* of the loveliest contrasted and
blended tints imaginable, bordered with rich patterns and threaded with gold and silver embroidery,
or inlaid with little flashing plates of glass and
pearl shell.   The bare feet of the women and children and the sandals of the men and boys create
no noise and the sleepy, patient animals in the ox-
carts go up or down the highway with broad, noise-
less hoofs and light loads of sugar-cane, fodder, or
cotton, disturbing the long and warm midday lull
with nothing louder than the chafing of the wooden
yoke beam or the creak of an ungreased wheel.   The
babies astride upon the hips of their mothers never
cry, and never have anything to cry about.   The
boys, being, as they are, not Christians, but Hindoos,
never want to be noisy, devilish, or cruel, but always
go about their games or errands gravely and silently.
Here and there a group of friends newly met con-

verse in elevated tones of pleasure, and there is, perhaps, a wrangle somewhere about a doubtful bargain
or a little harmless quarrel over a bad eight-anna
piece, which ends, as it began, in words. But the
traders in the open shops never vociferate, and never
madly advertise their goods, nor put up rival state-
ments of supernatural cheapness, nor struggle fiercely
and perpetually one with the other for the almighty
dollar or its Asiatic equivalent. Placid and digni-
fied and self-contained, with the established habits
of thirty centuries, they squat alongside their goods,
not pushing their sale, seeing that what is wanted
will surely be asked for when "Allah wills" or
"Purshuram pleases;" and meantime, while calmly
awaiting customers, they smoke the drowsily-bub-
bling hookah or leisurely balance their accounts with
a reed pen, or upon the abacus.

There may be hundreds, nay thousands, perambu-
lating a long street like that of the lively and famous
Chandnichowk in Delhi or the Moti Bagh in Poona,
and yet withal not more uproar or hubbub than in
a retired nook of the Central Park at New York.
Nobody is in a hurry, and for everybody alike it is
quite enough prosperity merely to live under such a
glad, bright, existence-gilding sun, and amid so many
sweet and pleasing sights of surrounding nature.
For nature is everywhere present around and among
these Asiatic communities, not terrified out of contact by business and the noise and smoke of big
cities, as with us and you. In every corner the palm-
tree lifts its stately feathered head and sings a hymn

from its waving plumes to the cooling breeze; the
banana hangs her broad green flags over the white
house walls and window lattices.   The Indian convolvuli, great bells of blue and white, with the splendid
yellow lupins and the tender lilac and gold sprays
of the Bougainvilliers, adorn the very meanest huts;
and upon the roofs and ridge-poles thus beautified
the animals take part in the general city life.   There
will be as likely as not monkeys sitting upon many
a housetop.   The four-handed folk come in from the
jungles to squat upon the highest tiles, all talking
jungle gossip, to the disparagement, no doubt, of
their bimanous and over-busy kindred.

The little striped squirrels run up and down the
doorposts of the grain sellers' shop; the sacred cow
from the nearest temple wanders by each store of open
corn and pulse, putting her privileged muzzle into
the rice bags; the green parrots flash up and down
the mid-street with a lively clamour, and the great
black bats—the flying foxes—hang in hundreds by
their hooked wings from the bare fig-tree.   You
can hear, amid the full tide of the city's traffic, the
" swash " of the clothes being washed and beaten at
the tank, and the scream of the kites as they circle
round and round in the pale, clear sky overhead.
The loudest sounds in the long, thronged, lively but
peaceful street will be the *ekka* rumbling along on
two ponderous wheels with some merchant's family,
its oxen and its red curtains all covered with bells
which jingle not unmusically, or some half-naked
religious mendicant blowing his big copper trumpet

or beating his cymbals for alms. Peace—the sustained, philosophic, contemplative peace of Asia—
broods over the people and the place. Life has of
itself become a luxury in ceasing to be a task, a
mill-grind, a never-ending work and worry. Ah!
if I could only transport some of the nerve-weary
workers, men and women, whose intelligent faces
and kindly eyes I see amid these many splendid
cities of the United States, worn with the fever and
the rush of daily affairs, to the quiet of my Indian
cities and fields, how quickly I could give them back
again *la joie de vivre*, that lost calm and gladness of
the healthy human soul, which cures everything, and
is an earthly side of the " peace that passeth understanding."

Prominent among the buildings of the city are
the temples and the palaces. These simple Asiatics
neither possess nor desire—nor, indeed, need—the
countless large institutions which fill your cities
with imposing piles of architecture. They want
no town-hall, because the tank, the temple court,
and the market-place serve very well for all the
purposes of such an edifice under weather which
never betrays. They want no vast hotels, because
everybody lodges with his kinsfolk; and they want
no big hospitals, because the Government looks to
that; they need no insurance offices, banks, asylums,
or manufactories, because they insure good luck by
giving the gods a cake or two or some flowers; they
bank by melting their spare silver into ornaments for
wife and children; they take care of and tenderly

protect their own imbeciles and indigent, and they
make everything needful with their own fingers.
But the temple will probably be gay, stately, and
beautiful, and the palaces of the Maharajah will
be objects of pride and joy to the populace, and
often very sumptuous, indeed, outside as well as
inside.

We will leave the temples and mosques alone
to-day, and penetrate a little within those palace
walls (which everybody, be it understood, may not
very easily do, seeing that the interior life and
domestic surroundings of a Hindoo prince of high
rank are not usually open even to such energetic
curiosity as that of American interviewers).

Let the visit which we are to pay be in a city of
Rajpootana, say, a very interesting and typical region
of India, and let us choose the court of one of the
Rajpoot princes, the Maharajah of Ulwar, as a specimen for respectful inspection. His Highness Mangal
Singh, the " Lion Lord of Good Fortune," as the
name signifies (albeit the title has since been sadly
reversed), was one of the immensely far-descended
kings of the great Rajpoot country, who rule their
own chivalrous, gallant, and high-spirited people
under the suzerainty of Her Mightiness the Empress
Victoria, to whom he and all his royal kindred are
most loyally attached. The Maharajah Mangal Singh
is (this was in 1887) a Knight Commander of the
Star of India, a magnate always saluted with a pre-
scribed salvo of eleven guns whenever he visits the
Governor of the Presidency. He is a young man of

perhaps twenty-five years, of an olive complexion, with eyes dark and lustrous, features intensely refined and delicate in tint, and indeed presenting the ideal of a Hindoo prince to look upon—such as

COURTYARD OF THE PALACE, ULWAR.

Eugene Sue tried to depict in his Djalma of the "Mysteries of Paris." His ruling passions are horses, the chase and war; but the last of these is of course a luxury impossible to indulge in, unless indeed the Maharani might some day be pleased at

need to ask her faithful Rajpoots for aid, and then
Mangal Singh would love better than his life to take
the field against Russian, Frenchman, or anybody else,
at the head of a band of fearless, magnificent horsemen.

Notice, as we enter the walls of his inner town,
how the heavy gate doors, hundreds of years old,
are studded with six-inch long spikes of iron. That
is a relic of pre-scientific and old-world belligerency,
such as was prevalent in Asia when elephants were
always first sent forward to batter down the portals
of fortresses with their foreheads; and the only way
of preventing the great beasts from bursting in a
four-inch oak slab was to put a set of sharp spikes
upon it. Even elephants, it was found, soon had
enough of ramming a front door equipped in this
style. The Rajpoot soldiers at the entrance of the
palace precincts—dark warriors of an unmistakable
fighting breed—wear the leaf of Rama's tree for
their badge, which the god plucked from the Indian
jungle when he was starting forth to recover Sita
from Ravana, the Demon King of Ceylon. Along
the road leading to the palace front you may see
several hunting leopards lying on their bedsteads
lightly chained.

It is a favourite sport of the Prince and of his
fellow-rulers to pursue the black antelope with a
trained cheetah, and I have myself often witnessed
that strange and exciting kind of hunting. The
leopard is carried, in a condition of sharp hunger, to
the open deer-country upon a peasant's bullock-cart,
and when the antelopes are sighted the cart is care-

fully driven in a circle nearer and nearer to some fine buck with good long horns, until the animal is brought within reasonable distance. Then the hood is taken from the beast, whose savage eyes roam round and round the plain, and soon fasten upon the deer, by this time some four or five hundred yards away, and not in the least suspecting what looks like a simple country cart with its rural people bent upon agricultural pursuits. The leopard, set free, slides down like a ferret from his straw bed on the cart, and worms his way unseen through rocks and bushes, until he has drawn near enough in rear or flank of his victim for a final rush, which he makes like a lightning flash, generally surprising and seizing the paralysed buck before it can gather itself together for escape. If the deer manages to get away, the cheetah puts forth no further attempt to follow it, but sulks in the thicket and is very difficult to catch again.

But if it succeeds in striking down its prey, the hunters hurry up, and while dragging the growling, savage jaws away from the bleeding haunch or neck of the deer, they slip into the crimsoned mouth of the brute a fresh-cut joint of a goat or calf, and the leopard, thus deceived and pacified, is soon secured anew and placed upon the vehicle.

In the Rajah's grounds you will see these royal cheetahs and the men who have charge of them peacefully sleeping together on the same " charpoy," but, all the same, the beautiful hunting beasts are in their evil moods fearfully ill-tempered and dangerous. Farther on we shall come upon a rhinoceros

roped up to a stout post and munching cabbage.
He is the survivor of the old, bad practice of beast
fights, in which all the Rajpoot princes, like other
Indian potentates, indeed, and magnates, used to
indulge ; but the Ulwar Maharajah was too well
educated and enlightened for any strong taste
toward this.　He has abolished the custom indeed.
Here is, nevertheless, the bygone " Bestiarium "—
the *janwa-khana,* the place wherein many and many
a combat of jungle gladiators has been beforetimes
bloodily waged—rhinoceros and tiger, rhinoceros and
elephant, elephant with elephant, &c., as well as com-
bats between rams, stallions, and buffaloes.　There
are princes and rich Zemindars who even now delight
in such barbarous pastimes, and I know of one who,
on a certain festive occasion, fastened a note for a
thousand rupees to the tusk of a male elephant mad
with " must," and another on the horn of a wild bull
buffalo, and offered them as prizes to the daring horsemen who, after two or three perhaps of their rivals
had been gored to death, could secure the tempting
wealth.

The palace at Ulwar offers a good example of
Hindoo architecture of the florid and latter modern-
day kind.　There is a rich, ornamental frontal wall
with little cupolas over the gates, as well as upon
each corner, the exquisite shape of which is directly
borrowed from the curves assumed by the bamboo
when it is bent to form a roof.　Inside the wall,
pierced by a vaulted and coloured entrance arch,
spreads a court, flanked on the right and left hand by

halls open on one side, with rows of beautiful sculptured columns, and leading on the far side by broad and sweeping flights of marble steps to an inner and highly decorated gateway. Through this we shall make bold to pass into the palace proper —that is to say, the public chambers of it and the audience rooms (*diwan'khanas*), for the zenana, or women's quarter, is of course only for very privileged and feminine eyes — and albeit a hundred pair of them, lustrous and gem-like, may be secretly watching the strangers who tread these sequestered Indian apartments, the lattice from which they survey us will betray nothing of the inspection.

It is a pity that the Hindoos should have adopted from their Mohammedan conquerors the custom of secluding their women, but this is now a firmly-rooted habit, which the great ladies themselves do most to keep up. A *purdahnashin*, a "curtain-dweller," that is to say, or Hindoo woman of the higher classes, would not be seen out of doors, to save her life, except at religious ceremonies and in the marriage month. I have myself talked on important business with a Mahratta princess of whose august person I only discerned the points of the toes under the edge of an embroidered curtain ; and when I was staying with the resident physician at Jeypore, in Rajpootana, a curious thing occurred. He was the old and trusted friend of the Maharajah, and the chief queen being taken ill, he was sent for from his dinner-table ; but when he returned, he stated to us that he had been obliged to put his head into a

green baize bag before entering the zenana of his
friend the King, and to feel the pulse of his illustrious patient and apply the stethoscope to her in
the absurd embarrassment of such an envelope, without which he could not have passed into the women's
quarter of the palace, firm friend and adviser as he
was of all its inmates.

We may have the good fortune to see the little
Prince of the reigning house, the heir-apparent
of the ancient realm of Ulwar, walking with his
hammals and attendants, who will sweetly say,
though it is only early morning, "Good evening,
sir," in order to demonstrate at once his politeness
and his mastery of the English language. And we
may even have the honour to salute the Maharajah
himself, if we find him seated in his simple little
chamber of justice, which gives by a carved window
upon an outer garden full of orange and pomegranate
trees, to the sill whereof suppliants and suitors may
come from town and country to ask judgment and
succour from His Highness. Do you perhaps think
that only the West knows what true justice is?
Observe over the arch above the writing-table of
the young Maharajah that Persian verse which is
inscribed from the Bostan or "Garden" of Sadi, and
which says :—

> Oh, King, take heed unto the poor man's sigh ;
> Unheeded, it can climb and shake the sky.

If it be not too busy a day among his somewhat
litigious subjects with the youthful and energetic

ruler of the Ulwar State, he may very possibly himself show the favoured visitors some of the wonders of his royal abode. There is, for instance, the
Shish'mahal—that is to say, the "Hall of Mirrors"
—entirely lined with dazzling plaques and fragments
of coloured crystal, which reflect the bright entering
beams of the Indian sun with such burning and
variegated lustre that it seems an apartment carved
out of some mountain-side where the native rock is
full of jewels.

The Hindoos love light. Those triumphs of Western manufacture and gifts of Western science which
they most admire are not our noisy locomotive
engines and complex mill machinery, which are too
restless and hasteful for them, but chandeliers with
a great many branches, and coloured lamps with the
electric light shining among cut glass. Every Indian
palace is apt, indeed, to be almost too much enriched
and illuminated by such foreign importations, for the
usually sombre and cloistered construction of these
abodes of Eastern quiet and luxury is better suited
to the soft gleam of oil-wicks burning in those
brass lamps which the native artificer fashions so
skilfully in the shape of god or goddess, of coiled
serpent or couching tiger, of the sacred bird called
"Hansa," or of the lotus and moonflower. But
even in Rajpootana they will all have immense
glass chandeliers and dropping crystal lustres, of
which, therefore, these Ulwar halls are all found
full. In one of them was to be beheld a remarkable instance of lavish and costly expenditure. It

was a long dining-room table, capacious enough to
seat fifty guests, made entirely—top, frame, and
legs—from solid silver. There must be a ton or
more of the precious metal in this piece of apparent
ostentation, which is, of course, as an article of
furniture, foreign to Hindoo habits, since everybody
in India sits on the floor to eat, as also in Japan,
or, if any tables be used, they are of the small
Turkish and Arab kind, about the size of a low
music-stool. That is why, when we want dinner
removed in Hindostan, we say "Mez lejao," that is,
"Take away the table." Upon and down the highly
expensive "mahogany" of His Highness run two
broad slots or channels, in which, by some ingenious
clock-work contrivance, a crystal current is driven
perpetually along, carrying with it little fishes of
all colours, fashioned in jewels and enamelled. And
very pretty indeed it is to see these artificial shoals
glide along in the miniature rippled river, between
its mimic banks of glittering silver. It must be,
moreover, understood, before American severity of
taste too much condemns such a use of solid treasure
as that of my royal friend, that it is the habit all
over India to put what you here call "hard money"
into similar tangible and visible shape. I have
seen in Baroda, at the armoury of His Highness the
Guicowar, cannon cast in solid silver, seven and ten
pounders, with wheels and carriages all to match;
and whenever a Hindoo artisan or peasant possesses
any rupees to spare, he takes them down to the *sonar*
—the goldsmith—who melts them into a bracelet or

a bangle for the wrist or ankle of the man's wife or daughter.

If I could only paint for you the inner court of such a palace, with its walls and alcoves, its galleries and minarets, its terraces and pinnacles all gilded by the burning sun above and reflected below in the still waters of the tank that fills up the middle of the square, all my disengaged readers would want to go to that picturesque and brilliant country. Sometimes, remembering the mere "joy of life" that such scenes give, I wonder why we all bear to reside so many weary and cheerless years in the chilly latitudes of the Northern United States of America or of Great Britain. At the moment when I am writing, in this otherwise cheerful town of Dubuque, Iowa, a heavy snowstorm is whitening all the world around. The bitter wind screams, the stinging blizzard drives, the house doors are blocked with great wreaths of snow; and the pleasant city and goodly hills around about it, which I doubt not are very fair and bright in summer-time, look as if only Polar bears could be content to dwell in such a locality. But, of course, the colder regions of the world are its real workshops, and the nurseries of its dominant races; while it is only the dreamy religions and the deep philosophies—not petroleum and lumber and notions —which come from the sunny East. Still, I think, as science develops, and as the restless breed of man realises how great a delight lives in repose and in those zones of our globe where nature, being largest

and loveliest, lends her aid to that repose, the tropics
and the subtropics will more and more be filled with
emigrant people from the North and West. It may
be reserved for your own mighty community, when
you have filled up the Mississippi Valley with a
hundred millions of prosperous folk, and made all
your Western wildernesses laugh with the harvest
which wells and irrigation works can produce, to
take in hand and civilise, as we have done in India
and Africa, some of the beautiful countries of the
Amazon and Orinoco, and those too sadly wasted
wonderlands of the South American States which
are to-day swarmed over by naked Indians and
jaguars, or by quarrelsome little hybrid Spanish
races, not much more profitable or peaceful.

I said the Maharajah Mangal Singh loved horses,
and he can show us, not far from this stately white
marble palace under the hills, his superb stud of
2000 Arabs and Arab half-breeds, some of them such
lovely and shapely creatures as are scarcely to be
seen elsewhere. An Arab horse is an absolute luxury
to ride, its temper is so sweet, its endurance so great
and its pace so pleasant, thanks to the low, springy
pasterns, which give elasticity to its dancing gait.

But let us now come away from Rajpootana and
go on the wings of fancy to a very different district
—that of Bhaonagar, in the region of Kattiawar,
another independent State, where Takhtaji Singh
is the great and enlightened chief. It shall be
evening, and when the fireworks have all been
finished, to the boundless pleasure of the vast crowds

outside the gates of the palace, we will enter and sit in the royal circle of the Diwan-Khana watching a Nautch or native dance.

It is a scene, this, very typical of India, where no festival or great ceremony is complete without the quiet and composing pleasure of the dance. Not that furious, gymnastic exercise in which we Westerns, especially our feminine section, rejoice to indulge, but the high and grave and distinctly fine art of rhythmical movement, accommodated to the lightest and faintest notes of the strange, wild music of cymbal and sitar, and to a harmony and subtlety of line and pace and waving limbs and robes to which the best ballet in Paris, London, or New York offers but a coarse contrast. The Prince, wearing rich and costly jewels, with a light evening coat of green satin, sits cross-legged at the top of the hall, having his guests and great officers beside him or ranged along the walls. His gorgeously dressed attendants, standing behind the royal cushion, are fanning the warm evening air from each face, or noiselessly bringing refreshments and the fragrant pipe.

Then Zanoub, the Persian girl, or Radha, the Hindoo nautchni, takes her *pan-soopari* (the betel-nut) from her mouth, adjusts her ample draperies, fastens the scarlet pomegranate-flower tighter in her hair, and rises to her feet, while the drum and tamboora begin " Taza-ba-taza " or " Jan-i-man." Lowly does she salaam to the great personage; piously does she touch the silver bells fastened upon her bare feet with a prayer for favour and

H

success, for dancing is a serious and solemn matter
with these people. And then she softly becomes
a living embodiment of music and of the poesy of
motion ; dancing true scientific dances ; expressing
the very language—by gesture, gait, and eloquent
sway and wave of hand and foot and arm and
body—of that passionate or sorrowful Persian or
Guzerathi song, which she sings in a high falsetto,
full of minor keys and minutely divided notes. Perhaps you will not admire it until you understand
it and have studied its marvellous antique grace
and emotional significance. Perhaps the Western
man will prefer, after all he sees and hears, to
encircle a tight-laced waist, bound in fashionable
silk or satin, and whirl it round to the better comprehended strains of Strauss or Godfrey. But the
indolent passions of the Indian blood find their
delight in this measured, sober, refined and sooth-
ing *pas seul;* and all night long, as dancer after
dancer salaams and sits down, to be succeeded
by another and another and another, these statesmen, warriors, merchants, and pundits of the strange
Indian world will watch with undiminished interest
the slow, quiet, musical passages of the Nautch.

I remember, in the days of the great mutiny, when
a famous native regiment, the Twenty-fifth Native
Infantry of Bombay, marched back to our station
covered with glory for faithfully fighting their rebel
brethren, I was commissioned to ask the senior
jemadar what form of entertainment the men would
best like to accept from the ladies and gentlemen of

the station. The answer was a "Nautch;" and
when we had hired the most famous dancing-girls
of the district, and had pitched great *shamiana*
tents on the plain, and had laid in plenty of betel-
nut to chew, they wanted no more. All night
long those veteran soldiers, fresh from fierce and
bloody battles, sat in large rings of scores and
hundreds under the moonlight, wearing their fatigue
dress of white cotton, and watching the dancers,
while softly smoking their "pipes of peace." How
different are the races of men !

What would gratify most, no doubt, such gracious
ladies as may honour me by reading these sketchy
recollections, amid all the picturesque surroundings of Eastern royal life, would be, I think, those
various Tosha'khanas or treasure chambers of the
Indian courts. If I had time and space, I would
also like to describe to American sportsmen the way
in which the Indian princes hunt; and what splendid,
varied, and exciting pastime in this line is afforded
by the jungles of Hindostan, with the grand studs
of trained elephants which such princes possess ; as
well as the really magnificent sport of pig-sticking,
riding the grey wild boar down with the keen spear
upon a quick and intelligent Arab horse. But I
must be content here merely to mention the jewels
of one particular Eastern potentate which dwell in
my memory.

Some of the finest gems in the world are still
to be seen in those Tosha'khanas of the peninsula,
where they are greatly prized and carefully guarded.

Many of the best pearls from Ormuz or Ceylon, of the choicest pigeon-blood rubies from Burmah, emeralds of extraordinary size, carved with long inscriptions in Persian, Arabic, and Sanscrit, with delicate and costly enamels after the style of the master art of Jeypore, were stored in the royal collection which I inspected at Baroda in Guzerat. There were swords there whose hilts alone were worth a large estate, so richly were they crusted with costly stones, while the blades of some among them were of such fine and perfectly tempered steel as to be occasionally more valuable than the handles. Certain among the choicest blades had slots cut in the damasked steel, up and down which ran costly pearls or rubies cut to a round bead, and certain of them were thrust into spiral scabbards, so faultless were their spring and elasticity. The old Mahratta custodian would suddenly open some old marmalade jar or sardine-box taken from the great barred vault, and turn out of this unlikely receptacle, rolled up in an ancient red or green rag, such a belt of sapphires and diamonds, such a diadem of Oriental rubies, such a bracelet or anklet, or ring for the nose or finger, as must have made the eyes of any lady who had a proper and becoming passion for beautiful things sparkle like the jewels themselves.

On high public occasions the princes and magnates of India vie with each other in a dazzling and gorgeous display of gems, with which they repair on their elephants to durbars or receptions.

The native classical name for such lovely baubles is *santosha*, the Sanscrit word for "contentment," as if their wonderful beauty were calculated to fill ordinary hearts and minds quite to the brim. It is better, however, for such as are not millionaires to talk and think as little as possible about the gorgeous contents of those Indian treasure chambers. But if you are millionaires, Tiffany in Union Square, New York, or the shops of Bond Street, London, can show you jewels better set and cut than those of India, though not so large, ancient, and historical.

VI

LOVE AND MARRIAGE IN JAPAN

A JAPANESE DINNER.

VI

LOVE AND MARRIAGE IN JAPAN

I HAVE been taken to task in a good-tempered way by many critics in England and America for venturing, in my " Seas and Lands " and " Japonica," to call the Japanese women " semi-angelic." The expression is a strong one, and it is never safe to generalise or exaggerate, least of all about such a subject. But, upon sitting down to write this article about the women of Japan, I find that I have nothing to retract. Upon maturest reflection, bringing together into one focus all the specimens I know of Japanese womanhood, in all ranks and circumstances of life, in all degrees of education, in town and country alike, I am still inclined to believe that the average or abstract Japanese female comes, all things considered, nearest among her sex, as regards natural gifts, to what we understand by an angelical disposition. This, be it stated, is not advanced in any idea of comparison or contrast with her sisters in other parts of the world. I would as soon, in my capacity as a writer, speak disrespectfully of the Gulf Stream or the Equator, and expect to be forgiven, as imply any disparaging parallel between various national repre-

sentatives of the fair sex.   All I find myself obliged
to maintain is that, taking into account her surroundings, this daughter of the Land of the Rising
Sun might pass, I really believe, into a celestial state
of existence with very few changes of nature, manners, or heart; and find herself, and be found there,
quite at home.

Everybody who has become really acquainted with
good Japanese women agrees more or less with what
I here so daringly repeat; and among feminine
opinions there is no better witness to the pleasant
impression made upon kindly and intelligent minds
by them than the admirable little book lately published by Miss Alice Mabel Bacon, every statement
of which I believe to be as accurate as its style is
graceful and its purpose high.   The only people
who do not appear to appreciate the Japanese
women are the Japanese men, and, no doubt, this
ought at once to make us pause before we praise
them too highly, since their own husbands, fathers,
and brothers must know a great deal more of social
and domestic life in the country than the best-
informed foreigner can ever learn.   But I am inclined to believe it is really a case where the
gods have been far more beneficent to a people
than that people well understands.   Still, since we
encounter in Japan a general absence of reverence
to the sex, and a lack of almost all those finer and
higher feelings which have found expression with
ourselves in chivalry and the literature of civilised
love, it is natural to ask why outsiders alone should

become enthusiastic about the virtues and merits of Japanese women. From the point of view of physical beauty it is not to be pretended for a moment that the Japanese woman excels her Christian rivals. Seldom or never, indeed, does one see among them any example of perfect feminine beauty. Compared to their stately sisters of England and America they are what a delicate ivory carving is to a marble statue. They are nearly all very small, with short lower limbs, with a little nose pressed into the face, with sleepy, slant-lidded eyes, an almost ridiculous gait, and for the most part a very limited education and very narrow ideas. How, then, shall we analyse and define the secret of the charm which this unique specimen of her sex exercises over all appreciative and cultured minds when they approach and enter her sphere for the first time ? It lies, no doubt, in her moral rather than her intellectual or physical nature. She is, in point of fact, the most unselfish, the most self-denying, the most dutiful and the most patient woman in the world, as well as the most considerate and pleasing; and, as I truly believe, more faithful to her own limited and ancient but earnest ideal of rectitude than any other of her sisters among the nations. The civilisation, immensely antique and rigid, which has not, with all its changes, produced so very great a success in the Japanese man, has, while placing the Japanese woman in a deplorably unfair and subordinate position, brought out from her being, by some strange spell, all the social virtues of which her race is capable, and made her, even in her subjection, so gentle, winning, and admirable, that the boldest advocates of Japanese reform in education and national development tremble when they ask themselves whether civilisation and "woman's rights" may not take away more from this tranquil, contented, and delightful creature than it can ever give to her.

There can be no doubt that socially and civilly the position of the Japanese woman is low to the point of servitude. An American woman, who sits at the top of the human tree in regard to the rights and privileges of her sex, would indeed shudder with sympathy or redden with indignation if the full truth could be told about the situation of her Japanese sisters. Practically they have no personal rights from birth to death. They belong throughout, in theory and to a great degree in fact, to some man or other : first their father, next their eldest brother, afterwards their husband and his male relations. They hardly ever hold property, since the family is perpetuated along the male line only, and real and personal estates pass to the boys. They have little or no voice in choosing their husbands, yet take one they must before they are twenty years old ; but that husband, whom they have not wanted, has an almost unquestioned right to divorce his wife upon the smallest reason, or for none at all. There exists really no true check upon this except what resides in the force of the opinion of neighbours. Out of

500 marriages, 200 at least end in some sharp and capricious separation; for the husband can get rid of his wife on the ground of too much gossiping or because of disagreement with the mother-in-law; and the worst of it is that the children afterwards belong to him exclusively. That is one reason why these Japanese wives are so divinely patient. Too patient indeed, we should all here say; but there hangs over their heads that perpetual sword of Damocles, the fear of dismissal; and to maintain their position they must please their lords and masters. In point of fact, there is no marriage at all in Japan. There are ceremonies, presents, family dinner-parties, puttings on and off of pretty dresses; but the so-called nuptial alliance is a matter of domestic arrangement, and has simply no legal or civil force at all. When the *nakodo* or agent has arranged a match, and all has been settled between the two houses, the bride and bridegroom drink nine little cups of sakë together, and the bride's name is transferred at the registry office of the Ken from her father's abode to that of her husband's father, where she will henceforth become her lord's constant body-servant and the humble attendant of his mother, who might make life a hell for her, and only seldom does so simply because Japanese natures are so much better than Japanese systems; wherefore for the most part the little brown people get on very well together. But the father parts with his daughter for good and all at marriage, except so far as visits of affection and compliment go; and for this reason, as in most Oriental countries,

daughters cannot be so much valued in Japan as
sons. The daughter, dear as she may prove by her
amiability, will some day or other disappear entirely
from the domestic roof; while the son or sons are
a permanent investment, carefully brought up and
treasured by the Japanese father and mother, because,
as old age approaches, it is the regular thing for
the parents to give up the business and cares of life,
and to lead an easy time, maintained entirely by
their male children. This is everywhere an accepted rule. The merchant, farmer, or householder so
retiring is called " Go Inkyo," and is treated with
most unbroken respect and indulgence; for it is
one of the central virtues of Japan unboundedly to
reverence old age. We might almost indeed forgive the vast mischief that Confucius has wrought
for China, and indirectly for Japan, by his abominable
philosophy of Opportunism, when one sees everywhere
in the two countries this noble and tender deference
paid to grey hairs. Truly writes Miss Bacon : " To
the time-honoured European belief that a young man
must be independent and enterprising in early life
in order to lay by for old age, the Japanese will
answer that children in Japan are taught to love
their parents rather than ease and luxury, and that
care for the future is not the necessity that it is in
Europe and America, where money is above everything else—even filial love. This habit of thought
may account for the utter want of provision for the
future and the disregard for things pertaining to the
accumulation of wealth which often strikes curiously

the foreigner in Japan. A Japanese considers his provision for the future made when he has brought up and educated for usefulness a large family of children. He invests his capital in their support and education, secure of bountiful returns in their gratitude and care for his old age. It is hard for the men of old Japan to understand the rush and struggle for riches in America—a struggle that too often leaves not a pause for rest or quiet pleasure until sickness or death overtakes the indefatigable worker." The Japanese woman herself gets an immense benefit from it, for when she comes to be Obăsan, that is, " auntie," or Obâsan, which is "grandmamma," the hard part of her life is over, and she rests among her children, honoured and cared for, without complaint. On the whole, I am afraid that the two happiest periods in these gentle and self-denying lives are childhood and declining years.

The early years of the Japanese girl are, in truth, pleasant enough. Although not so welcome on her first appearance as her brothers are, she is sure to be dear both to father and mother: and in the latter of these she is equally sure to find a nurse and guardian truly " semi-angelic." She will be born into an atmosphere of gentleness, grace, and kindness, and after five or six weeks of infantile existence will pass into the outer world upon the back of some sister or little female servant, where she will learn insensibly to grow up like other Japanese babies, demure, restrained, silent, polite and self-respectful. When able to toddle about in her *geta* or *waragi*, she will never be slapped or put into a corner or told "not to do so and so." The sternest possible moral medicine of reproof will be administered to her with the sugar of gentle voices and tender faces, but at the same time she will be instructed daily and hourly in the duty of suppressing herself, and absolutely obeying her elders and betters, as well as of being ready on all occasions to sacrifice herself for the sake of others. Of course the English or American idea would be that abjectness must result from all this; but positively that is not at all the case. The Japanese woman, like the Japanese man, brings out of all such early education in a marked degree the virtues of self-respect, high spirit, and resolution; the fact being that she sees in all this the ideal of her duty, and that which ensues—the submission of her whole life to her father first, to her husband next, and then to her grown-up male children—is the willing and eager compliance with a duty, not the acceptance of a bond. Japanese history is full of the most heroic proofs of the nobleness of soul possessed by the women of the land, from the great queen who conquered Corea to the lovely Oto Tachibani Himë, who died by leaping into the sea to appease the tempest and save her husband the Emperor. In private life, also, the Japanese woman displays no qualities of the slave; she is steadfast and heroic in sickness, danger, or poverty. Always a lady, in whatever rank of life she may be born, she permits herself no expression of impatience or revolt, which would compromise her own ideal of the *Nihon no onna.* She can die as well and bravely as she can live; and often, at a crisis, recalls in her own simple way the example of Lucretia, of whom the poet says that in sinking to the ground she carefully arranged her garments, " ne non procumbat honeste."

Nor truly do the Japanese men show themselves so much demoralised by Confucius as openly to regard the female sex as inferior. The proof of that fact is here, that when a family contains only grown-up daughters, and is at the same time of high position, so that to preserve the name and estates of the line becomes important, it is the custom to adopt into the house a bridegroom for the eldest daughter, who takes her name and passes into almost the self-same position of subordination as does the ordinary Japanese wife. Such a young man is named Yoshi, and lives all his life completely under the thumb of his well-born wife and her mother and father. Moreover, no nation has ever yet been able to make slaves of its women. The function and mission of woman is to rule, not by outward symbols of authority, but by the far stronger and subtler control of the inner affairs of human life; and Voltaire was never so wise a philosopher as when he wrote under the " portrait d'une femme " at Versailles :

> Quiconque tu sois, voilà ton maître ;
> Elle est, elle fût, ou elle va être.

The Japanese woman, like all her sex everywhere, in dealing with the blundering laws of men, has

I

known how to take advantage of the deplorable legislation due to Konfutze, and to mould it into a state of things which furnishes her with an ideal, and leaves her free to rule the house, and to become in very many cases indispensable for it. But there is no denying the fact that they live from birth to death upon the good-will of those to whom they practically belong, while they owe the pleasures and the independences of their generally blameless existence to their own sweet, patient, and self-contained natures.

What has been said will help to show the American or English reader that there do not enter into the life of the Japanese girl any of those ideas of flirtation, love-making, courting and the rest of it which count for so much in a European or American girlhood. In the middle and lower classes she is fairly free to come and go, to see her friends, male and female, and to mingle with the gay crowds of holiday-makers in festivals and at Matsuri; but she will have so little to do with the choice of her husband that her light and gentle mind leaves the subject entirely alone. Nor is her physical nature in any degree whatever a passionate one. The Japanese temperament is too artistic, too measured, too tranquil, too constantly governed, for wild flights in direction of the desire or imagination; and I should be inclined to say that in actual bodily and spiritual nature the Japanese woman is one of the purest and most refined on earth. Nevertheless, it is not to be concealed that her views upon many questions

that are called "moral" would startle her civilised
sisters.   There are always two moralities, in truth—
the eternally established code of right and wrong
which makes fidelity of mind and purity of thought

A GEISHA.

eternally divine, and those more or less conventional
systems which different nations have constructed
in different ways, and which especially, and often
very stupidly, touch upon the details of the relations

between the sexes.   All depends upon the point
of view taken by each race, and it will go far to
help outside peoples to understand the Japanese
woman if they get firm hold of the fact that she
regards life and its conduct from a standing-place
wholly diverse from that of her English or American sister.   Physical honour is for these last the
supreme virtue, and all the perspective of their moral
landscape is more or less constructed with that for
the foreground.   Wholly otherwise is the view of
the Japanese maiden.   She looks at life from the
eminence of a perfectly ingrained loyalty, of an
obedience which she has trained herself to make
unquestioning ; and when these counsel her to face
any danger, to accept any dishonour, nay, to perpe-
trate any crime, she assents sooner than fail in devotion to father, husband, and family.   Naturally to the
last degree nice in her habits ; delicate, refined, and reserved ; she will not hesitate, and never has hesitated,
to sacrifice herself—as we should say—" body and
soul" to the dictate of this devotion and of these
duties.   That is, of course, a very exceptional necessity in Japanese families, but it does sometimes
arise ; and when it does arise, though the Japanese
woman is by nature as proud of her purity as the
little ermine which dies under the stroke of the
hunter rather than enter a refuge that has been
soiled, she sets utterly aside those dictates of chastity
which are imperative with us, and accepts conditions
of existence justly considered here improper and
repulsive.   Yet even these, be it said, cannot alter

the original elevation of her nature, and Japan presents the only examples known to my experience where women who would be called and thought " outcast " in any other country remain " ladies " in spite of leading a life of the lowest type. It is as if their placid souls passed through the mire and dust of depravity on some invisible *geta* like those that lift their little feet high out of the mud of the Tokyo streets during a rainstorm. To go deeply into such a subject is, however, not possible for me in these pages. For myself, if I have sometimes bitterly said that the Japanese men do not deserve from their gods the splendid gift of the Japanese women, it is when my mind has been full of incidents like the above; yet, precious as are the qualities of the sex in that gentle and pleasant land, I would rather see Japan again wildly revolutionised, and all her old manners disappearing before the waves of our modern civilisation, than that the system should continue which year by year immolates these high-hearted victims.

If anybody wants to know how deeply the motive of such self-surrender is blended into the thoughts of the nation, he should read the story of The Loyal Ronins, told in Mitford and summarised by Miss Bacon in her admirable book.

From our point of view, it seems indeed absolutely discreditable that a noble family like that described in this ancient tale could possibly consent to such domestic infamy; but what I have written above, and what Miss Bacon says as well, must be borne in mind, that the point of view in their moral landscape is wholly different to ours ; that enormous value is attached to fidelity of soul and comparatively little, except as its token and touchstone, to fidelity of body ; and that the father looks upon his daughter as something born to serve him, and eventually to pass from his hands into the possession of others, without his retaining any except the slightest hold upon her. Positively, the self-dedication of children to parents is so complete in Japan, as also in China, that the wholesale acceptance of it by the daughter, as well as by the son, naturally tends to draw the father into taking the execution of it for granted to the fullest extent and the farthest point. The Japanese unmarried girl in the middle and lower classes makes all the clothes for her parents, sweeps and cleans the house, cooks the food and waits at meals ; and many of these acts are still performed out of tender filial feeling even in the houses of the upper classes. The odd thing is, that this devotion is not accompanied by any particular personal respect, apart from the universal decorum and etiquette of Japanese domestic life. I have seen a Tokyo girl who would have done all that has been alluded to for the sake of her aged father, send him out in the rain to buy fish and rice ; and it cannot be too often repeated, in order to understand the Japanese moral code, that it is with the children an ingrained standard of action which has to be and must be observed, rather than that personal passion of affection which springs up in our households and might prompt English or

American girls to any and every filial service that was not dishonourable. Let me add that among most of the educated and respectable Japanese, especially in the families of noblemen and ex-samurai, the feelings that we ourselves experience of horror and disgust at the selfish complaisance of parents are largely shared, while the public sentiment daily grows in Japan which condemns, and will eventually, let us hope, abolish the possibilities of such a perversion of one of the noblest of human virtues. Curious it is also to notice how this intense devotion of the children thrives in an atmosphere uncheered by any of those signs and tokens of parental love to which we are accustomed. Children are embraced ; never grown-up daughters. But then it is to be understood that Japanese affection is wholly undemonstrative. In that land, even with lovers there are no hand-shakings, no ordinary tender expressions, no caresses. Kissing is as unknown in Japan as waltzing ; and is thought, indeed, when witnessed among Europeans, to be a very animal and low-minded way of express-ing attachment. You might intimately know a dear friend of either sex in the land of Japan for twenty years without once touching them, and perhaps it is this singular, universal immunity from bodily contact which helps to keep alive the proud and sustained reserve of the Japanese woman as regards her person. Let it be added, that the habit of fidelity and devotion thus cultivated toward parents passes into the mind of the Japanese woman and characterises all her social relations. She is naturally and by education the most faithful creature imaginable. No infidelity on the part of her husband or her lover leads her, for the sake of revenge or despair, to imitate the evil example. A breach of duty on her part as a wife is really almost unknown, and she will extend the same habitual and established faithfulness to relations less binding than those sanctioned by such marriage forms as do exist in Japan. So long as she is well treated and not perforce obliged to look for the necessities of life elsewhere, she makes it a point of honour to maintain her part of any temporary and irregular alliance, and so long as she can possibly put up with bad conduct on the part of him who ought to be equally faithful to her, she tries to meet every vexation with patience and silence, uttering with gentlest lips the constantly heard phrases : " *Damatte*," or " *Shikata ga nai*."

There are many who think that the spread of education will put right what is wrong at present in the social and civil life of these quiet and dutiful beings. Just now, it is not very much that the average Japanese woman knows, although schools and colleges are everywhere increasing. They learn to write in *Katakana* and *Hiragana*, and acquire enough of the Chinese characters to read the signs on the shops and the commoner phrases used in correspondence. Then, also, most of them master the strings of the samisen and kôto, and perhaps learn the arts of arranging flowers, of keeping accounts, of the special etiquettes of social existence, and above all, needlework. They make, unmake,

and remake all their own clothes; and that is about
the only form of property which the Japanese woman
generally owns. Fashions never change in the
country, and since a girl gets at her marriage a
complete outfit from her family, augmented by presents from her husband, she is provided to the end
of her existence with materials for unpicking and
remaking. Almost the only occupations which a
woman can take up with are those of dressmaking
and teaching, but for the last she must have passed
through some of the new schools and colleges, which
teach Eastern and Western learning together, to the
sad fatigue of many a youthful feminine pupil, who
brings home at night from them a headache as heavy
as the books that her musumë carries. Moreover, it
is a fact not to be denied, that this foreign education
does affect in a rather disastrous way the graceful
manners of the girls; and whether it be desirable or
not, you can always tell the scholars of a missionary
school, or Daigakko, by some slight lack of that
perfect grace and ancient decorum which is observ-
able in the unsophisticated Japanese maiden. This
new education, it may be added, too often produces
discontent without providing any way of allaying it.
The instructed Japanese girl knows too much to be
contented any longer with her career, and yet is
utterly unable to find any means of obtaining the
independence that could alone rescue her from it.
As matters stand, it is safe to say that she does not
gain as much from Western learning as she loses in
regard of old-world tranquillity and sweetness of

manner, with that soft acquiescence in the traditional
state of things which made her pass this life on the
whole so easily, from the hour of the *miya maèri*, when
she went first into the temple as a baby, to the hour
when they burn her cream-white little body and nothing is left of the gentlest of human creatures except
a handful of grey ashes. There is another sort of
education, however, which does great good, and that
is the presence and the frequent society of English
and American ladies, who, I have always thought,
as wives of missionaries or as residents of the land,
effect more solid amelioration than all the sermons
and all the school-classes put together. In meeting
the best of these, the Japanese girl sees for herself
how perfect freedom may go with grace, goodness of
heart, and humility ; and in such sweet instances she
sees also how the European or American husband
can preserve towards his wife a chivalrous submission and a daily tender attention without forfeiting
his manliness or the natural rights of his sex. This
influence is working steadily for good on the minds
of the people, and it is a curious illustration of it
that a Japanese gentleman in European dress behaves
in public with much more regard and politeness to his
Japanese wife than when they both wear the native
costume. Still, it was no farther back than the 11th of
February 1889, that the Emperor for the first time
made his progress through the streets of the capital
with the astounding sight of the Empress riding in
the same carriage. And even his Majesty, enlightened
and progressive as he is, when I had the honour of

being present at the imperial garden-party last year, came upon the lawn where the ambassadors and invited guests were waiting his appearance, not arm in arm with his august consort, but preceding her by many steps.   Let me pay the tribute of an admiring sentence to that smallest and sweetest-natured of all Japanese women, the good and patriotic Empress.   Childless and disappointed, and doomed to see the diadem of Japan pass to the offspring of another who is not married to the Emperor, even as Japanese marriages go, she has taken the whole country to her motherly heart, and is as true and dutiful an Empress as she is a tender and faithful wife to her august lord.

Japanese legislation is slowly seeking to do more justice to Japanese women.   A law has been passed making it impossible for the son of a concubine to succeed to a noble title, and that will apply in future to the imperial household itself.   Another law has been established granting to wives the right of claiming a divorce ; but this, in the nature of things, will almost never be availed of, because there is literally no future in ninety-nine cases out of a hundred for the woman who should act upon it. Outside the law, nevertheless, public opinion is a considerable force in Japan, and it is this more than any statute which at present in many ways protects the Japanese wife from too great wrong.   A man who capriciously turns his wife away, or is unkind or violent to her (a thing, to tell the truth, almost unknown in the country), will find his neighbours and friends making things decidedly hot and unpleasant for him.

Side by side with education many foreign friends of Japan rely upon the spread of Christianity in the country. No doubt, as far as it does spread, it carries with it ideas of woman's rights and woman's true mission immeasurably higher than those which Confucianism has promulgated far and wide in Mongolian Asia. Eventually I hope it will win a great, if gradual, social victory on this ground, but as a creed J believe it will find the necessity of amalgamating much of the Buddhism which it sees occupying nine-tenths of the area of Japan. There is nothing to my mind fundamentally hostile between Christianity and Buddhism, nor do I think it impossible that Christianity may do what Buddhism itself did when it first entered Japan, and take possession of the hearts of the people by silently adopting many of their national ideas. Shintoism, the religion of the Emperor and the court, is not a religion at all, but a cult of ancestors derived from the ancient nature-worship of the land. The Japanese people themselves are, in matters of theology, the lightest-hearted in the world. Their religion has been well defined as " a mixture of fun and fear," but the women are, all the same, sincerely pious, and there is no Japanese home without proofs of this ; while one sees in the streets the laughing musumë, the gaily-attired geisha, and the hard working coolie woman stop all alike at the gate of the temple, to enter, to pull the altar bell, to mutter the little devout prayer, with closed eyes and head bent down, and then to drop into the temple chest the hard-earned coin, while the small palms are clapped together to let Heaven know that its "honourable attention" is no longer requested. Certainly, if missionaries only knew how to be enlightened and adaptive, there could be no richer or better soil to cultivate than that of all these simple, sweet, and impressionable hearts.

One point in which the Japanese women are above and beyond all their Christian teachers is in the tender regard they pay to their dead, and in the ceremonies, full of a strong and sublime faith in the future life, which they make at their graves. One of the duties of the Japanese wife and daughter, never neglected, is to visit from time to time the tombs of her husband's ancestors or of her own parents, and to place there fresh branches of the pure *sakaki*, and to see that the little resting-places are kept neat and clean. Nor has any religious teacher, however exalted, a single page or line of any lesson to teach the Japanese woman about the perfect fulfilment of her duty to her children or to her parents. There is no Western lady who might not rather take example by the ceaseless grace of these domestic relations. Never do the Japanese children leave or return to the house, in any rank of life, without prostrating themselves before the tender mother, and softly asking permission of absence, " O itôma." Never does she return, but all the

children and servants throng to the threshold, and
with foreheads upon the mats and soft ejaculations
of welcome, salute the " O kaeri," the "honourable re-arrival." It is to the mothers that is due
the passing onwards from generation to generation
of that gentle inheritance of Japanese good manners,
and for the most part the children repay this rich
affection. There is almost no end to the indulgence
with which they are treated. The story is told of a
sick girl who had the passion to give a garden-party
under cherry blossoms in the month of December,
and rather than disappoint her wild wish, the father
and mother hired artificers to cover the branches
of the bare trees in the garden with innumerable
delicate blossoms of pink and white tissue-paper,
so that the wilful girl might carry out her fantastic
purpose.

That which would most of all make the Japanese
woman mistress in a larger degree of her destiny,
and perhaps bring this about without spoiling the
matchless charm of her devotion, her self-denial, her
inexhaustible grace, her endless delicacy of speech
and act and bearing, would be to reform the laws of
property in her favour. If there were a statute, as
exists in France, obliging the father, under certain
proper conditions, to provide for his daughter as
well as his son, we should see a large number of
Japanese women made independent of the vicissitudes of life, and soon a new state of things would
arise. If, again, it were possible to extend to Japan
the movement which in England and America has

LOVE AND MARRIAGE IN JAPAN   143

provided so many women with honourable and lucra-
tive employments in public and private offices, that
also would open a wide door for the escape of many
a gentle Japanese maid from the stern necessity that
confronts her now of marrying without love, and
depending all through her life upon her father, her
husband, and her children.

All comes to this, therefore, that in larger and
more generous laws respecting the endowment of
female children, and in the opening up of new fields
of employment to the sex in general, seem to dawn
the best hopes of justice for the Japanese woman.
But even while one breathes such aspirations of
change and new times for her, a chilling fear comes
upon the mind lest, in touching with the coarse
hand of Western civilisation that consummate pro-
duct of the isolated faiths and systems of Japan,
we find spoiled for ever the old-world charms of
her nature, and see depart beyond recall virtues
and qualities never to be replaced, as they have
never been surpassed. This same Japanese woman,
with all her shortcomings, ignorances, littlenesses,
and absurdities, is like the brilliant and flower-
loving butterfly whose existence she often imitates.
One rash touch upon the light and glad wing
leaves her still flying, perhaps, but may destroy the
dainty delicacy of that jewelled embroidery upon
its delicate vans. On the whole, she has been up
till now very placidly happy, like her mothers and
grandmothers before her, and that is more than I
quite dare to predict for her daughters and grand-

daughters, when, as seems inevitable, all around her must alter, and new times bring her new manners, while in her astonished little ears "the great world spins for ever down the ringing grooves of change."

THE EMPEROR OF JAPAN.

VII

JAPANESE WRESTLERS

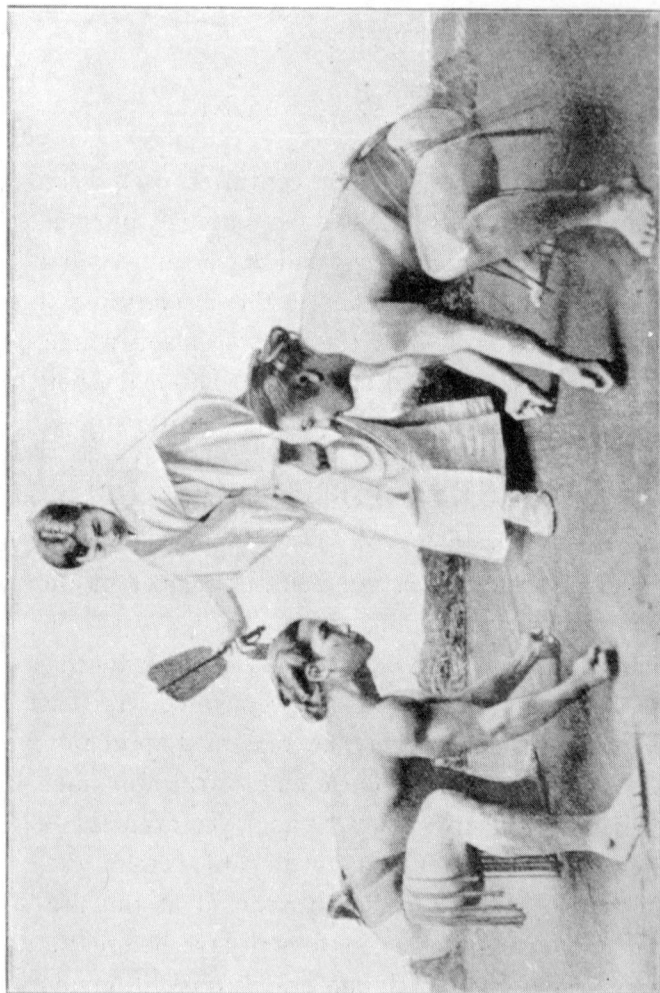

JAPANESE WRESTLERS.

P. 147.

VII

JAPANESE WRESTLERS

WRESTLING in Japan has, for centuries past, been cultivated as a high athletic science, seriously pursued by a large professional class, and extremely popular throughout the Empire. This is the special time of year when, and Tokyo is the central place where, the chief annual exhibition of the national sport comes off; and thus, for more than a week past, nothing has been talked about so much as the great contest going forward between the champions of the Eastern and Western side of " Dai Nippon " at Ekoin. Ekoin is in a north-western central quarter of the vast Japanese capital, and there, twice a year, the all important *Sumo Banzuke*, or wrestling tourna-ments, are held. The number of registered wrestlers —*sumotori*—in Japan may be reckoned, probably, by thousands, but only picked and certificated men are privileged to appear at Ekoin; yet even these, on the present occasion, amount to no less than 371. Their status has been solemnly decided at the pre-ceding January contest, and, a few days before the summer trials, long catalogues are published, giving the names of the combatants in the rank settled by the elders of the Wrestlers' Guild. These catalogues also arrange and notify in what order the contestants shall be coupled, although a certain element of chance enters into that. The professional status of each man remains fixed hereby until January next, when he will be promoted or degraded in accordance with the prowess displayed during the present exciting days.

Exciting, indeed, they are ; for no Derby Day at Epsom, no University Boat Race, no Waterloo Coursing Cup awakens at home more widespread interest than this prolonged encounter of the West and East in Japan. Everybody has his favourite side, everybody marks his list of cherished champions ; and during the *Banzuke*, on all the fine days, the Ginza and Nihombashi roads are thronged with jinrikshas trundling down to the scene of action. On the fine days only, because just at this part of the year the *ume-no-ame*, or "rains of the ripening plum," are frequent, and the management wisely notify that they will only open the wrestling theatre when the weather is good. The funds of the great association are maintained from the show, and it is therefore necessary to utilise thoroughly its popularity. Twice, accordingly, this past week, the "Garden" has been closed ; but we have had several brilliant days of sport, despite the weather, and metropolitan enthusiasm is just now at its height, since the time has come for the deciding matches. It would hardly be tolerated if I should inflict on the British public a complete catalogue of these Tokyo *lutteurs*, but, for a sample of the titles which they bear, the couples of the first class shall be here appended. They stand as follows :—

WRESTLERS OF THE FIRST RANK.

	East.	West.
National Champion .	Nishinoumi .	—
Champions . .	Konishiki .	Yawatayama.
1st Sub-Champions .	Hibikimasu .	Otohira.
2nd Sub-Champions .	Ichinoya .	Tanino-oto.
1st	Asashio . .	Wakaminato.
2nd	Hokkai . .	Onigatani.
3rd	Datenoya .	Tomonohira.
4th	Dewanoumi .	Hiranoto.
5th	Imaizumi .	Shitenryu.
6th	Chitosegawa .	Ozutsu.
7th	Odate . .	Shinrlki.
8th	Takanoto .	Onigake.
9th	Sotonoumi .	Chiyenoya.
10th	Orochigata .	Hibikiya.
	Ayanami †	Tsurugizan. †

The Japanese ring-names for the first four are respectively Yokozuna, Ozeki, Sekiwaki, and Komusubi —all technical appellations. Yokozuna, for example, means the "wearer of the Emperor's belt." The athletes with a mark to their titles were ill at the last match, and hold their high rank provisionally. The Eastern "crack" Nishinoumi has no compeer, being champion; and the first on the Western list, Yawatayama, has been absent, having sprained one of his mighty arms. These names, so strange to your eyes, with scores of others like them, are as familiar to Tokyoites as those of Orme and Flyaway at home; and, if you would know what true "fame" is, you should listen just now to the talk in the tea-houses and 'riksha-stands about Nishinoumi and Otohira and Ozutsu. These and Konishiki, who fight with Nishinoumi for the East, are the four chief favourites.

Very grave and firmly-established are the rules of the Japanese wrestling ring, and not the slightest departure is permitted from them by the judges or the public. There are forty-eight legalised "falls," divided into classes of twelve each. One encounter, unless a draw occur, settles each combat. The regulations as to where, when, and how each man may "clinch" the other are sternly laid down, and the language of the wrestling garden is, in every particular, as clear, positive, and authoritative as the Code Napoléon. The professional wrestlers are a class apart, albeit drawn from all ranks and localities. They are selected for their bulk and muscle; and amid a people so nationally small as the Japanese, the average *sumo-tori* towers like a giant, and swaggers through the crowd like an orange junk among a fleet of fishing sampans. They live like "fighting-cocks"—being huge feeders and drinkers, whom a wire-drawn British pugilist would indeed batter into breathless helplessness in a round or two; but the same skilled pugilist, if clasped in the ponderous embrace of Nishinoumi or Konishiki, would feel like a filbert in a nutcracker. They have patrons who train and feed them, and when they have once taken a good rank in the Tokyo *Sumo Banzuke*, they fill up the year by "starring" in the provinces at local matches. Like all their race, they are, for the most part, good-tempered and honest Titans, who wish to win, but seem to have no desire to do it by cruel or unfair means, albeit there are times and situations when the victor, if he likes, can easily kill

his man.   I myself saw a leg broken in an encounter,
but it was obviously by accident.   The major portion
of the bouts seems to be decided chiefly by sheer
weight ; for, as has been remarked, the men cultivate
flesh, and even fat, to the point of vast obesity; but
there is displayed a great deal of solid and educated
skill besides, and one of the most adroit and successful of the Eastern representatives, Katsuhira
—who in my sight hurled over his knee a colossus
of flesh and bone—was quite a small man, with
muscles of living steel under his smooth brown
skin, and little hands and feet which might have
become a fashionable lady, concealing enormous
strength.

But now let us repair to the Ekoin, and see
how the great bi-annual tournament of the *Sumo
Banzuke* is carried on.   Whirling through a maze
of busy Asiatic streets, behind the twinkling legs
of our "*kurumaya-san*," we reach at last the scene
of action, easily known by thousands of fluttering
flags on all sides and the concourse of bare-headed,
bare-legged Japanese thronging to the entrance.
This is up a narrow lane, where in England nothing
but a large force of police could preserve any
order ; but the Japanese holiday public polices itself.
Everybody is good-tempered, smiling, and willing
to be jostled ; and even if pushed into the tray of
fried bean-cakes, or upon the pan of sizzling star-
fish, is readily comforted by a " Go busata " or a
" Go men nasai."   No carriages could well approach,
and there are no regulations for any, but my riksha-

man dexterously thrusts his vehicle in between the
stall of an *ameya* blowing sugar-birds out of paste
and the shop of a dealer in flags and lamps, and
promising the obliging tradesman a penny—two *sen*
—for taking care of it, passes in with me to the
arena. This is at once the most democratic and
the most conservative land in the globe. The
good fellow, who has pulled me five miles at the
speed of a trotting pony, takes his seat on the
mats in my box with as good a decorum and as
just a self-regard as anybody, and having assumed
charge of my boots and placed at my side the tobacco-
box and the "honourable tea," proceeds to read to
me from the Chinese characters the programme of
the afternoon, with many enlightening comments.

The building, if it can so be called, is a vast
improvised circular structure of pine stems and
bamboos, roofed with cotton cloths, and walled
with the same. Its countless tiers of rude seats rise
interminably one above another from the wrestling
stage in the middle. This is the most carefully
constructed feature of the edifice—a low, circular
floor, strewed thickly with fine black dust, and
surrounded by a ridge of rice-bags, firmly fastened in
their places. At four points of its circumference rise
as many poles, bound round with different coloured
cotton cloth, and under each sits an umpire—-one
for north, south, east, and west respectively—very
correctly attired in high-class Japanese fashion,
with *hakama*, *kimono*, *obi*, and all the rest. The
wrestling-ring measures about fifteen or sixteen feet

in diameter, inside the rice-bags ; and there are two
other officials seen within its sacred limits, the umpire
and the herald.   Both are attired in the ancient
Nippon style of a *Samurai*, with projecting shoulder-
pieces, hair tied back in a cue, and fans with long
strings of purple silk.   Round the ring, on the floor
of the building, which is perhaps a foot or eighteen
inches lower than the ring, you see squatted a dozen
or fifteen nearly naked men, of immense bulk in
body and limbs, who are the next batch of combatants.   Scattered about the circles of expectant
people you may discern a good many more of the
same sort, distinguishable by their topknots and
their huge size; but these, as being for the time
spectators, wear the *yukata*, an ordinary bathing-
dress of stamped cotton, over their brawny frames.
The place will hold 4000 people, and is full almost
to the fluttering green and purple cloths of the roof.
If we should have a really business-like earthquake
just now to shake down the massive beams of fir
above our heads, there is here the precise arrangement for such a sweeping catastrophe as might
almost get into history.   But nobody thinks of that.
There are very few women present, since it is not
the "mode" for the female sex to assist at such
spectacles, though you may note here and there the
wife or mother of a champion, or some family party
comprising a Japanese lady or two.   There is,
however, plenty of the Japanese *beau monde.*
Here may be recognised to-day, for example, the
two Princes Tokugawa and Konoye near the stage,

with the Marquis Date, and there, opposite, Count
Tsugaru, with many of our foreign notabilities.
Everybody smokes; everybody reads the list of
the champions, if they only know the crabbed
Chinese characters. A placid chatter fills the
huge interior, mingled with the cries of the
"tea-boys," "*Yoroshii? yoroshii gozaimas?*"—"Is
it well?" "Are you all served?" Empty lunch
boxes go out and full ones come in from the neighbouring tea-houses; 4000 painted fans flutter in the
hot afternoon air, and four little light-blue tangles of
smoke curl upwards from the pipes of the four um-
pires sitting cross-legged upon their silken cushions.

But see! The umpire reads from a long roll
upon a red stick the names of the successive
couples who will next contend before us, and then
the herald, in a high theatrical voice, proclaims
the style and title of the forthcoming pair. This
official is known as the *yobi-dashi*, or "caller-forth;"
and, as his loud-pitched falsetto terminates, two
massive athletes step from below upon the stage,
slightly raised above the floor of the hall. They
ascend from opposite sides, for one half of the
building and of the arena is for the East, the other
for the West, and in the contests there is always a
Western and an Eastern man. Two of the same
party are never matched at Ekoin. Each champion is stark naked, save for a linen rag and a
black silk girdle, from which hangs a fringe of
silk cords, much resembling that of leather worn
by the women of Upper Egypt. Each, as he

slowly and ponderously mounts the platform and
steps within the rice-bags, turns his face round to
his own side of "the house," and, stretching his
left leg high and far into the air, brings down that
foot with a thud upon the earth, smites a resound-
ing blow with the flat of his palm on his squared
thigh, stretches forth the right leg in balance,
slaps that also, and then, without deigning a glance
at his adversary, who is going through the same
performance behind him, stalks to his corner, wets
his lips with water, rubs his mouth with salt,
brushes off the sweat from his arms and breast
with a square of paper, spits, and swaggers to his
place over against his opponent. As they confront
each other, each man squats down upon his heels,
letting his huge dark carcass descend upon the
elastic muscles and ligaments of thigh and calf with
a resilient movement, like a barouche settling upon
its springs. Upon this the umpire, in an ancient
costume of green and gold and purple, with fan
in hand, and hair dressed "to the nines," after
the old *Samurai* manner, approaches, nicely
measures the distance of his men, and, standing
with his white stockings astride, levels his fan,
and says, "Proceed." The two brown giants lean
forward on their hands, now like two gamecocks,
pitted almost nose to nose, and, with eyes fixed
eagerly upon eyes, watch each other. The inflexible
rule is that the "clinch" must be made simultaneously. Neither must get the better of either
by any premature motion, and thus, when you

hear a yell and see the giants fly at each other, you are at first disappointed to find that after all, time upon time, it is "no start." One or the other will let his arms drop, or the umpire himself will call out "*Mada! mada!*"—"Not yet! not yet!" The fierce embrace is unlocked, the brawny rivals saunter to their corners, where again they wash out their mouths with water, sakë, or soy, take a little salt for purification, wipe themselves over with paper, expectorate, and then anew crack their huge joints, and crouch down face to face. Again and again this will be repeated. The umpire shouts the disappointing "*Mada;*" one or the other drops his arms; the audience patiently fill their little pipes, but shout "*Sa! yarè*" — "Come, now; begin!" An often-baffled rival will also be heard to exclaim tauntingly, "*Yarè! Yarè!*" At last it is really a fair grapple. The pride of the West, Osutsu, and the glory of the East, Konishiki, are now locked together in the long-expected and decisive struggle. The umpire, letting fall his fan to the very end of its purple string, has cried aloud "*Agatte!*"—"A good grip!"— and walks round and round the enlaced combatants, keenly noting every movement of the strife. The usually placid Japanese public is now all alight with emotion. When young Konishiki has been lifted bodily from earth by the prodigious Osutsu, the West shouts "*Hora! Hora!*" until the bamboo rafters tremble. When the young champion of the East twines his leg round the giant's thigh and slips out of his difficulty into a new and commanding position, the other side of the house roars mightily "*Konishiki San banzai*"— "Ten thousand years of life for Konishiki!" Nor, truly, is it otherwise than a good and manly sight to see those splendid frames matched so fairly in bloodless battle; the dusky skin and flesh trained so hard that you mark the other wrestler's hand slip from it as from brown marble; the muscles working underneath like snakes beneath a blanket; the feet so desperately planted, the grasp so implacably kept, each man glaring through the eyes of the other to catch at his next mind, or the coming moment of his weakness. There arrives sometimes an instant when, perfectly equipoised in the strife, deadlocked and simultaneously become quite breathless, the watchful umpire will, by a movement of his fan and the word "*Yoshi!*" part the gasping combatants. But generally—and often very quickly—the match is clean wrestled out. In the bout I am describing the younger athlete conquered, to the greater glory of the East. Ozutsu's vast brawn was laid low, and even thrust outside the rice-bags, and the air rang with the name of Konishiki, while dozens of delighted backers flung their hats and caps upon the stage, exclaiming "*Ageru-zo!*" ("I give you this!"). Such votive head-gear is, of course, all duly brought back again to its owners, and the habit is really a relic of the ancient times, when it was considered becoming to strip yourself to the waist before a superior.

In this way combat succeeds combat during many hours, and the victors of to-day meet each other inside the rice-bags on the morrow. Each conflict presents, of course, its special incidents, but they follow the general character described. Almost all of them are interesting, but when the chief champions meet, the excitement becomes extraordinary, and the foreigner himself cannot keep quite clear of the prevailing enthusiasm. At present it seems that the Eastern side must carry off the glories of this Ekoin summer meeting. It possesses three doughty fighting men who have not yet sustained a fall, to wit, the unconquered Nishinoumi, the gigantic Ho-o, and the lighter but dauntless Konishiki. The West can only boast of one representative whom none has compelled hitherto to bite the dust, but he is a very famous wrestler indeed, the colossal Otohira. It may seem strange to have to apply Titanic epithets to Japanese-born men, but, in truth these *Sumo-Tori* are a special race. There may be a sprinkling among them of strong pure-blood Nipponese drawn from the ranks of sailors, jinriksha-men, and the like, but the majority appear a breed apart, and are said indeed to be of Tungensian extraction, originally from the province of Idzumo. Many are six feet and upwards in stature, and of a great natural bulk, artificially increased. Altogether, the bi-annual *Sumo-Ban-zukes* of Tôkyô are most certainly " a sight to see."

Tôkyô, *June* 10, 1892.

VIII

AT AN INDIAN CHRISTMAS-TIME

"AT THE LIPS OF THE BLACK FIELD-PIECE."   P. 161.

VIII

AT AN INDIAN CHRISTMAS-TIME

IT is natural to think of Christmas-tide as we see it in England—in most years wintry and white, as if the earth decked herself in a new and pure mantle to celebrate the birthday of the Divine Teacher of "peace and goodwill." But if one travels a great deal, or reflects only a very little, it will soon be experienced how there are Christmas-tides of all sorts, and of every variety of weather, upon this globe. Christmas Day in the Holy Land, where Christmas Days began, is, as often as not, very warm indeed. If it were not so, the shepherds would not have been watching their sheep out of doors when they heard that heavenly music. In Cape Colony and at the Antipodes, December the twenty-fifth, as likely as not, will prove the hottest day of the Southern Hemisphere ; and in India, though the universal festival of Christendom falls in what is called the "cold season," the Anglo-Indian has to make an effort of imagination, amid the sights and sounds of tropical life, to realise that it is indeed Christmas-time, and that, although climate, prudence, and the doctor may unanimously forbid, he and his household must eat plum-pudding and mince-pies, and make believe to be amid the old surroundings.

As one lives, and works, and wanders about the
world, a vista of Christmas-times is gradually formed,
down which the mind casts retrospective glances,
recalling some that were silver with snow, some
which were golden with sun-glare, some which were
of the old homely type, and some which were spent
in wild places ignorant of English ways and English
faces.   There is no reason why there should be anything sad in the retrospect.   All of them were interesting in their way; all brought some fresh reason
to be grateful for the rich delight and beautiful
variety of life; and if, as is probable, there are more
to come in this existence, or else in a series of much
better existences, why should so much ado be made
by any of us about transient troubles?   It should
not in the least degree affect well-ordered minds
with melancholy to look back along the avenue of
fifty or sixty Christmas Days, even though they will
wistfully remember at what points in the long road
this or that true companion turned aside to a higher
but hidden path.   It is good to live and good to
die, and the stupidest thing in all philosophy is
pessimism, as the most foolish belief on all the earth
is unbelief.   Let sensible folk rather learn to say
with Chaucer :

> Unto this day it dothe my hertë boote
> That I have hadde my worlde, as in my time.

I for one recall with a quiet and grateful pleasure
all the particular stages of the vista—the Christmases in England, the Christmases upon the ocean,

the Christmases in India, the Christmases in Egypt, in Bulgaria, in America, in Greece, in Algiers, in Japan. Which Christmas-time shall I write about to-day? Shall it be one out of the hot and sunny Yuletides? An Indian Christmas Day, with perhaps a story to it, not the less useful if it contrasts stormy epochs of the past with present peace, and primitive passions with the things which are "lovely and of good report"? An Indian Christmas-time let it be !

I was in India during all the dark days of the Great Mutiny in 1857 and its following years. That seems, and truly is, a long while ago—so long ago that another Hindostan has since arisen. At a very early age I was appointed Principal of the Government College at Poona, in the Deccan, and the Sepoy rebellion was in full blaze when I landed at Bombay with my wife and child. The siege of Delhi was in progress; scanty but precious reinforcements were pouring in from various points to the hard-pressed British troops. Our own vessel—an old paddle-steamer called the *Pottinger*—carried out 300 soldiers and officers of all sorts; and during the voyage to Bombay constant practice with pistols and other weapons went forward. At Cairo, whence we had still to cross the desert in vans, we met wounded officers and men returning home from the first Indian fights. All kinds of ugly news encountered us on the way, yet it was a very light - hearted ship's company on board the old paddle-steamer, albeit many among us were destined never to see England again. I especially remember a young civilian who was soon afterwards murdered in the South Mahratta country by a rebel Rajah, and also an engineer officer named Glastonbury Nevill. The latter repeatedly assured me that he had a fixed presentiment he would fall; and, too truly, the first round shot fired at Rajgurh cut him in two.

We landed; and how beautiful, and new, and wonderful India seemed, despite the desperate crisis which was pending. Never shall I forget that first Christmas season in the Deccan, nor, indeed, my first morning in India. Everybody had to be at his post, and even I, a mere teacher, was ordered up by " John Company Bahadur " to my college within an hour of arrival. Thus all night long we journeyed through the Concan, and up the Ghâts, and over the table-land of the Deccan in a mysterious darkness, meeting long lines of cotton carts, and files of sepoys, and groups of country people with their heads swathed up in cloths, but seeing nothing of India except the white dust and the phantom figures in the starlight, until the dawn broke over the flat-topped hills of Poona. But then how bright and strange, and full with delightful novelty of bird and beast, of tree and flower, of men and women and children, and their ways and words, this Eastern world appeared! I could hardly be persuaded to go in to breakfast out of the great hot Indian garden, so absorbed had I become in the realisation of what I had read about. The kites circling round and round in the cloudless pale blue sky; the mynas, with their yellow beaks and legs, chattering and strutting; the bee-eaters,

bronze and green, darting about in chase of the
gorgeous butterflies, whose wings—crimson and black
or blue and silver—they strip away before devouring
the body, until the ground beneath their perch was
like a painter's palette; the mongoose sniffing around
the snake's hole; the lively-coloured lizards glancing
in and out among the great blue blossoms of the
convolvuli; a swarm of rose-necked parroquets flashing with loud screams through the mango-trees, and
settling in a green cloud upon the silk-cotton tree;
the red and emerald "coppersmith" hammering away
on his branch in the tamarind; the sun-birds, with
plumage of canary and purple, plunging their tiny
bills into the trumpet-flowers; the vultures grimly
perched in black rows on the wall; the incessant
crows everywhere busy and noisy; and also everywhere scuttling up and down, in and out, those little
striped squirrels, which you see all over the Indian
Peninsula. Do you know why they are striped with
five long dark grey marks? It is because the god
Shiva saw one of them once dipping his bushy tail
into the Bay of Bengal time after time, and shaking
it out over the shore. "Absurd little geloori!" the
god said, "why do you do thus?" "Oh, Thousand-
Handed," the squirrel replied, "the palm-tree holding
the nest which contains my wife and children has
fallen into the water by reason of a typhoon, and I
am trying to bale the Bay of Bengal dry with my tail,
to save my dear family." Upon that the deity smiled
graciously, and, stooping down, stroked the tiny
beast, leaving on its back five marks of his finger and

thumb, and afterwards commanded the ocean to retire until the little squirrel had recovered his nest and belongings.

Yet, although the glories and wonders of nature in India absorbed me a great deal more than the slight personal dangers of the time, even my quiet and learned retreat was not entirely outside the troubles of that period. The Government of Bombay has since built a spacious and splendid edifice for the Deccan College; in my time we were housed in an ancient but picturesque palace of the Peishwas, the old Maharatta kings, in the heart of the city. Its carved teak columns, green quadrangles, and shadowy Oriental halls used to make me very proud of being "Principal," and from the very beginning I liked my dusky students—of whom there were some 500—and wished sincerely to be good friends with them. Yet at the commencement an awkward thing occurred. I used to repair in the hot morning by bullock-cart or palanquin to the college, returning every afternoon on horseback; and one morning I saw a notice in Marathi writing, unsigned by me, upon the gateway. I ordered it to be taken down and read to me, whereupon it proved to be an offer of 10,000 rupees for the Principal's head. To treat this seriously would have been a sad mistake; so, knowing that Hindoos are as susceptible as children to badinage, I assembled the classes, had the rebellious document read aloud, and then made a little speech, saying how glad I was I did not know the authors of the offending paper, since if I did they

would have to be denounced, and blown from guns,
or hanged. Not knowing them, nor wanting to know
them, I was free to express my satisfaction at having
my head estimated at a sum so handsome, and I
thanked my anonymous enemies for the delicate
compliment. At the same time, I added, my hope
was strong that that head would prove more useful
to all of them on my shoulders than off, and I invited
such as were disaffected at least to try the experiment. As a matter of fact, even the peaceful Deccan
College, being full of Brahman students, was also
full of foolish and windy elements of rebelliousness,
and a high police authority sent a private application
to me to admit as scholars into the institution two
or three young natives, who, seemingly intent on
learning, would watch and overhear and eventually
report to the department. I indignantly refused.
I had gone there to teach my pupils, and to be taught
by them—not to betray their temporary follies and
see some of them perhaps cast into prison or executed. I was reported for my obstinate refusal,
but Lord Elphinstone—then governing Bombay for
the Company—privately upheld me, only intimating
that I would have to be personally answerable for
the good behaviour of the students, since I was so
inflexible in their protection. And I think this got,
somehow, to the knowledge of the young Brahmans,
for we did become great friends, and days as happy
as any in my life were afterwards passed in that
ancient Mahratta palace, among my dark scholars,
while outside us the thunder of war rolled, and the

gallant English regiments held up against fierce and
frightful odds the flag of John Company, which was
soon afterwards to be transferred to Her Majesty the
Queen, Kaisar-i-Hind ; Adhirajni.

I well remember that particular Christmas, and a
strange and moving story of the Great Mutiny,
which I picked up in the jungle, upon one of the
many hunting excursions I was in the habit of making from Poona.   For many years past I have given
up gun, rifle, and fishing-rod—not because I was,
or am, weary of carrying them, for the passion of
woodland wandering is as strong as ever with me,
but because the beauty, wonder, and delight in life
of the wild creatures grew upon me so much that
I can no longer kill any of them.   Yet, although
Emerson justly praises the man who " catalogues
the birds without a gun," it is certain that nothing
makes any one a naturalist so quickly as a sincere
love of the spear and rifle, which lead the sportsman
into recesses and private places of the jungle and
mountain, where neither he, nor any one else, would
otherwise roam.   So, in those Indian days, I was up
nearly every dawn before the morning star, and away
on horseback to the river to shoot snipe and duck ;
and when a day or two of holiday arrived, off into
the open country, round the city, where antelopes
abounded, and where you were as likely as not to
come across panther, wolf, hyæna, or even bear, and
possibly an occasional tiger, while thinking only of
florikan and quail.   In the darkest days of the Mutiny,
when even some of our faithful Bombay regiments

were rebelling, and mutineers were being blown
from guns or otherwise executed at Satara, Bombay,
and the surrounding stations, the country proper
was always fairly safe and quiet. The agricultural
people neither understood nor heeded the political
storm. Their grievances were not against the Saheb-
lôk—the Government—but against the *marwarries*,
or money-lenders. If the peasants ever rose anywhere, it was to cut the throats of those *banias* and
burn their books; after which they would come
back to their oxen and wooden ploughs as tranquil
as good little children who have been to wash their
hands. We rode, therefore, in much calm and comfort all about the Deccan plains in the very midst
of the great mutiny, though its leaders — Nana
Sahib and Tantia Topee—were both Mahrattas, and
although, in old Mahratta phrase, "the fire was on
the hills."

Glad, and free, and rich in sights and sounds
to rejoice one who loves this beautiful earth, were
those plains of the Deccan at Christmas-time. It
is not a tropical vegetation there, but rather resembles the sub-tropical flora of Japan, except that
no fir-trees ever mingled with the bamboos and
acacias. Between the flat-topped trap ranges, which
ran round and round the horizon like castles of
giants, vast level tracts extended covered with sheets
of smooth rock and bushes of corinda, dwarf thorns,
and cactus, with long dry yellow grass, all inter-
sected by deep or shallow *nullahs*—watercourses—
then quite dry, but full and flowing in the rainy

season.   Here and there a village nestled within
its mud walls, and here and there a green garden would shine amid the arid plain, from which
came pleasantly the creak of the well-rope dragging
up the dripping *mussuks* to irrigate the enclosure,
and the song of the bullock-boy, keeping his slow
white cattle to their lazy work.   Pleasant it was
to pitch the tents in such a spot, and to ride forth
at daybreak for a long morning's shooting, while
the peacocks screamed in the thicket, and the
monkeys, newly awakened, scratched themselves by
way of toilet, and went about their four-handed
business.   I learned more than any books have ever
taught me from those delicious Indian dawns, noting
the marvellous life of the waste, and the ways of
its living things.   Is there any sight more full of
the *joie de vivre*, the ecstasy of existence, than a
string of black deer—bucks and does and fawns—
pacing at early morning over the unpeopled plain,
the sun sparkling on their sleek golden backs and
shining ringleted horns—wild with perfect physical
health, and vigour of slender limb and shapely
muscle ; leaping, circling, gambolling, ready to jump
out of their velvety skins for pure pleasure to breathe
the warm air, and feel the good ground under their
little jet-black hoofs ?   Keenly as I then loved the
rifle, I have over and over again laid it aside, to the
disgust of my shikari, when we had stalked within
shot of such a troop of lovely and happy creatures, and
from behind a clump of lemon-grass watched their
pretty jealousies and coquetries one with another.

It was about Christmas-time, on one of these rambles, that I came at night, with Luximan, my *ghora-wallah* and constant attendant, to a far-off village in the Deccan. Long ago have the funeral flames consumed what was mortal of that faithful old Mahratta, who knew all there was to know about horses, except that he would insist on painting their tails and manes red at Christmas and other festivals. We had shot hard and ridden far, and, the tents not coming up, I was lodged in a temple of Mahadeo, my cot being placed close beside the red-plastered image of the god. Thus the villagers, male and female, approaching partly to make evening offerings to the deity, partly from curiosity to see the saheb, came, one after the other, close in view, and I noticed among them a comely woman having a singularly sad, refined face, dressed as a widow, with her black hair cut short, and wearing no bangles, nose-ring, armlets, head-disc, or ornaments of any kind. Yes, there *was* one. As she lifted her hands in worship to the god, I observed upon her wrist the slender iron braclet worn by Mahratta wives, which, by a kind of instinctive movement, she hastily pushed back, out of sight, upon her brown arm. Next morning, again, it was she who brought the milk in a brass lota, out of which we sahebs could not drink without defiling it, so she poured the milk forth into an earthen pot, and once again I saw the iron bangle slide down from her forearm to her wrist, and the woman nervously thrust it back into her sleeve. This puzzled me, because she was in Hindoo widow's dress, and yet carrying the mark of a married woman ; but I am glad I did not ask questions of her for the reasons which will be seen.

The next night was cold, and I was warming myself at the camp-fire, where Luximan was also seated, when my thoughts reverted to the sad-faced woman at the temple, and I asked my faithful groom if he knew her by name, and did he understand why she wore the bracelet of a Hindoo wife, being evidently a widow ? Luximan looked anxiously about to see if anybody was within earshot. Then he said very seriously, "*Han, main samajhtá hun, Saheb*"—"Yes, sir, I understand—but it is a hidden thing, which holds the lives of men in its silence. Only if the Presence will promise never to speak of it may I tell what I know of Sita, the milk-woman." I readily undertook to respect his confidence, and then, in his own way, which must be made here much briefer and plainer, he related to me what follows :—

Sita was a very pretty Mahratta girl of low caste, who had been betrothed and married to a sepoy in one of the Bombay regiments, named Govind ; and this young man, for his good conduct and soldierly qualities, rose to be a havildar, or non-commissioned officer, and was popular alike with the rank and file and with his superiors. Govind had a half-brother named Wittoba, almost exactly like him in features and figure, so much so that people not of the village would easily mistake one for the other ; and whether from this similarity of nature, or whatever cause,

Wittoba also became deeply enamoured of Sita. He was, nevertheless, very much attached to his half-brother, but, knowing his love to be sinful and fruitless, after vainly endeavouring to overcome it, which the daily sight of the beautiful Sita rendered impossible, he left the village, and enlisted as a soldier in another regiment of the Bombay army. Thus matters stood when the summer of the year 1857 brought the great Mutiny, and Govind, who had been punished and degraded for some trivial fault, was angry, and allowed the emissaries of Tantia Topee to undermine his loyalty. He became "faithless to his salt," attended the secret meetings of the disaffected in Bombay, and was one of those whose treasonable designs were overheard and denounced by Mr. Forjett, the Police Commissioner. When the regiment moved up into the Deccan, half of it was ripe for mutiny, but the ringleaders were narrowly watched, and at a fitting moment were disarmed and arrested; so that, the proofs of guilt against Govind two others being overwhelming, he and they were sentenced to be blown from guns at Sattara.

Wittoba's regiment, like most of those composing the Bombay army, remained loyal, and a wing of it was quartered in the same station. Thus it happened that on the night before the execution, when Sita was sitting in her hut, rocking herself to and fro in her wifely misery, after the manner of Indian women in deep grief, a sepoy in his white undress uniform of cotton, with the red Mahratta turban, entered her house, which had the usual two rooms divided by a

bamboo screen and curtain. It was Wittoba. He
sat down ont he floor opposite to the weeping wife,
and for some time no word was spoken. Then this
dialogue ensued :—

"Evil hath come to thy threshold, Sita! and
sorrow upon thy heart. To-morrow they will kill
thy husband."

"Alas! it is so. Oh, Shiva! Shiva! why did he
listen to those wicked men who bade him betray his
salt ? "

"They were foxes who tricked him, and he was
a hare to be beguiled. It is a dreadful death, Sita!
You will not have his body to burn upon the wood
and the cow-cakes. The breath of the cannon blows
it into dust and air. I have seen it; the end is
terrible."

"I know, Wittoba, I know. Why do you talk
thus? What is the use of breaking a broken
chatty? My heart is heavy enough already."

"*Dilbur mut ho !* Don't let your heart be heavy !
I have come to lighten it ! "

"You? How ?"

"Sita! I can save Govind from the mouth of the
big gun."

"Why will you talk lies? Nothing and no one
can save my husband."

"I speak no lie. I can save him. He lies to-
night in the chowki by the artillery-ground, chained
and alone. I am one of the relief guards in the
early morning. I can enter, on this or that pretence,
just before they parade for the execution. I can

open his fetters, can put upon him my uniform, and give him my musket and bayonet—taking his own prison clothes ; and we are so alike in face and form that no man will know, in the early light, and in the trouble of the hour, that Govind has become the sentinel and Wittoba the prisoner. The gun will boom ; I shall be like the chaff you shake from that winnowing fan, and my brother will come here to you at night, and you can go away into the hills together."

" Brother of my husband ! why do you say all this ?"

" Because I love you, Sita, more than life ! Because I would buy with my life one hour of your love. Listen ! This is what I am come to speak. Let me stay with you here to-night, till the wolf's tail comes into the sky, and then what I have told you I swear by the cow that I will surely do."

" Wittoba ! This is deadly sin."

" It is not sin for you to save the life of your husband."

" It is deadly sin that you should desire his wife."

" I will abide that. I have weighed it all. The three worlds are less to me than once to hold you in my arms. I say this shall be my sin, not yours. Will you have your husband live or die ? "

" Govind ! Govind ! "

" Only one hour — then you shall have saved him."

"But, Wittoba, if it could be—if it might be—and afterwards you did not keep your promise?"

"I am mad with love of you, Sita; but I am no liar. I swear to you, by the Great Mother, that I will do this deed, and stand at the gun's mouth to-morrow morning instead of Govind. Decide! Say yea or no, for the night weareth away."

"Yea, then! For my lord's sake I will do this grievous wrong to my lord. May Heaven forgive, for well I know he never will! But if thou dost fail in thy pledge, the curse of Chittore light upon thee."

"I shall not fail."

* * * * * * * *

When the last jackals were stealing homewards in the grey of that fatal morning, Govind, the havildar, was awakened by a hand upon his breast. It was Wittoba, the sepoy, in regimental uniform, armed, and bearing a bowl of hot conjee and some chupatties. "Rise, brother," he whispered, "and be silent! They bade me bring to thee the last of thine earthly meals, but while thou dost eat I will break apart these chains, and take off *kapre* and *juta*, and change apparel with thee. We are as like as two leaves of a milk-bush, and thou shalt fix bayonet and march forth to keep the ground, while I take thy place at the gun. Nay! no refusal, and no thanks. This has to be. Afterwards shalt thou know why." With hurried explanations

Wittoba half forced, half persuaded Govind to comply, and—once thrust forth free from the guard-house, dressed in uniform, the bugles sounding, and muffled drums beating—bewildered, wondering, rejoicing, remorseful—the redeemed man went mechanically through the duty of the day.

They brought forth Wittoba, supposing him to be Govind, and would have bound him, like the others, to the gaping cannon-mouth. But he saw his brother mournfully regarding; and desiring, perhaps, that Sita should know how faithfully he had kept his guilty bargain, he walked directly to the front of the gun, and, standing close to the muzzle, erect and proud, waved away with his hand those who carried the cords, saying, "*Bundhun nuko*" ("Do not tie me"). Something irresistibly heroic in his fearless air made the British officer nod a chivalrous compliance, and they left him there unfastened, at the lips of the black field-piece, while the artillery-man pulled the lanyard.

When Govind and Sita were resting that night at a temple, on their way to the village in the hills, she asked what her husband saw as the smoke cleared away, and he replied, "I saw only a red turban, rolling, and a waistband which twisted and twisted along the maidan—if, indeed, I saw so much, for my eyes were dim."

And Luximan said that the wife told all to her husband, and that he left her, neither beaten or cursed, neither praised or blessed; for he said, "Until we come to Swarga I know not to which of

M

us thou art the wife." And afterwards Sita lived alone, in widow's dress, but always keeping on her arm the mark of her marriage. So that was how I had chanced to see at Christmas-time in the Indian village the hidden iron bracelet of which I have never spoken until now, when there is no longer the slightest danger in speaking.

IX

SOME JAPANESE PICTURES

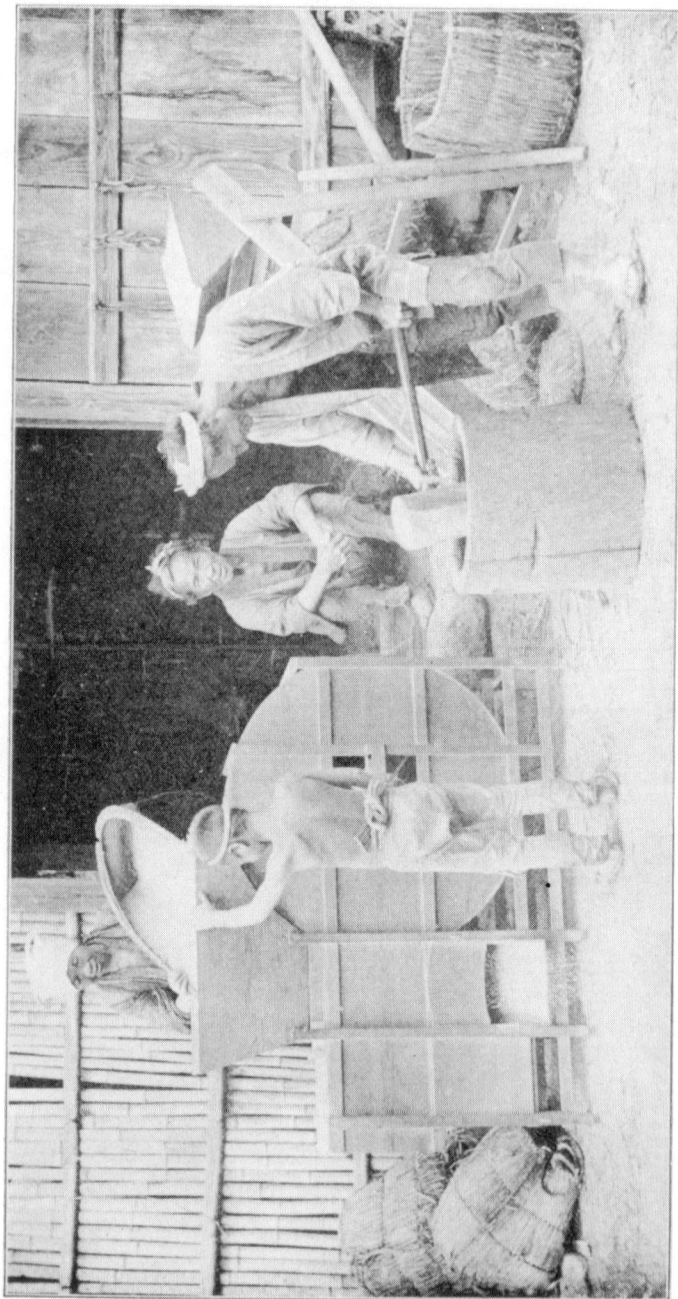

RICE CLEANING IN JAPAN.

IX

SOME JAPANESE PICTURES

THE children of Japan charm everybody who visits the country. From the highest to the lowest ranks, and almost without exception, they are the best-behaved, least mischievous, most sedate, demure, correct, amusing, and unobnoxious specimens of minute humanity to be found on the globe. The average American boy, especially if born in well-to-do homes, is an egotistic, noisy, restless little tyrant, who makes a railway saloon or a drawing-room a place of torture to his elders. The average English boy, more shy and silent, is yet by nature full of mischief and suppressed devilry, and is too often capable of the most fiendish cruelty. As for girls, they are everywhere, of course, more docile and gentle than their brothers, and seldom provoke the sensitive or nervous mind to thoughts of infanticide. But the Japanese babies and children—boys and girls alike—delight and comfort the foreign visitor by their ideal propriety. The streets, the houses, the temples, the gardens, the railway lines are free and open to them, for their playground is "all out-of-doors;" yet they never seem to be in the way, or to damage anything, or to forget their good manners, or break flowers and shrubs, or put stones on the track. They are so preternaturally and prematurely reasonable! This does not imply that they are dull, or indifferent, or lifeless. On the contrary, nowhere is youth so joyous as with "young Japan;" these little ones chirp like sparrows at every corner, and flit from pleasure to pleasure like butterflies in a flower-garden. I think such a pretty state of things is due, first of all, to their gentle, tender, dutiful mothers. Nowhere in this world have small boys and girls more affectionate, patient, devoted bringing-up than the little Japs get on the breasts and at the knees of their *okkâsan*. And this, in after years, they richly return, the reverence for father and mother being the very keystone of the national arch. Filial piety is, next to loyalty, the cardinal virtue of the land, even carrying the people occasionally to extravagant or even criminal lengths. The classic picture of a good son in the Japanese print-shops represents a certain young man who, in the season of mosquitoes, stripped himself bare at bedtime, and so lay down near his parents in order that the mosquitoes might feed on him, and let the honoured elders alone. And lately there was a dreadful case in Tôkyô, where a man actually killed his wife because he had been told that nothing short of that would bring back to health his sick mother. Such a deed, of course, shocked public opinion nearly as much in Japan as it would do in England, but it illustrates the force and prevalence of parental and filial dutifulness in the Empire.

Another reason why the Japanese children grow up so good, so charming, so candid, so amenable, is, I think, because they never heard of such a thing as "original sin," and are never treated on the system which belongs to it. By Buddhist belief, no doubt, every little Jap comes into the world with the mistakes of a previous existence to atone for and to cancel—it is the doctrine of *Karma* or *Ingwa*. But parents, friends, neighbours, and teachers leave all that to Destiny and to the *Kami-Sama;* their part is to treat the small being as a new-come guest into the garden of life, to be received with grace, kindliness, and consideration as a stranger, and not to be bullied and browbeaten into correctness. "Go and see, Jane! what Master Reginald is doing, and tell him not to do it!"—such was the legend of one of Mr. Du Maurier's child-pictures in *Punch*—but a Japanese mother and a Japanese child could never even have comprehended the joke. They do not slap, or thwart, or forbid and constrain the little ones in Japan, although they very strictly train them to make bows, and to be silent and submissive and respectful; and it is a great recommendation of what may be called the anti-Solomonic plan that the children repay courtesy with courtesy, and consideration by consideration. Moreover, they see so much of their own world in very early days that they do not break forth, like those of Europe, into its wonders and excitements fresh and frisky from the nursery. At five or six weeks of age the Japanese baby goes out into the open air, lashed

on the back of its mother, sister, aunt, or nurse,
and there it rides all day long, except at necessary
intervals of refreshment, taking its slumber in this
peripatetic cradle, and, when awake, seeing everything which goes on in the streets with its little
slant-lidded, beady, black eyes, so that, when it
comes to the point of being able to toddle for
itself, nothing is strange to the observant babe.
It owes, also, to that early life in the open air
and perpetual motion on the back of some relation
or other, a large part of the generally robust health
enjoyed by its kind. Japan is of all countries,
except England, that wherein the fewest children
die between birth and the age of five years, albeit
another point in favour of Japanese babies is that
they are nursed at the breast until they are two,
or even three years old. In every way their world
is made very pleasant to them at starting. The
towns and villages are full of toy-shops, where the
most grotesque and ingenious playthings are sold
for their benefit, at the lowest possible cost. When
there happens a temple feast—a *matsuri* or *ennichi*
—the precincts of the holy shrine are crowded with
toy-stalls and the portable shops of the *ame-ya*,
blowing, out of bean-paste, all sorts of "sweeties,"
shaped into dragons, snakes, birds, demons, and
the like. Nobody is too proud or grand to carry
a baby, or to be seen bearing home through the
streets ridiculous creations of fluffy tigers, feathery
cocks and hens, or balls of wool and tinsel. At
the great wrestling-match this year in Ekoin I

watched a huge *sumotori*, the champion of his class, overthrow his opponent after a tremendous struggle, amid the delighted plaudits of some three thousand spectators, who flung a hundred hats and caps into the ring. Ten minutes afterwards I met the same gigantic hero, outside the wrestling theatre in the street, carrying a bit of a baby on his back, by the side of his little glossy-haired wife, and feeding it over his brawny shoulder with salted plums.

The Japanese children have, by the way, a vocabulary quite their own—just as the jinriksha-men talk their own *patois*, and the Court people use a special form of speech; while even Japanese women employ many words and phrases never heard from the lips of men. One distinguishing feature of the children of Japan are their sleeves. After much observation and meditation in the streets and roadways of the country, one arrives at last at an explanation of the extreme dignity which the little ones exhibit under almost all circumstances. It is due, you perceive, to the long flowing sleeves which they wear. Nothing in respect of dress gives so much importance and presence to the human figure, grown or ungrown, as wide and hanging sleeves; and all the little Japanese, when habited at all, go about in tiny gowns very much resembling those worn by Masters of Art and Doctors of Divinity at Oxford and Cambridge. If ladies only knew how much that is graceful and imposing depends upon deep, long, flowing sleeves, they would abandon the tight fashions of the present time, and go back in this

regard to the beautiful costumes which English
dames wore in the days of the Edwards and
Henries, and which have been universal in Japan
for two thousand years. A whole book might be
written about the æsthetic and social value and
dignity of long sleeves.

Special days are set apart in the Japanese year
for the boys' and girls' festivals. The great day of
the girls is March 3, when all the doll-shops in
Tôkyô, Kyôtô, and the other large towns, are full of
what are called *o hina sama*—models on a tiny
scale of the Emperor and Empress, with their court
and domestic belongings. These toy establish-
ments are handed down from mother to daughter,
and I have seen high-born children playing with
hina sama three hundred years old and more. The
special day for the boys falls on May 5 every year,
when the air is full everywhere of great, hollow,
floating fish made out of coloured and gilded paper
(which the wind inflates), hoisted high upon a tall
bamboo pole in front of each abode where a male
child has been born. The fish is the carp (*koi*),
the universal emblem of courage and perseverance,
because he swims so stoutly against the stream,
and hardly consents to die when he is cut into thin
slices for *sashimi*.

In early years, and, indeed, until the age of
eighteen or nineteen, nothing can be too gay and
brilliant for a Japanese damsel to wear. The little
Nippon maids go about far outvying in splendour
the great butterflies of crimson and gold, or of

saffron and silver, which flit around their heads in the gardens and bamboo-groves. Parental affection seems to exhaust itself in devising gorgeous colours and attractive patterns for their little *obi* and *kimono*, while the *jiban*, or underskirt, cannot possibly be too magnificent. If these garments be only of cotton, the mother and father will have them gay; but even the poor children generally manage to wear fabrics half of silk and half of cotton, and the well-to-do always have their clothes composed of silk, or the beautiful silk-crape known as *chirimen*. This last takes the most brilliant dyes quite perfectly, and admits of very lovely decorative effects, in obtaining which nothing is feared except inharmonious combinations. You see young maidens in the streets and the temple-gardens literally glittering with gold, silver, vermilion, sea-green, sky-blue, rose-red, and orange; some wearing an upper dress covered with fans, birds, waving woods, bamboo boughs, or fish; and at a garden-party given by the Princess Mori at Takanawa, I was presented to a young lady—the lineal descendant of the great house of Tokonawa Shoguns—whose *jiban* of azure silk was an embroidered pool of lotus-blossoms, while her *kimono* of tender, creamy *chirimen* had on it Japanese landscapes of rising moons, rice-fields, Fuji-yama, with the snow upon its crest, and suchlike. When the mature age of twenty or twenty-one is reached, these dazzling glories of the toilette are exchanged for sober-hued dresses, grey, dove-colour, tea-colour, fawn, and brown; but even then the *jiban* may always be as glorious in colour and patterns as fancy dictates, and the *obi* a splendid piece of figured satin. The attire of the boys is in every case quieter and more restrained, and elderly people cannot be clad too soberly.

Japanese girls grow up to be Japanese women without change in their gentleness, docility, or good manners ; and Japanese boys continue to appear attractive, candid, free from *mauvaise honte*, and altogether delightful, until they reach the awkward and gawky age, which for a time spoils most lads. The Japanese boy is delightful; the Japanese man is generally intelligent, polite, and, in his degree, worthy; but the Japanese youth, especially in the middle classes, is wont to prove a hobbledehoy and a social nuisance. As scholars and students they are almost faultless. There are no rules of discipline or punishment in the schools and colleges, because none are needed. The pupils are only too anxious to learn, and are always in their places before the master is ready, and keen to continue work when he is tired. They are too apt to think they know a subject when they have only commenced to understand its rudiments ; and although always deferential to their *sensei*, the teacher, they will dictate to him, if he permits, the course of study. But a certain number of them, mingling very imperfect modern education with very crude political theories, leave their schools and colleges full of ambitions and desires which are beyond their range, and instead of accepting humble and useful walks in life, turn into detestable and dangerous agitators, whose want of sense would be contemptible if their inherited disregard of personal risk and their passionate *entêtement* did not render them evils to be reckoned with. These are the *soshi*. Like our own young "baboos" of Bengal, and "reformers" from the Indian Government College, they have got the wind of personal and political conceit in their heads ; but, unlike the "baboos," they are not in the least timid. For want of other and better employ, they hire themselves out to unscrupulous politicians as boyish "swashbucklers," to break up public meetings, intimidate nervous statesmen, dominate the voting places with noise and menace, and sometimes even to commit assault or murder. It was one of these unlovely youths who, brooding fanatically over a supposed offence against the *religio loci* of a temple at Ise, assassinated my enlightened and illustrious friend Viscount Mori ; and another such threw the bomb which deprived Count Okuma, the Japanese Prime Minister, of a limb. The worst of them are well known to the Government and the police, and when any rather exciting time is coming forward in Tôkyô, and popular disturbance has to be feared, it is not unusual for the Administration to clear them out of the capital by scores or hundreds, obliging them to spend a little of their ill-used leisure at Yokohama or elsewhere, until the temporary excitement has died away in the seat of Government.

The outdoor games of the Japanese children are

much like those of other small folk in various parts
of the world; though the ingenuity of the race
refines upon them. The *tako*, or kite ; the *koma*, or
top ; the playing-ball, *tama;* the stilts, *take-uma;*
the hoop, *taga;* the swing, *bu-ranko;* the skipping-
rope, *nawa-koguli;* prisoner's base, *o nigoko;* and
oyama-no-taisho, king of the castle, are just as
popular, with many other familiar pastimes, in
Tôkyô as in London. But the natural skill and
adroitness of the people improve upon the Western
forms of these sports. The kites are much more
scientific than ours, with long streamers at the
lower corners, and strange little contrivances to
produce sounds, explosions, and illuminations in
the sky. Japanese tops, which will spin ever so
long on a string or a knife-edge, are well known ;
and as for Japanese ball-play, there is not a little
maid of five or six years in the streets who cannot
keep two or three of them in the air at once with
one hand, while the other holds the umbrella over
the bald pate of the rocking baby. Some of their
indoor games might be very well introduced among
English children, being graceful and merry, yet free
from boisterousness. For example, there is the
pretty sport of *tsuri-kitsune*, or "fox-catching," at
which many may play at once. Somebody unwinds
his or her silken sash, and ties it in a half-hitch,
or a reefer's knot, so as to make a running-noose,
of which two players hold the opposite ends, balancing the noose vertically on the floor. Then any
little prize—a sweetmeat or what-not—is laid on

the floor on the far-side of the noose, and one by
one the outsiders try to snatch the object safely
through the trap, the two players seeking to catch
the fox's paw just as it goes into the noose. Great
fun is elicited from this, and when a fox is caught,
he surrenders all his prizes and takes one end of
the snare. Or this is sometimes coupled with our
English game of forfeits. Again, there is a quiet
and amusing Japanese form of blind-man's buff,
me-gakushi, where the fun is had with a large
soft ball, not hard enough to break anything or
to hurt; and the blind man—after turning round
three times—throws this very suddenly in a direction as unexpected as possible, any person struck
being obliged to take his place. Another form of
me-gakushi is where the blind man sits in the
centre of a large circle made around him by the
other players, after he has had his eyes covered,
and he is then allowed to talk, make jokes, say
anything he can to provoke a giggle or an ejaculation, so that he may specify the exact position in
the circle of somebody, and oblige that one to take
his place. This is called *ocha-boji*, and admits of
the most charming developments.

The "grown-ups" have, for their indoor pastimes
—to leave aside music, singing, and, in cultivated
circles, the ever-absorbing composition of *uta*,
Japanese poetry—two principal games. One is *go*,
properly called *gomoka narabe*, which, albeit played
on the same board, and with the same counters or
"men" as *goban*, is a very different game from the

childishly easy one hitherto known and played in this country. It is much more difficult and elaborate than chess, and admits of deeper and more complicated combinations. Everybody plays it, especially at the hot springs and bathing-places, and there are *go*-clubs and professors of the art and mystery of *go* in all the larger cities, while, what is more remarkable, blind players and teachers of remarkable skill may oftentimes be met with. Mr. Chamberlain has partially described the game, but it must be taught, and, being taught, would be a very valuable addition to the sedentary pleasures of English homes. He says :—

" *Go* was introduced into Japan from China by Shimomichi-no Mabi, commonly known as Kibi Daijin, who flourished during the reign of the Emperor Shômu (A.D. 724–756). In the middle of the seventh century a noted player called Honnimbô was summoned from Kyôto to entertain the Chinese Ambassador, then at the Court of the Shôgun, from which time forward special *go* players were always retained by the Shoguns of the Tokugawa dynasty.

" *Go* is played on a square wooden board. Nineteen straight lines crossing each other at right angles make three hundred and sixty-one *me*, or crosses, at the points of intersection. These may be occupied by a hundred and eighty white and a hundred and eighty-one black stones (*ishi*, as they are termed in Japanese). The object of the game is to obtain possession of the largest portion of the board. This is done by securing such positions as can be most easily defended from the adversary's onslaughts. There are nine spots on the board, called *seimoku*, supposed to represent the chief celestial bodies, while the white and black stones represent day and night, and the number of crosses the three hundred and sixty degrees of latitude, exclusive of the central one, which is called *taikyoku*, that is, the Primordial Principle of the Universe. There are likewise nine degrees of proficiency in the game, beginning with number one as the lowest, and ending with number nine as the highest point of excellence attainable.

"In playing, if the combatants are equally matched, they take the white stones alternately; if unequal, the weaker always takes the black, and odds are also given by allowing him to occupy several or all of the nine spots or vantage-points on the board—that is, to place stones upon them at the outset. Very few foreigners have succeeded in getting beyond a rudimentary knowledge of this interesting game. Only one, a German named Korschelt, has taken out a diploma of proficiency. The easy Japanese game called *gobang*, which was introduced into England a few years ago, is played on the *go* board with the same *ishi*, and the only art here is to see who can first get five pieces into a row diagonal, vertical, or horizontal."

The other popular indoor-game of the Japanese is a card-game, called *hana-awase*, played everywhere, always, and by all classes. On any day, at any jinriksha-stand, you may see the *kurumaya-*

san squatted down, deep in the delight of *hana-awase*, the well-thumbed cards laid on the footboard of a "ricksha;" and just before I left Tôkyô a grave scandal arose, because a whole bench-full of judges had been caught playing this fascinating game with *geishas* at a tea-house. It is a really fine game, and deserves to be introduced among us as a quite possible rival of whist, skill and chance mingling in it as they do in that classic recreation of the middle-aged. *Hana-awase* means "the matching of flowers," and it is only lately that it has become universally popular in Japan, though probably far more ancient than any of our European card-games. The pack consists of forty-eight *karuta*, generally no larger than a visiting-card, having twelve suits of four cards each, these suits being named after various flowers, leaves, or trees, which are symbolical to the Japanese of the twelve months. The following list exhibits the suits and their symbolism, with the native names :—

Pine (*Matsu*)	January.
Plum (*Ume*)	February.
Cherry (*Sakura*)	March.
Wistaria (*Fuji*)	April.
Iris (*Negi*)	May.
Tree Peony (*Botan*)	June.
Lespedeza (*Hagi*)	July.
Eularia Japonica (*Tsuki, Bozu*)	August.
Chrysanthemum (*Kiku*)	September.
Maple (*Momiji*)	October.
Willow (*Shigure*)	November.
Paullownia (*Kiri*)	December.

Hana-awase is a card-game where the cleverest

sharper cannot cheat, because it is impossible to foresee the end. It is a game fuller of vicissitudes than poker or bézique, and repaying attention and calculation more than écarté or nap, while for the gambler its capabilities are as prodigiously ruinous as its chequered flow of good and bad luck is fascinating to the player for love. I shall, therefore, in hope of its ultimate acclimatisation among us, summarise below an account of the game, derived by the late General Palmer, of Tôkyô, from two accomplished players, Messrs. Yokoyama and Mori. Describing the cards the General says :—

"The method of decoration was representative of the twelve names of the suits, and might either be rudely printed or hand-painted, in which latter case cards may cost several *yen*. As a rule, the greater the face-value of any card the more elaborately was it decorated. The first in value were the four *shikomono*, or 'brilliants,' namely, the commanding cards of the *matsu*, *sakura*, *bozu*, and *kiri* suits. These were usually more highly decorated than the others, as, for instance, 'the blossoms in the Palace garden,' *gotenzakura*, the *kiri-no-oo*, and so on. The commanding card of the *shigure* suite, *o-ame*, was equal to a brilliant in counting the hand (that is, having the value of twenty chips of one point each), but had no other property of a brilliant. The commanding cards of the *ume*, *fuji*, *negi*, *botan*, *hagi*, *kiku*, and *momiji* suits, and the second cards of the *bozu* and *shigure* suits came next, having a value of ten points each, except for the process of reckoning in *teyaku*, in which the *shigure* second card only counted one. These were called the *ike-mono*. Next came the *tanzakumono*, distinguished by having a coloured bar across the decoration to represent a strip of paper, which, with other cards, have a value of five points each ; and lastly there came the *kasu-mono* (trash or refuse), twenty-four in number, consisting of the last two cards of the first ten suits, the fourth of the *shigure* and the second, third, and fourth of the *kiri*, which have a value of one point each."

The paper goes here into the difficult matter of counting the played cards. It says :—

"The peculiarity of the *shigure* hand was that while its cards, for counting the players' hands at the end of the game, reckoned respectively 20, 10, 5, and 1, they were only valued for the *teyaku* as *kasumono*, counting one each. The value of the 48 cards in all is 264, 3 times 88, or 22 times 12. As many as seven persons might sit down, but only three could come into the game at one time, and each player played his own game. The deal and the dealing went round from the right towards the left. The sitter on the dealer's left acted as 'pony,' and shuffled the spare pack for the next deal. In all, seven cards were dealt to each player, and six were placed on the table as banco. In the matter of declaring to play, a complicated system of forfeits was practised. If there were more than three players, say five, only three could play, and the third in order must wait till the two before him had declared, and then negotiate with Nos. 4 and 5 with the view of buying them out, in which case they were exempt from forfeit. Coming now to the *teyaku*, each player must at the outset declare whether he held *teyaku*, that is, one of twelve specific combinations, in which each of the four cards of the *shigure* counted simply one, as *kasumono*. The object of the play was for each player to match as many cards as possible of the same suit, and to gain as many high-value cards as possible. *Dekiyaku* consists in the holding of the four Brilliants and the *o-ame*, or one of a limited number of other combinations. In counting the value of the cards for *hana-awase*, every point above 88 counts to a player's credit, and every point under to his debit. In each case the deal passes to the highest score in *hana-awase*, and twelve deals make the game. The counters are of two kinds, *kwanki* of twelve points each, and chips, value one point each."

Obviously these particulars can give only an outlined idea of *hana-awase*, but it is truly a first-class card-game, requiring good memory, good judgment, skill in calculating chances, and great readiness in counting, all being affected by the element of luck to about the same extent as Western card-games. Japanese who are most familiar with poker, declare that *hana-awase* surpasses it in its combination of skill and luck. An ingenious person who had learned the Japanese cards and way of counting, could very readily introduce the pastime here, substituting the rose, oak, snowdrop, violet, &c., for the

native names, and adapting the native represen-
tations.

Until recently all funerals in Japan were conducted
by Buddhist priests, even those of Shinto dignitaries
themselves; but now the Shintoists bury their own
dead, in a coffin much like that used in Europe.
The Buddhist " casket" is small and square, and the
corpse is doubled up inside it, in a kneeling or
squatting position, with the head bent down to the
knees—some say in order that the dead man may
repose in an attitude of prayer, others that he may take
again, on being born into a new world, the folded-
up form which he had before his mother gave him
birth.   Observe that, notwithstanding the Japanese
reverence for ancestors, the man on the horse by the
side of the procession does not lift his hat off as the
dead body passes.   It is not the custom in Japan
to do this, because of the ingrained Buddhist idea
that the earthly tenement is nothing, and the spirit—
the *tamashi*—all; and yet that same man would not
dream of speaking to an equal or superior without
uncovering his head.   One of the funny sights in
Tôkyô is to see a countryman struggling with the
strings of his big sun-hat, while he wants to talk
ever so much, but cannot, to the friend or master
whom he has just encountered.

Buddhism did good service throughout ancient
and mediæval Japan in the matter of funeral obser-
vances, besides introducing to the Empire tea-drink-
ing and other excellent novelties and noble doctrines.
Formerly, as Mr. Chamberlain tells us in his "Things

Japanese," the horrid custom prevailed of burying the living with the dead. It is related that in the twenty-eighth year of the Emperor Suinin (B.C. 2 of the Christian chronology) his brother died. All his attendants were buried alive round the tumulus in a standing position. For many days they died not, but day and night wept and cried. The Mikado, hearing the sound of their weeping, was sad and sorry in his heart, and commanded all his ministers to devise some plan by which this custom, ancient though it was, should be discontinued for the future. Accordingly, when the Mikado died in A.D. 3, workers in clay were sent for to Izumo, who made images of men, horses, and various other things, which were set up round the grave instead of living beings. This precedent was followed in later times, and some of these figures still exist. The Ueno Museum in Tôkyô contains several specimens, and one (of a man) is now in the British Museum.

The vast tombs of the ancient Emperors and Daimios of Japan were called *misasagi*. The *misasagi* vary greatly in size. One measured by Mr. Satow in Kozuke was 36 feet in height, 372 feet long, and 284 feet broad. But this is a comparatively small one. That of the Emperor Ôjin, at Nara, measures 2312 yards in circumference, and is 60 feet high. Huge stones were reared inside them, and the industrious inhabitants were forced to labour unpaid to pile up the rude but costly burial-places. All this gave way before Buddhism. Mr. Chamberlain writes :—

" In the eyes of a Buddhist, vast costly structures were not only a burden to the people, but were objectionable as tending to foster false notions of the real value of these mortal frames of ours. Many of the Mikados were earnest devotees of Buddhism. Beginning with Gemmyô Tennô in A.D. 715, a long series of them abdicated the throne in order to spend the remainder of their lives in pious seclusion. In several cases, by their express desire, no *misasagi* were erected over their remains, and some even directed that their bodies should be cremated and the ashes scattered to the winds."

Cremation and burial are both practised in Japan, the former most extensively. A Japanese cemetery is full of narrow laths of wood, styled *sotoba*, set up round the very narrow grave of the deceased, and displaying his " death-name," which is quite different from that borne by him during life. The customs of the people are very graceful and tender as regards their dead. For fifty-nine days after the demise of a parent the children must set fresh flowers every day at the well-kept tomb, while afterwards frequent visits must be made. But all the dead of a household have their funeral tablets put up in front of the little family shrine inside the house, and every daybreak the inmates softly say their names with folded palms and heads bent down, and light a *senko* stick for each, so that its fragrant odour is the first thing in the morning which tells you that the Japanese household is up for the day.

The Japanese methods of taking ducks by decoy

do not greatly differ from the methods employed in Norfolk and our fen-regions, except that the Japanese never employ dogs. That is for want of the proper breeds, not for lack of skill in training, for the Japanese sportsmen and fishermen are most patient and adroit, as witness their extraordinary success in educating cormorants to catch fish. This, which always takes place at night, and by torchlight, is one of the strangest and most interesting forms of sport. It has been faithfully described by the late General Palmer, to whom I have previously been indebted in this article. The best place to see cormorant-fishing is on the river Nagara, near Gifu, in the province of Owari, and the system is thus explained :—

There are, to begin with, four men in each of the seven boats, one of whom, at the stern, has no duty but that of managing his craft. In the bow stands the master, distinguished by the peculiar hat of his rank, and handling no fewer than twelve trained birds with the surpassing skill and coolness that have earned for the sportsmen of Gifu their un-rivalled pre-eminence. Amidships is another fisher, of the second grade, who handles four birds only. Between them is the fourth man, called *kako*, from the bamboo striking instrument of that name, with which he makes the clatter necessary for keeping the birds up to their work ; he also encourages them by shouts and cries, looks after spare apparatus, &c., and is ready to give aid if required. Each cor-morant wears at the base of its neck a metal ring, drawn tight enough to prevent marketable fish from

passing below it, but at the same time loose enough
—for it is never removed—to admit the smaller prey,
which serve as food. Round the body is a cord,
having attached to it at the middle of the back a
short strip of stiffish whalebone, by which the great
awkward bird may be conveniently lowered into the
water or lifted out when at work ; and to this whalebone is looped a thin rein of spruce fibre, twelve feet
long, and so far wanting in pliancy as to minimise
the chance of entanglement. When the fishing-
ground is reached, the master lowers his twelve
birds one by one into the stream, and gathers their
reins into his left hand, manipulating the latter
thereafter with his right as occasion requires. No. 2
does the same with his four birds ; the *kako* starts
in with his volleys of noise ; and forthwith the
cormorants set to at their work in the heartiest and
jolliest way, diving and ducking with wonderful swift-
ness as the astonished fish come flocking towards
the blaze of light. The master is now the busiest
of men. He must handle his twelve strings so
deftly that, let the birds dash hither and thither
as they will, there shall be no impediment or fouling.
He must have his eyes everywhere and his hands
following his eyes. Specially must he watch for the
moment when any of his flock is gorged—a fact
generally made known by the bird itself, which then
swims about in a foolish, helpless way, with its head
and swollen neck erect. Thereupon the master,
shortening in on that bird, lifts it aboard, forces
its bill open with his left hand, which still holds the

rest of the lines, squeezes out the fish with his right, and starts the creature off on a fresh foray — all this with such admirable dexterity and quickness that the eleven birds still bustling about have scarce time to get things into a tangle, and in another moment the whole team is again perfectly in hand.

The cormorants are caught young, and very carefully educated. They become almost as humanly intelligent as their masters, and know exactly their distinguishing number, and the proper order in which they should enter the water. If cormorant No. 5 attempts to go in before cormorants Nos. 3 and 4, the chatter and squawking become terrific. The leader of the team is always an old grey bird, called *dai ichi*, and most jealous of his privileges. Some of these veterans have taken fish for their masters during periods of twelve and fifteen years, and truly comical it is to see them returning in the early morning, ranged on the gunwale of the boat, shaking their wet wings, preening their soaked feathers, flapping their tails, and stolidly digesting their share of the fish, with a running chorus of yelps and squawks, wanting nothing to seem like the blue-coated fishermen themselves, except a little brass *kiseru* smoking in their big beaks.

I must say something about those hard-working fellows, the *kuramaya-san*, or jinriksha-men. Without the ever-present aid of the class to which these belong, locomotion in Japan would be difficult or impossible. You begin by laughing at the ridiculous

vehicle which he draws, and end by almost living
in the convenient little trundling-machine, which is
seen everywhere now, in the remotest villages of
the Empire as well as in its towns and cities. The
"ricksha," as it has come to be called, is indeed spreading all over Asia. It forms the common conveyance
to-day in Hong-Kong, Shanghai, Singapore, Penang,
the Dutch colonies, the Indian hill-stations, and elsewhere, but will never come, I think, into European
use, partly because of the white man's prejudice
against turning draught-animal (albeit, he will pull
a bath-chair at a walking pace), partly because of
horse-traffic, which, in any excess, is fatal to the
"ricksha." Yet this thoroughly acclimatised Japanese conveyance has only been in vogue for twenty
years. It was invented in 1870 by an old gentleman of Kyôtô, who was paralysed, and went about
in a little cart, or perambulator. Now there are
over 60,000 of them in Tôkyô alone. The outfit
of a jinriksha-man—coat, drawers, hat, lantern, all
complete—is set down in the Tôkyô police regulations at five *yen*, about eleven shillings. His lawful
rates for pulling you along at five or six miles an
hour are from seven to fifteen cents, the Japanese *ri*
equalling two and a half miles English. And on
that modest twopence per mile the brave fellow
will keep himself and his family, his average daily
takings being about fifty cents.

A British cabman or labouring man or artisan
will justly scorn such an ill-paid and patient life,
but there is one point about the low-class Japanese

which might be profitably imitated in this country
or in America. I mean the perfect and scrupulous
cleanliness of the people—one and all, from the
highest to the meanest. There are many enviable
traits in the Japanese which we can never hope to
introduce or imitate. We cannot import their delightful politeness, which renders existence a softer
and pleasanter thing for all concerned. We cannot
equal their deep respect for age and profound filial
devotion, which make life quiet and easy for every
parent, since he is sure to be maintained in honour
and comfort by his sons, so that no one struggles to
save, and every one looks forward to old age as the
safest and sweetest period of his years. We cannot
have their artistic perceptions of the simpler beauties
of Nature, nor reach their perfect joy in a cherry-spray,
a maple branch, a stream, or a seaside grove. We
cannot live so refinedly or die so cheerfully as these
children of the far past, whose religion is a fairy-book
and whose social system resembles that of birds and
butterflies. But, oh! we might be clean! I love and
honour my countrymen and countrywomen of the
working and middle classes beyond words, and think
them, what they think themselves, the chief of all
races—but, as a people, do they habitually wash?
Will anybody be bold enough to say that the average
tradesman, or artisan, or handicraftsman, or labourer,
or railway man, or cabman in England, always or
often, or, in many cases, so much as even sometimes,
bathes after his day's labour? Do they even in-
variably wash their mouths and hands before kissing

the mistress and children and sitting down to meals ?
Alas! we know that they do not, and, with the
miserable provision made for them in their houses
and towns and villages, that practically they cannot.
But these Japanese—men, women, and children—
would rather go without their food than without their
tub. They could not, and would not, sit down at
home with dirty fingers or unwashed feet. A ricksha-
man's hands or a maid-servant's hands are just as
beautifully kept in Japan as a Minister's or a Court
lady's. The feet of the people are fair and sweet and
symmetrical to behold, and in a crowd they have no
odour because of their superlative purity of skin. If
we suddenly saw bare all the feet and limbs of our
working people—ay, or of many among their betters
—what would they look like in the way of personal
neatness and propriety? Ask the hospital surgeons
and the attendants at our workhouses! But you
could not strip the humble dress from the poorest in
Japan and fail to find his skin clean, his hands and
feet trimly kept, his person proudly pure. It is not
due to the climate, for Japanese winters and springs
are as cold and damp as ours. It is due to the noble
and elevating love of cleanliness for its own sake ;
and I wish with all my heart I could make England Japanese in this one point. Hard work never
spoiled a housemaid's honest hands if gloves were
worn and proper care were taken of them, and with
clean feet and limbs a man can do as much toil as the
one who goes like a pig. In Tôkyô alone there must
be 2000 public baths where adults can bathe for a

halfpenny and children for a farthing. It is true they use the same big tub and the same water, but then the real washing is performed outside the great *oke*, with little tubs, and the bodies of the bathers are kept so clean that a dip in the general water does not soil it. It is a medical fact that the Japanese escape typhus and many forms of European maladies by their semi-divine cleanliness—which is part of the self-respect characteristic of this gentle and gifted people—so that if I had the power, and might offer to my country one precious and universal gift from the "Land of the Rising Sun," it should be the Japanese warm bath-tub, at a halfpenny a head, universally accessible out-of-doors or indoors.

X

AND NOT ASHAMED

BEN BOOTH B?

"NEAR THE LITTLE QUAY WHERE THE TRAWLERS LAY."

P. 211.

X

AND NOT ASHAMED

It all happened in a village of the West Coast which I used to know, and to haunt: and I heard it from an old coastguardsman, as I sate in the hollow of the red cliffs near to the little quay where the trawlers lie. I had been reading a noble passage of Mr. Ruskin's "Modern Painters," which I will hunt up and quote, because then, whoever peruses these lines, whether they like my story or not, will be sure to get something worth their trouble.

The passage was that in Part III., sec. i, ch. xv., of "Modern Painters," and it was good and pleasant to read such wholesome words in the placid hollow of the cliff, with the Channel Sea rippling underfoot, beyond the furze and blackberry bushes, in curves of green and silver, with the goldfinches flitting among the thistles, the larks carolling overhead, and the gulls flying hither and thither, more for pure delight in the power of their wings than for any hunger. Wrote Mr. Ruskin:

"It is not possible for a Christian man to walk across so much as a rood of the natural earth, with mind unagitated and rightly poised, without receiving strength and hope from some stone, flower, or

leaf, or sound ; nor without a sense of bliss falling
upon him out of the sky. And if it be not always
so, that is partly the fault of even holy men, who in
the recommending the love of God to us refer but
seldom to those things in which it is most abundantly
and immediately shown. Though they insist; much
on His giving of bread and raiment and health
(which He gives also to the inferior creatures), they
do not require us sufficiently to thank Him for that
glory of His works which He has permitted us
alone to perceive. They bid us often meditate in
the closet, but send us not enough into the fields
at evening. They dwell on the duty of self-denial,
but they do not half enough inculcate the duty of
delight. No doubt many an earnest mind has often
little time or disposition to heed anything more than
the mere toil and obligations of life ; but I think
that of the weaknesses, distresses, vanities, schisms,
and sins which ofttimes in the best men diminish
their usefulness and mar their happiness, there would
be fewer if, in their struggle with Nature fallen, they
sought for more aid from Nature undestroyed. It
seems to me that the real sources of bluntness in
men's feelings towards the splendour of the grass
and the glory of the flowers are less to be found
in ardour of occupation, seriousness of philanthropy,
or heavenliness of desire than in the turning of the
eye at intervals of rest too seriously within ; the
want of courage to shake off anxieties and leave
the way of the world to Him that rules it. . . . I
believe the root of almost every failure Christian

teachers make has been the effort to force men to earn rather than to receive their salvation . . . and to call on men oftener to work for God—who needs it not—than to stand by and see God working for them."

The same high idea is to be found in the poetry of the Sufis. Their subtle and melodious Persian bard sings—as I have transcribed him in my " Sàdi in the Garden "—about

> *Ma'arifat*, the State divine,
> Where the Soul dwells in light beyond this light,
> Nor sees alone *Jalâl*, Greatness of God,
> But *Jamâl*, Beauty, Grace, and Joy of God,
> For which dear splendour we desire Him most,
> Not for His terrors nor His majesties,
> And so doth Sàdi inculcate in song.

It was the right place to sit in and to realise the meanings both of the British prose-poet and of the Persian mystic, while admiring how Nature had led them both to the same great and comfortable doctrine. The cliffs, ruddy as blood with the old red sandstone of which they were built—made a natural amphitheatre of peace and beauty, whose far vast stage was the Channel, upon which went and came the "peoples of the sea." Veronicas with wild roses and the golden sprays of the gorse adorned its clefts and ledges ; while families of rock-pigeons, living in the recesses of the cliff, filled the air with pretty noises of love and bird business, which mingled with softened sounds of boat-building and of human doings from the village lying just beyond the head-land. A narrow and steep path wound along the

mid-way bosom of the hollow, down which I presently
perceived an old friend of mine (the coastguardsman)
approaching, his telescope under his arm, and handling an empty pipe. Sitting down beside me, and
borrowing my tobacco-pouch, he cut my philoso-
phising short, just as I drop it here ; but something
which he told me then and there about that particular
spot of the coast has made me always remember the
scene, and the page in Ruskin, and the thought that
it is good to be natural, and to get from Nature those
lessons of simplicity, and trust, and truth which she
can impart.

He began out of a little incident which occurred
while we sat there together. A good-looking young
woman, with a pretty boy toddling by her side, came
down the path, carrying a heavy basket—for it was
a short cut to the village—and the grey-headed
sailor and I helped her with her load over a difficult bit of the descent. I noticed she had a
face so comely and frank as to compel observation,
and was struck by the honest directness of her
glance and the fearless look of her beautiful grey
eyes.

"Nothing contraband in that big basket, Mrs.
James, I hopes," said the old Bluejacket, making
a semi-official joke.

"La! Mr. Brown," says the handsome young
matron, "just look for yourself;" and with that
she threw back the napkin from a whole poultry-
yard of chickens and eggs which she was carrying to
the little shop where she sold such commodities, and

where her husband kept the post-office, and dealt in stationery and dry goods.

"'Taint the first time, Mary, be it, as I've had to have my eye on you here?" said the coast-guardsman, with a kindly softening of his seafaring tones.

I couldn't imagine why the rich blood should leap as it did into those pretty cheeks. I should have thought—merely from passing her now and then, and exchanging a few friendly words—that she was too composed, and happy, and self-satisfied a wife and mother ever to have any need or power to blush. But the wild roses that her skirts brushed against, as she shook her head archly at the old sailor and passed away down the path, were pale in their warmest crimson compared to the burning glow which went over her cheeks and brow; and down, indeed, to her neck and bosom.

"Why, Brown!" I said, "you have managed to set that handsome Mrs. James's face on fire with a word! What did it mean?"

"It don't mean anything agin the goodness and the sweetness of her, sir! You may take your davy about that. A better and a truer woman don't walk these parts. But it do mean something out of the common that happened in this wery spot and to that wery Mary James, and what might, p'raps, have been ever so much worse than it turned out, except for the chance of my keeping my weather-eye lifted that day."

And then my marine friend—salted down into

sagacity and kindliness by many a hard but useful year of life—told me the little story which sticks in my recollection along with that nook in the sandstone cliff, that passage in Mr. Ruskin, and the reflections they started about town life and country life. I must take leave to translate him out of the Devon vernacular in at least the greater portion of it.

" You've seen James, sir," he began, " him what keeps the post-office ; and you've seen what a quiet, proud, self-respecting sort of young man he is. He was always the same, and no honester don't live, and no uprighter ; but the silent ways of him was nigh to costing him Mary yonder." Whereupon he narrated to me in his own style, and with many an intercalated cloud of smoke, how Mary was the daughter of a farmer—a widower—in a neighbouring inland hamlet, and how she grew up the prettiest little maid of the district from her childhood ; and how, out of many admirers, the one she secretly liked most—almost without her own knowledge— was this same John James, who was son of the owner of a trawling vessel, a good-looking fellow and excellent sailor, but shy and reserved. The one she liked least—with very full consciousness of her reasons, for he was a noisy, selfish, self-willed person, rich as people are reckoned in those parts, and well-built, and rather finely-featured, but given to drink, and otherwise objectionable—was the lawyer of the market-town, named George Barker. And to understand the matter rightly, he must give me to know that James had never spoken, nor never dared or dreamed to speak, one word to Mary about the love of which his heart was full, and had only once, indeed, gone so far as to ask her, at a dance, for a yellow rosebud which was in her hair. George Barker, on the other hand, was always persecuting her with his undesired attentions, and saying bitter and bad things about everybody else who ventured to cast an eye in her direction, trying in every possible manner to worry her into marrying him. John, who knew a good deal that had been shameful about George Barker's life, was far too honest a fellow to speak against him behind his back; and this was the state of things when a bad season came and Mary's father made lee-way in his farming accounts and got behindhand, and had to borrow money by bills at heavy interest; until at last the prospect was that he would end by losing his farm for a matter of £200, where his father and grandfather had lived before him. This came to be known to most of the neighbours, and to John James and George Barker among those; and the two of them, each for himself, took characteristic resolutions. John, who had never ventured to speak to Mary while she was reputed rich, was inclined to do so now that her father had no money and might be ruined. But what he determined upon was to sell his share in the trawler, realising about one hundred pounds, and go to sea in a pilot-cutter, where the pay for a mate is fairly good, saving every penny of his

wages, until he could put it to the £100, and offer
it all to Mary's father before the crisis ripened.
Barker, on the contrary, who had money and to
spare, secretly bought up whatever bills he could
lay hands upon, signed by Mary's father, and prepared a *coup*. He went to the old gentleman and
demanded his daughter, acquainting him with the
fact that, holding most of the bills, he meant to
sell him up if Mary was refused to him, or to burn
them the day she became Mrs. Barker. There was
a painful scene afterwards at the farm-house. Mary,
who was a dutiful child devoted to her father, was
informed of the alternative, and with her heart
hankering after John, doubted sorely whether it
was not, after all, love lost, because of his silence.
She could not, however, bear to think of her father
bankrupt, outcast, perhaps in prison. George might
turn out better than he promised—he must have
some regard and respect for her to be ready to
tear up £200 in bills for the sake of her hand.
She would marry him—if it must be; and the
old coastguardsman hit his pipe so hard upon
the bench when he told me this, that the bowl
flew off.

That same day, he said, John had put £135 into
the bank towards buying off Mary's father from his
creditors ; and was walking home by the beach full
of gentle pride and hope. Mary had been to the
village to sell chickens and eggs and butter—and
was coming the other way, in a very mournful
mood, by this same upper path. "And as it hap-

pened," said the old sailor, " I was on duty at the
top of the cliff, a-carrying this wery glass. And
what did happen, sir, was most rum," whereupon he
proceeded to recount a certainly remarkable episode.
John James, it appears, was a wonderfully clever
swimmer, and fond to excess of a sea-bath. The
little bay being free of people, the afternoon divine,
and the green water bright and laughing enough
to tempt a tired mermaid, he stripped, and plunged
in from the rocks. After a half-hour in the waves
he was climbing back to the ledge where he
had placed his clothes when that occurred which
often befalls along these Devonian cliffs—a slight
landslip. A ton or two of rock, detached by the
summer rain, rattled down, and one fair-sized frag-
ment caught the unfortunate John on the side of
the head and laid him senseless, half in and
half out of the water. " It was just in that nook
down there, sir! which you can spy from this
seat; and if you'll look up you'll see the clift is
a fresher red right above us than along the rest
of the brow."

At that moment Mary was slowly pacing down
the path, wrapt in miserable reflections; having
the day before given herself away, also having that
very day learned in the village that John had
signed articles to cruise in the pilot-cutter *Good
Hope*, which looked as if he never had cared
for her, and cared less than ever now, since her
father was on the point of bankruptcy. "Now,
sir," said Brown, "what I tells you now is what I

seed with this here glass, though not till it was
half over." Arrived at the place where the bench
is planted, she suddenly observes something pink,
something unmistakably unusual, at the foot of
the rocks. It is half in the wash of the waves,
half leaning against the seaweeds and stones. Ah!
it is a man, a drowned sailor! She must approach
—she must examine—if possible, if there be any
life, she must help! Sturdy and healthy as one
of her father's heifers, it is nothing to her to
scramble down the steep face of the slope and to
reach the body. At the last few steps she passes
a heap of clothes upon a stone, and recognises
the pattern of the neck-handkerchief lying upon
the pilot-jacket; recognises the silver cable-chain in
the waistcoat! It is the man she secretly loves!
It is John James! One glance at the pallid face,
down which a thin thread of crimson blood trickles,
confirms what the clothes have told her; and—
country girl, sea-coast girl, as she is—all is quite
clear to her in an instant. He has been bathing
under the cliffs, a stone has fallen and struck him;
he may not be—he need not be—dead! Before
her maidenly eyes he lies, who was too shy to
tell her that he loved her, and, "I allow," says old
Brown, "there's plenty of fine London misses who
would have fainted or screamed, or called for salts
or somethink, with that to look on." But being
as pure as rain, and as simple as sunshine, and
as natural as the flowers, Mary bends over her
lover very tenderly, and feels for his heart. It

beats! it beats! and—oh, token of truth stripped
bare!—right over it, on the white skin, is tattooed,
as sailors use, the word "MARY." Moreover,

" SHE SUDDENLY OBSERVED SOMETHING PINK AT THE FOOT OF THE ROCKS."

hung about his neck in a length of white sennet
is a little silk bag. Being daughter of Eve, she

must look—she does look, into that bag.   It is
only a tiny string to pull, and inside—"La!"
there is the yellow rosebud he begged from her
hair at the dance; faded, and soaked by the waves,
but, oh! the rosebud!   Now, for twenty times
better reason than mere humanity, must she show
herself heroic.   If John James lies here many
minutes longer, the incoming tide will choke and
kill him; nor is there any help to be had except
what she can give.   "You'll understand," says
Brown, "that it's only just after this p'int that I
comes into the play; for I hadn't clapped eyes yet
upon what was going on below."   She bends down
over the swooning man, and, placing her great
shapely arms under his, and getting his helpless
chin upon her shoulder, heaved his body up with the
majestic power resident in the loins of country-bred
English girls; and clasping him tenderly but firmly,
mounted the stones, step by step, until she could
lay him on a place of safety amidst the grass and
sea-poppies.   Then, woman-like, the danger being
gloriously conjured, she succumbed, and broke
into tears and weakness—having just force enough
remaining to fetch John's coat and shirt from the
rocks below, and dispose them over her strangely-
confessed sweetheart.   " 'Twas so I saw her, sir,"
Brown went on, "sobbing and laughing by turns
by the side of the man that loved her; and, at
the first, I allow, I didn't understand it.   But
when all was made clear, and we wiped the blood
away and see him coming to, I says, 'You're a

right good girl, Mary!' I says, 'a rare good brave girl! and, as this young chap's getting round, you run off home, and don't say nuthen to nobody, no more won't I; then no one won't ever be able to arst about it—not even John himself.'"

Her face, he said, became red again like a cliff-poppy, when this counsel was being given. But she took it gladly, and went off, leaving Mr. Brown to bring John to, and to take the business on himself, which he did. As to the advice of absolute silence, she did not quite follow that, insomuch as, full of her new and tender secret, she told her father that night that he must ask her no questions, but that it was quite impossible she could ever marry George Barker. Which piece of sudden news made the old gentleman deeply perplexed, and George savagely angry and jealous.

Afterwards, to make up the money wherewith he intended to aid Mary's father, John—recovered, and unaware of his rescuer—went off in the pilot-cutter, and was away for a fortnight or more, during which time a violent summer storm burst upon the coast. He went off in his proud, silent way, with only just a hand-shake of farewell to his beautiful love, never dreaming that those quiet, limpid eyes had read the inscription above his manly heart, and that Mary had borne him, stark naked, in her faithful, fond arms, like a baby. Men are such fools, for the most part! The interval was a troubled one up at the farmhouse, because George Barker went there again and again to plague Mary and to threaten the old gentleman, whose bills were soon falling due. Then the bad weather came, and one afternoon—when the worst had blown over, but still no boat could as yet put out, and the villagers were gathered on the sea-front looking to windward, as coast-folk will, for the waters to bring their own tidings—presently they spy some wreckage coming in, and then, outside, a boat, bottom upwards, and, outside that again, what the look-out man allowed to be a corpse driving. All this quickly spread into the countryside, and brought everybody down to the shore ; nor was the excitement small when the swamped boat rolled into reach, and was found to have *Good Hope* painted on the stern. Had the pilot-cutter gone down, then, and would the poor human flotsam and jetsam prove to be some one they all knew—John James, perhaps ?

It came ashore, bare to the waist, sorely disfigured by the fish and the waves, so that the features were wholly indistinguishable. It came ashore, and was reverently laid on the shingle, amid a crowd containing Mr. Brown, George Barker, Mary, and a hundred others, among whom the rumour ran—no doubt because of the dark hair and strong frame—that it was indeed John. And poor Mary, seemingly, for just one agonised moment, thought so too ; since, obeying an emotion entirely irresistible, she sprang forward, knelt by the sad relic, and, laying open the chest of the corpse, exclaimed, " Ah, dear God ! no ; it's not John ! there's no mark upon his bosom ! "

I had lent the coastguardsman my pipe, well filled,

but—at this point—he let it go completely out, so absorbed was he in finishing his story; which he did in the following words, as well as I can recall them :

"They was all, sir, pretty much startled-like to see Mary do such a thing as this—all 'cepting me, that is to say, because, in course, I wery well understood. But it might have gone off quiet, and only have made gossip, hadn't it been for that man Barker, who, with the ugliest face you ever see, burning alive with disappointment and spitfire jealousy, breaks out, before everybody, at Mary, saying, 'What do *you* know, that you *ought* to know about the marks on John James's bosom—you——?' Sir, he never got the evil word more than half-way out before he was clouted on the mouth with three or four rough sleeves at once, for Mary was the favourite of the village ; and while they was half for ducking him and half for letting him go, I sings out, 'Hold that 'ere gentleman fast, lads, till I clears this fog up,' and then and there I says the whole story over to 'em all, and how Mary come to know what was wrote upon John's bosom, and the courage and goodness of the girl."

"They thought more of her than ever, didn't they?" I asked.

"Lord, sir, they'd have give her the moon out of the sky if they could, so proud they was of her, and pleased. But it's a rum thing, too, what happened soon afterwards."

"What was that?"

"Why, a message came from John, saying he was all alive and jolly, and he and his mates, after losing a boat and having a poor fellow washed overboard, had done a very pretty piece of salvage in the Channel-mouth with their pilot-cutter, helping a treasure-ship into Plymouth, which was going to be worth to them more than a hundred pounds a man."

"Well, Brown," I said, "I can guess the rest, as if it was written out on the log-slate."

"Don't doubt you can, sir," responded the old sailor, demurely lighting his pipe—my pipe rather—anew. "John came home, and paid the old man clear, and flew where he had been before, without knowing it—into Mary's arms—and there was a wedding and grand doings, and you may judge it's five or six years ago by the size of yon little toddler that went down the path with Mrs. James just now. She won't let John go to sea any more, if she can help it, and there ain't no need, for the Squire got him the post-office, and that salvage job turned up trumps to the tune, I'm told, of four hundred pounds."

"And George Barker?" I inquired.

"Oh, George! oh, he cleared out. We didn't want him any more, and he didn't want us."

XI

A LUCKY NEWSPAPER

"IN JIBING, THE BOOM KNOCKED THE SKIPPER OVERBOARD."   P. 229.

XI

A LUCKY NEWSPAPER

In beautiful old-time May weather those butterflies
of the sea, the yachts of our pleasure-navy, began
their season this year, and all lovers of the noble
pastime were glad that the Prince of Wales, with his
splendid new cutter, the *Britannia*, carried off two
first prizes in the earliest matches of the spring from
such antagonists as Mr. P. Donaldson's *Calluna*, Lord
Dunraven's *Valkyrie*, and the out-classed *Iverna*.
Mr. A. D. Clarke's cutter *Satanita*, while stretching
her fresh canvas on the Solent, had sprung her boom,
and could not take part in these contests, which were
otherwise in many respects so memorable.   To what
perfection has not the art of shipbuilding for pastime
been brought, when we can see two such exquisitely-
modelled craft as the *Britannia* and the new *Valkyrie*
reach and run all the way from Gravesend to the
Mouse Light and back, and again from the Nore to
the Goodwins and Dover, and scarcely ever from first
to last have more than a ship's length or two of
distance between them !

I was myself afloat in my own vessel, the *Harelda*,
a yawl of 80 tons, in the delicious weather of that
opening week, and cruising over those same waters

where the matches were sailed, that is to say, at and
beyond the Mouse Light and North Foreland.   How
little do those ashore who are unacquainted with
the estuary of the London river understand what is
implied by such a spot and beacon as the Mouse
Light.   To the eye of one who simply inspects a
small-scale map, or passes in a passenger-ship down
the river, and out at its mouth, in this or that direction, for foreign travel, those outer waters where
the two estuaries of Thames and Medway melt into
ocean seem to be merely one equal and simple expanse.
But, in reality, they constitute such a labyrinth as
might have puzzled the Minotaur.   From Orford Ness
on the northern coast, southwards, right across to the
North Foreland, that watery waste which the two
rivers make is a perfect maze of sands and shoals, of
knolls, oozes, and shifting shingle, which guards the
royal river and the imperial city better than the best
fortifications and strongest war-ships.   If in time of
conflict with an alliance of formidable naval enemies,
we could afford to remove, and did remove, the buoys,
beacons, and lightships from all those intricate passages that lead through and along the tangle of
shallows, no foeman in his senses would dream of
bringing a heavy squadron to bombard Sheerness,
Gravesend, or Greenwich, letting alone the forts that
fringe the river.   Or, if any one had the desperate
courage to make such an attempt and succeeded in
it, that could only be by the assistance of some
thoroughly qualified English Channel pilot, supposing
such a traitor were to be found.   There are, no doubt,

men, and even plenty of men, salted down by sea
business from their youth, and conversant a thousand
times over, in every sort of weather, with that marvellous network of deadly dangers, who, asking nothing
but the deep-sea lead in their hand and a trustworthy
compass, could bring the largest vessels through the
baffling intricacies of South Channel or Queen's
Channel; the Knock Deep, or the Black Deep, or
the Barrow Deep; the Sledway, or the Shipway;
going clear of the Inner and Outer Gabbard and the
Galloper and the Kentish Knock and Alborough
Flats, the Tongue, the Shingles, the Girdler, the
Knock John, the North Knob, the Middle Sunk, the
Shipwash, Buxey, Columbine, and Cant; to say
nothing of the outlying and ever-dreaded Goodwins,
the South Falls, and Sandettie. These are only
some few of the titles given to that wilderness of
wild water and hidden land which constitutes so
formidable a defence for the mouth of our principal
river. But we dare not ever use them as a defence.
To remove the buoys and beacons, planted by the
hundred in this maritime maze, would be to render the
Thames impenetrable to our own commercial fleet,
and to all the innumerable small peoples of the sea—
smacks, schooners, brigs, barges, and borleys, which
come and go at the mouth of Father Thames. The
consequence is, that those endlessly involved water-
roads, with all their turns and windings, have to be
learned by heart, not only by those who follow the
profession of pilots, but by the fishermen, yachtsmen,
and others who frequent them. The knowledge dis-

played by London cabmen of the names and localities of metropolitan squares and streets is very often
remarkable ; but it comes to nothing as an effort of
automatic memory and proof of the bump of locality,
compared with what a really experienced and qualified
navigator will carry in his head about such an estuary
as that in which the yacht races of last month were
held.   The streets—for all their intricacy—are ever at
the same level and of the same width ; but the rise and
fall of the tides in those waters alter all their aspect
and character, so that for the pilot, who has been
compared to the cabman, there are two or three or
four salt-water Londons to learn by heart.   There
is Thames Mouth at high tide, when the flat-bottomed barges and vessels of small draught go gaily
over almost everything, and the broad sea-ways are
brimming full, and free and plain even to the ships
of heavy burden.   Then there is the low-water
Thames Mouth, when half-a-hundred important
gateways are quite shut by some narrow but dangerous ridge of sand which dries nearly bare, and
upon which in bad weather the sea breaks and
thunders as if it were a Pacific coral-reef.   Then
there is the Thames Mouth at half-ebb or half-
flood, most deadly of all, because of the currents
and eddies of the in or out running tide, which will
often lift an incautious navigator upon the brink of
a sandbank, rising abruptly like a railway embank-
ment from water six or seven fathoms deep.   In
winter-time and wild seasons nothing can be more
mortally perilous than the position of vessels caught,

like flies, in the spider's web of these treacherous under-water puzzles. If they go aground when heavy seas are running, she must be a stout ship that does not quickly bump in her bilge, and crack and shatter her timbers with the repeated shock of her blows upon the hard knoll. And if the weather be fine, she is often left by a spring tide so high that nothing the crew can do will get her off. There is a class of men called Hovellers, of whom many live in and near Harwich, whose business in winter, when there is no yachting or other light work, consists in going out in powerful rough-built cutters to salvage, where they can, all sorts of craft caught upon the banks and shoals of the Thames. They live in constant familiarity with deadly danger, and earn an occasional windfall by many a narrow escape and hardship almost unimaginable to the landsman. I have heard one of them say that the stoutest mariner afloat, who has been through every ordeal that the sea could inflict upon the human spirit and the human stomach, cannot long withstand the terrible sensation of standing upon the deck of a stranded ship when the sands below, with awful shock following upon shock, are beating the masts out of her like loose teeth from a broken garden-rake.

Immense ingenuity has been devoted by those in authority to the duty of elucidating the marine puzzles which such a coast offers; but to learn to read the sea-signs of the Trinity House is almost as long and difficult a study as that of a new language.

The accomplished steersman must know why the buoys on one hand are conical, and those on the other flat-topped; and what their colours mean, when they are painted white, or black, or green, or red, or striped vertically, or striped horizontally, or surmounted by a staff, a ball, a cage, or a bell. Notable among recent improvements are the large, ever-burning, automatically-supplied gas-buoys, from time to time carefully filled with gas at high pressure, which constantly burns in a well-guarded lamp. By day, an experienced mariner of such an estuary picks his way from buoy to buoy—if it be clear weather— as easily as a cabman taking the right turnings in town. By night, a succession of these floating lamps and heedfully-planted lighthouses leads him with reasonable safety through the intricacies of the place. But if the sky be thick, by day or by night, it is to the lead that he must chiefly trust. Nor is there any monument of faithful human service, to my mind, more striking and more illustrative of how man may help man by true discharge of daily duty than the figures on the coasting-charts, which here-abouts, and in a thousand other localities, register the painstaking and accurate soundings made by maritime surveyors. All over such an area as this deadly expanse of sea-traps and tidal perils every spot on the huge map will be marked with figures faithfully representing the exact depth of water at low tide. If, therefore, you only know how to read intelligently the otherwise bewildering multitude of marks, you can hardly take three or four consecutive casts of the hand-lead without knowing to a nicety where your ship is situated. A special danger, however, arises from the fact that these sands and mazes are perpetually shifting their position, closing up old passages and opening new ones. Eighteen years ago I well remember sailing in a little cutter which I then owned through the Spitway, that leads between the Buxey and the Gunfleet Sands, out of the Wallet into East Swin. Then, at low water, we had fifteen feet at that spot, and came through carelessly; while only last week I sailed the *Harelda* through the same difficult gut within an hour of flood, and for a dozen casts in succession the utmost that the leadsman got was "quarter less three," so that, at the end of the ebb, there would not be five feet of water in that passage now.

Desolate beyond expression in the winter months are these winding water-paths and coasting-lanes by which the commerce of the world feels its way into the river. Weird and uncanny to any except the surest navigator in the strongest ship is it to hear through the fog or the pitch-black darkness those particular buoys that are armed with a heavy bell, against the sides of which the rolling of the sea sets four or five ponderous hammers for ever banging. Melancholy in the mid November or December— beyond the scream of the seagull, the whistle of the wind, and the seething of the seawaves, is that dirge-like note always pealing from the edge of the sand or shallow where cold Death sits waiting for the imprudent crew. Nor is there one of these bells

which has not in its time tolled the funeral-knell of
some hapless ship's company. But in the summer
weather all is different. The breeze, if it blows fresh,
seems to have no spite in it; the waves, if they roll
free, appear to be at play, like the pleasure-craft that
dance over them with their white sails and glittering
topsides and dainty rigging. It is fun and not danger
to scud or beat from mark to mark and down the
winding water-lanes of green and silver; though only
by some such hard winter experience can any just
sense be had of the wonderful skill of our coastmen
and mariners, and of the excellent work done all
round our perilous shores by the Admiralty and the
Elder Brethren.

The Mouse Light — so gallantly rounded on
Thursday and Saturday, the 25th and 27th, by the
Prince of Wales's beautiful ship, the *Britannia,* and
her consorts—is a point not very far advanced into
that complicated Thames labyrinth. You run down
to it from the Nore through the Warp and the West
Swin with great facility, so that it makes an excellent
goal for a river-yacht race; and all the coasters
coming up from the North and the East reach it by
a road which landsmen could never find—along the
Shipway, the King's Channel, and the Middle Deep
—yet one that is as plain to mariners as Piccadilly
to Londoners. It was a pretty sight to see the fleet
of grand new cutters sweep round the red markship,
of which I for one must always retain a special recollection because of what I saw happen there once,
when a lady's kindly thought, and a copy of the

Daily Telegraph, between them saved the life of a man. On the occasion in question, now many years ago, I was on board a club-steamer watching such a match as that of last week. The yachts had one by one approached the Mouse Light, and I had happened to mention to a lady on board how lonely was the life of the lightkeepers, and what an event for them would be even the temporary excitement of the passage of the yachts and excursion steamers. "I wish I could send them my newspaper," she said; "there is something in it so very interesting!" and upon that offer, starting with her own copy of the *Daily Telegraph,* we collected a whole sheaf of newspapers and magazines from the passengers, and, waving one of them, hailed the lightship to send a boat for the bundle of literature. It was fine quiet weather, and they were glad to do this—just before the yachts rounded the Light. The last of the competing pleasure-craft—a powerful cutter—steered by a famous yacht-captain, was just turning to run home, when, in jibing, the boom knocked the skipper overboard. He could swim, but badly, if at all, in his heavy pea-jacket. His own vessel had shot far ahead before she could come to the wind and lower a boat, and all the other yachts in the race were well out of the range of rescue. But by the good fortune of that gentle lady who had hit upon the idea of sending her paper to the Lightship men, there was their boat just halfway back to the Mouse ship, in exactly the proper place upon the water; and it only cost two or three strokes of her oars to come to the spot where the poor skipper was sinking, and pull him into the boat with nothing worse than a ducking and a scare. And so it was, according to the heading of this paper—that a "lucky newspaper" saved the life of a man.

THE "HARELDA."

XII

THE TIGER'S VILLAGE

BEN. BOOTHBY

P. 241.

"LIES A CORPSE UNDER HIS CLAWS."

XII

THE TIGER'S VILLAGE

" *Ghora ki badli karna hoga ?* "—"Do we change horses here ? "

" Nay ! it is only a miserable village, Protector of the Poor ! where we may stay a little to buy milk and get fodder for the cattle."

This conversation took place between an English Sahib and his servant towards evening upon a country-road in the Deccan, that wide tableland of the Bombay Presidency which was called in old times " Maharashtra." The particular spot was on a jungle-path passing from Sattara along the lower slopes of the Ghâts, where they rise towards the fashionable hill-station of Mahabuleshwar. The country thereabouts is very pleasant to see, and to travel through, in the right season. Dense masses of dark-green foliage cover the rolling hills, which have a soil of rich red clay, contrasting well with the clumps of sâl and tamarind trees and the thickets of corinda. The vegetation is not tropical—at least, to the hasty observer; there are no palms or bananas, that is to say, and not many bamboo groves upon the uplands I am recalling to mind. An ordinary English bracken flourishes freely upon the bare rounded elevations which here and there rise among the more thickly-wooded heights, and the pansy and balsam, the lupin and marigold, will be perceived in the jungle, along with all sorts of flowers more strange to the European eye, the white and deadly datura, the wild indigo, the coral-lily, and delicate parasites festooning the trunks and branches of the forest-trees, some of them of singular loveliness and variety of form and colour. Although not far removed from main and well-frequented roads, this jungle-country of the Western Ghâts is as wild and sequestered in many parts as the heart of a wilderness. From the lonely pools that lie at the foot of the hills the Indian plover rises, as you pass, with its strange cry which sounds like "Did you do it? Did you do it?" Now and again a family of monkeys, the grey Hanumans, will cross the forest path, the old man of the four-handed household angrily chattering at the sight of strangers, while the child-monkeys jump upon the backs or breasts of their hairy mothers, where they will nestle quite securely while she jumps down a precipice or up into the fork of a tree. In the sandy patches you may come upon a mongoose or a porcupine, or see that strange beast the *paradoxurus*—"ood," as the Mahrattas call it—stealthily grubbing about the cactus clumps for rats or snakes. The button-quail and rain-quail start from almost every tuft with sharp whirr of their little mottled wings, as if they were cricket-balls exploding; and the jungle-dove, cream-coloured with jewelled neck, coos soft love-notes in every milk-bush. You will sight no black buck in these uplands, but, possibly enough, you may start a ravine-deer, and perhaps a sambar or *barasingh*. Yet the underwood conceals many other and fiercer animals, some of which are the real lords of the manor here-abouts. The bison roams the neighbouring hills, and the bear is a permanent tenant of them; wild cats and leopards live in many a hidden cavern of the rocks; while at night you will not pitch your tents in any region of the district without knowing by their cries that the hyenas reside there, and the red hill-fox, and as a matter of course the jackal. But the true owner and landlord of many a tract of country in the parts I am revisiting in thought is that gold-coated and dark-striped tyrant of the woods, the tiger. There are large ranges on the ghauts—one might almost call them estates—which are owned, at least temporarily, by a pair of tigers, or, it may be, by an old male tiger singly, or by a tigress which has been left alone to take care of herself and her cubs, and so develops all the worst virtues of her fierce maternity. It is one of these last that has come to my mind in connection with a summer evening in India, when along the lonely jungle-road the Englishman with his attendants was approaching the village, and asked the question with which this paper commences.

In such a country as I am describing the villages are few and far between, partly because of many difficulties as to agriculture and markets, partly because of the resolute way in which the more courageous wild beasts dispute with man hereabouts his pretensions to call himself " lord of the creation." On the plains, where the country is open and easily traversed, tigers never stay long in one place, or are likely to pay with their hides if they do ; but on the shoulders of the hills, surrounded by thickets which are the fringe of an interminable forest, the striped Rajah of the forest is oftentimes master of the situation, and takes tribute from the cattle, goats, and dogs of the community, till he can be trapped or poisoned, or until he departs for some personal reason elsewhere. It is not so bad for the country people as long as he retains his natural dread of man, which is so instinctive that the Indian herd-boy will often fearlessly save his oxen by shouting at the attacking tiger, and even flinging his stick at him ; nor do the slender Indian girls shrink from leading their goats to the stream or fetching home wood and grass because a tiger has killed a cow or kid just beyond the village fields. But at one time or another a tiger who has been, like the rest of his kind, terribly afraid of man in any shape, lays this dread aside on a sudden and for ever, and then becomes truly formidable. It is perhaps in most cases the result of an unintended experiment. The courage of a tiger is the courage not of pride, but of desperation, like that of a cat. He will get between the roots of the trees or the cracks in the earth to escape, but if escape be cut off, he will attack an elephant with armed sportsmen upon it, which is as if an infantry soldier should hurl himself

against the masonry of a fortress. In some fatal
moment the Hindoo girl going with her pitcher, or
the native agriculturist, or the local postman with
his jingling bells has passed some spot where a tiger
lay in wait watching the distant cattle grazing, or
waiting for night-time to visit some tigress who
has amorously responded to his roar. The beast
has thought himself perceived, has feared to be cut
off from his usual retreat, or the victim has shouted
in terror, making the tiger hysterical with fright;
and then in a paroxysm of rage and fear, it has
snarled, and sprung forth, and dealt, in frenzy rather
than design, that terrible blow with the forepaw
which will stun a wild boar and dislocate the neck-
bone of a bull. Before his roar of angry surprise
has well echoed through the jungle, the man, or
woman, or child lies a corpse under his claws, yet
instinct forces him to go on, and to crunch the soft
neck with his yellow fangs. Then the secret is
out: the tiger has learned what a " poor forked thing "
this lord of the creation is; how feeble his natural
forces; how useless for self-defence that eye that was
so dreaded; those hands that were so crafty; those
limbs that bore him so haughtily with his head to the
sky. Moreover, the tiger has tasted man, and found
him as savoury to devour as he is easy to butcher,
and from that time forth the brute neglects no
further opportunity, but becomes step after step a
confirmed " man-eater."

There appeared the other day, in an Indian newspaper, a letter from an English official who had

come across an instance where a young tigress, in
the manner alluded to, had depopulated a district,
killed dozens of men and women, and taken actual
possession of a forest-road and tract.   She began
her career in July by killing two women near a
woodland village, and at the end of the following
December had slain at least thirty persons, becoming
bolder and more cunning with each fresh murder.
Her beat lay in some foot-hills, and she roamed over
an area twenty-five miles long by three or four broad.
The country was such that she could neither be
tracked for any distance nor driven forth by beaters.
She would not kill a tied buffalo, nor would she go
back to a corpse if once disturbed.   She became at
last so bold that she ventured, in open daylight, to
carry off men and women when cutting the crops in
the terraced fields, stalking them from above and suddenly springing on them.   The terror of her fero-
city spread through the country.   The villagers left
their homes for safer regions, yet even in the forests
the tigress learned to stalk the sound of an axe, and
made many victims, before the woods were proved to
be even more dangerous than the fields had been.
The method of attack adopted was so sudden as
to prevent any possibility of escape ; the blow dealt
so deadly as to render even a cry for help impossible.   The victim was dead and carried off before
his companions knew what had occurred.   Constant
efforts were made for her destruction—poison, spring-
guns, and dead falls were ineffectually resorted to,
any number of buffaloes were tied down at night, and

many a time the fresh trail of a kill was taken up in hopes of obtaining a shot at the tigress, but with no result. At last a file of soldiers were requisitioned to see what force could do to remove this horrible animal, cunning having been found of no avail. The beast was killed, and was found to be a young tigress, in perfect condition; the pad of her left forefoot had at one time been deeply cut from side to side, but had thoroughly healed, leaving, however, a deep scar, which proved her presence wherever she roamed. The same account mentions one instance in which two cowherds, living in a small grass hut in a somewhat wild forest, were cooking their food in the evening when this tigress suddenly sprang upon one and carried him off. His companion intimidated the animal with shouts and threats, and succeeded in making him leave his victim. Carrying his wounded companion into the hut, the trembling *Koombi* closed the entrance and waited for daylight. But this he never saw, because after a time, the tigress, emboldened by the increasing darkness, returned, and forcing her way into the hut, carried off the uninjured man, who was doubtless doing all he could to prevent the approach of the brute. The other, who had been first seized, died of his wounds and of sheer shock the next day, after relating the story to those who had found him.

The party of the Sahib that Indian evening came across just such a scene as is here spoken of. All Indian villages in this part of the Deccan are pretty much alike. The larger ones will, perhaps, have rather imposing ramparts and towers made of mud, with a gateway regularly closed at night, which keeps out robbers and wild beasts, and may sometimes even be defended by armed men against troops. But the ordinary jungle village is either open to the plain and forest, or has at best a fence of dried thorn-bushes cut and piled around it, through which there will probably be many gaps. The huts within, of mud and wattle, ranged in a long dusty lane, or perhaps in a square, possess very flimsy wooden doors, sometimes only a hatch and a curtain. There will generally be seen an old tree in the middle of the village, and a little temple, perhaps only a mere porch, or *mandal*, built of sun-baked bricks and timber, approached by steps and open on one side. In the front of the temple will be a pole with a yellow flag; within the simple shrine probably a conical stone painted red, or an image grotesquely cut in marble or basalt of the monkey-god, Hanuman; or of Ganesha, the deity of wisdom. Ordinarily you would know you were coming to the village by the buffaloes trooping home, and as likely as not by lines of villagers entering with wood or fodder, as well as by the sounds, from the little abodes, of cotton bows twanging in the hut, where the peasant is fluffing his cotton before cleaning it in the gin; of the blacksmith beating his copper into shape for a *lota*; of the women singing the mill-stone song at the *chark*; or of the housewife driving backwards and forwards the beam of the hand-loom. If nobody should be at work, you would be sure to hear the monotonous but

exact rhythm of the tom-toms from somebody's house
or kinsfolk feast; there would be a wall-eyed, shiny-
hided buffalo wallowing in the village tank, a few
white egrets stalking about its edge, a vulture
perched upon the tree in the square, and much
cawing of the crows watching for bits of chupatty
from the hands of the little naked children.

But as that Sahib's party came down the hill-side
by the widening path to the jungle village no sound
whatever arose from its few and humble habitations.
Nobody came out to make salutation or to offer
supplies; no cattle were perceived wandering about,
no children, no birds appeared, except indeed many
vultures upon the tree in the square and on the
temple roof. The pots in the grain-dealer's shop were
empty and overturned, a piece of cloth just begun was
left with broken threads upon the loom in the next
hut. On the other side of the way the chatties at a
potter's stall were tumbled and broken, and a sheet of
copper lay at the blacksmith's forge half-bent to make
some vessel, but precipitately abandoned. Wherever
one gazed there were signs of a hasty flight on the
part of the inhabitants, who did not seem to have
left anybody to represent them. Yes! there was one
silent and melancholy representative, and the sudden
appearance of her would have startled the party very
much more than it did but for a discovery made by
the Sahib's *ghorawallah*—the groom—close by the
silent and empty temple. There was a muddy patch
there in the square, from which the last of the rain-
water had but recently dried up, and, in the black

slime so left, were deeply imprinted the "pads" of
an evidently immense tiger. It was, of course,
evident now to the Englishman, and to those with
him, that the striped Terror which left those foot-
marks had given the villagers notice to quit, and was
somewhere or other near at hand, in practical possession of the fee-simple of the village. Desolate
beyond expressing was the little unpeopled "place"
of the hamlet, and the look of that helpless red god
staring from his portico upon the huts that he could
not protect, along with the excitement of the hungry vultures perched on the cotton-trees, aware, no
doubt, of the deadly secret of the place. For, round
the corner, by the dyer's shop, where two or three
newly-stained turban cloths still hung upon ropes to
dry, they came upon that secret. Across the threshold
of a mud hut, evidently dragged away from the
broken charpoy on the earthen floor, lay the body of a
woman, torn on the brown delicate neck and along the
shoulders and breast, with long red claw-marks. A
dead infant, also mangled by a savage bite, and with
one of its arms nearly torn off, lay half concealed
under the corpse, the appearance of the bodies showing that they had been only lately slaughtered. No one
could doubt what had killed them. The sign-manual
upon their bodies was obviously that of the royal
beast, who often in this way disputes the right of his
human rival in India, roaring to scorn the illusion that
man is master of created things. The Sahib's party
was badly equipped for tiger-shooting, and passed on—
not without anxiety and the closing-up of the three

or four servants and coolies—through the outskirts of this evicted village. At any moment her ladyship the tigress or his lordship the tiger, who had taken possession of the spot, might emerge from a grain-

"THE LOOK OF THAT HELPLESS RED GOD STARING FROM HIS PORTICO."

store or a cow-pen, or even from some milk-bush or jowari-patch, to ask the travellers what business they had upon the royal property. The Englishman hastily put bullets into both barrels of his shot-gun and walked his horse as quickly as his men could follow out of the ill-fated *gaum*. At its outskirts they were astonished to hear a voice high above their heads, which came, as they afterwards found, from a young Hindoo low-caste man sitting concealed in the branches of a large mango-tree, from which could be overlooked both entrances of the village. He had made a rude platform in a fork of the tree, and watched on it with the long barrel of a matchlock protruding, and by his side an earthen jar of water. They invited him to come down and to tell them the meaning of the extraordinary spectacle they had witnessed. He descended, and informed them that for weeks past his village had been infested and persecuted by a tigress, which, after killing cattle and goats, had slain and partly eaten three or four children outside the hamlet, and had taken, during the past eight or nine days, to entering the village at night and carrying off somebody or other sleeping, as Hindoos do, outside their huts under the verandahs. The woman slain that morning with her baby was the wife of the poor matchlock-man, and he had perched himself in the tree, hoping to avenge her death when the Sahib's party passed.

It was too serious a case not to be reported in the proper quarters, and an expedition of practised tiger-shooters was equipped among the officers at the nearest station. The beast was tracked, and was killed after receiving eleven bullets, and then it turned out that she had a half-grown cub which had lost a limb, so that the maternal affection of the

ferocious parent had driven it to such desperate
ways. Indeed, the spectacle of that village was full
of philosophical suggestiveness. The dead human
mother had been slain by reason of the very same
instinct which had made her seek in vain to
preserve her child from the attack of the tigress,
driven to its wit's ends to find food for its own helpless offspring. The tigress was in her way as tender a parent as the loving mother whom she murdered : and then, besides, there was the whole village
depopulated, to make one wonder what sort of a
world it would have been if, as might well have
happened, tigers had evolved as masters of the globe
instead of men.

XIII

WILD BOARS

P. 257.

"HE AT LAST PUTS ASIDE THE BUSHES AT THE EDGE OF THE PATCH AND EMERGES."

XIII

WILD BOARS

In days when I used to fish and shoot and hunt, and variously kill the beautiful or interesting wild creatures of the woods and fields—which now I would not do—I came to know a good deal about the wild boar. And you cannot know much about him without very deeply respecting him. No beast has a higher pride or finer courage, and none becomes the savage surroundings of his home with better lordliness. He is afraid of nothing, armed as he goes with the twin scimitars of his gleaming tusks, and cased in bristly hide, which is a span thick over the withers. The Indian boar will do battle against the tiger itself, and not always get the worst of the contest, for one good rip with those sharp moon-shaped tushes—such as I have seen slash through saddle-girths and numdah, letting out a horse's entrails—will start a scarlet stripe among the black stripes of the tyrant of the jungle, out of which he quickly bleeds to death. And if sportsmen must and will slay—nor can it be maintained that slaughter is not the present way and law of Nature—then there is surely no sport in the world so entirely entrancing and exciting as "pigsticking" —to have tasted which is to despise evermore all

257

R

milder and more commonplace delights of the chase.
In this pursuit, also, the wild hog often shows a
magnificent courage. He hates to come out of the
sugar-canes or the *jowari* field, where he has put
up with his wife and family for the day. He more
than half suspects the presence of those grey-coated
men on the Arab horses, who are waiting in pairs
outside the cover, with their bright spears balanced
in the right hand, and the left restraining the fidget-
ing mouths of their steeds. But the beaters make
such a tumult with sticks and drums and crackers,
that his wife and children have bolted across the
open already, and it is clear that he too must go. It
is at a surly trot, however—disdainful and reluctant
—when he at last puts aside the bushes at the edge of
the patch and emerges—emerges to see with half an
eye that his enemies are mounted and about to pursue him, now that they have got between him and
his shelter. Well, he must make for another; but
he does it with dignity, for he has supped heavily
on the village crops all night, and the old grey boar
values his digestion. What is this, however? A
horseman on either side presses hard and harder after
him, with the point of a glittering spear held close
and low. It is abominable, but it is serious ; he must
change his trot for a gallop, and lead these insolent
disturbers of his peace into the broken and rocky
ground. Looking back out of the corner of his
small eye, of which the white shows like a speck of
mother-o'-pearl, his pig's heart rejoices to observe
one of his foes come headlong down upon the smooth

trap-rock with a crash which will put him entirely
out of the hunt, at any rate until the friendly thicket
can be reached into which the sow and her litter are
just now safely entering. Meantime the other spear
has approached as the boar slacked a little on the hill-
side, and, before he knew it was quite so near, the
sharp point, slightly misdirected, glides on his skull-
bone and goes right through the high-cocked ear.
It does not damage the boar nearly so much as it
infuriates him ; and then you see that grim, grey
dookur set up his bristles like a fence of aloe-stalks,
and champ his foaming jaws, and swing round to
charge the daring pursuer. You have need of a
horse who knows his business at this moment, and
you should well understand how to manage and
recover your disappointed spear. If the Arab is
thoroughly well trained, and you do not chance to
come out of your stirrups with the sudden swing
round—in which case the boar will probably end the
chase by ripping you in a manner to make the doctors
look serious—then the jungle-hog starts off discon-
tentedly again for his still distant refuge, and you
may add to the glory of "first spear" the joy of presently feeling the willow-leaf steel slide in a foot
deep behind his gallant brisket ; with a curious ease,
too, as if the great pig were made of butter. It is
the pace which does that—you need not thrust !—but
in the small closing eyes of your victim as he rolls
over on the rock you will still see the glare of an
unconquerable and defiant courage.

The mention of any special wild animal which he

has long ago studied and followed usually brings back to the votary of the woodland and the waste some particular scene of his remembrance and experience. When anybody speaks of tigers, for example, I chiefly recall, as it were by instinct, a wonderful picture in the Indian jungle, when I saw from a *machan*— or platform of boughs, in a tamarind tree—two young tiger-cubs playing with a peacock which they had killed. Fortuny himself even could never have reproduced—for all his superb command of the palette—the splendid play and savage combination of colours which that hidden corner of the Indian forest furnished to the eye. The burning evening sun lighted with mellow gold the coats of the fierce little tiger-kittens—orange silk with stripes of black velvet—the broken amethysts and ruined emeralds of the poor bird's train cruelly scattered over the trampled grass; the blood-stained sapphires of his breast; the scarlet and silver jewels of his crest; his russet and black wings—all framed in by the waving boughs of the korinda bush and the long flags of jungle-grass. We did not interfere with the little monsters, because we were waiting just then for their mamma, who was more than suspected of having lately killed a village-girl, and had certainly slaughtered the dead cow over whose carcass the *machan* had been established. But that jungle-picture, with its blaze of sunset colour and wild beauty of death and passion and destruction, always comes again to my mind when there is talk of tigers.

As for the boar, he brings to recollection an especial scene of the Eastern wilderness. Of course, in
India, we did not shoot the *dookur*—at all events,
not near a station, or where he could possibly be
" ridden." That would be as bad as to kill a fox with
gun or poison in any English hunting shire ; and how
nefarious such a deed would seem, of course, no words
could tell. Sydney Smith said once to a friend who
was talking freely about a new clergyman's opinions,
"Oh, don't call him a Socinian, please ! They think
hereabouts that that means netting pheasants or shooting a fox." I myself, on one sad occasion, killed by
accident a dog-fox in some English turnips, not seeing him, and taking the movement in the leaves for
the passage of a hare which we had started, and while
we secretly buried Reynard where he fell, the feeling
of remorse was exactly as if we had put to death a
churchwarden ; such is the force of tradition ! But
on that evening, and in that spot which I so well
remember, I was positively obliged to slay a boar
with lead instead of steel, to save a native and myself. It was amidst the pretty broken country round
Poorundhur, not far from Poona, in the Bombay
Presidency—a country of trap-hills, and vast plains
of black soil, which splits open in summer-time,
with innumerable wide fissures, into which the
lizards and field-rats take headers as you walk, and
where the snakes glide back and forth. I had been
shooting quail, with none but native attendants,
and as the sun touched the western horizon we
came to the edge of a deep glen, wooded with

rounded clustered bushes, between which showed patches of yellow grass.

"Down in that nullah, Gharib-parwar!"—(Protector of the Poor)—"there are plenty of deer and hares; and perhaps a leopard," remarked my Mahratta shikari.

"Get fifty people of the village," I answered, "to-morrow morning early, and let us beat the nullah from top to bottom. We can do it if——"

"*Dekho! dekho!*" interrupted Raghu; "look, Sahib, look!" And where he pointed I saw something in the upper part of the valley moving downward, which might be hyæna, leopard, or anything. Obeying a not very wise instinct—for the light was rapidly failing—I snatched my rifle from Raghu's hand and ran down the slope, he following. What a lovely and lonely hollow it was in that silent Indian waste, with its smooth tables of sand and grass, its green bushy sides, and cascades of wild parasitical flowers growing on the tree-stems, while the tiny grey ringdoves flitted cooing from bush to bush, and from the thin string of water at the bottom the Deccan peewit, who cries "Did-you-do-it? Did-you-do-it?" rose, aware of our presence. Soon, a button quail bustled out of a cane thicket higher up, and settled almost at our feet—sure sign that something was coming. And something did indeed come! We were standing on a level patch of clear ground with dense cover above and below, and the twilight, which lasts so briefly in India, was already growing dim, when out blundered a big jungle sow, followed

by a pack of piglets, bent, no doubt, on a drink of
water in the bottom, and afterwards the nightly
forage. Motionless although we stood, she saw us
from her little eyes, and grunted something perfectly

"I SANK ON MY KNEE, AND FIRED QUICK."

intelligible, beyond doubt, to her little ones, for they
all immediately scurried hard across the open,
hustling their lumbering mother. It was intelligible, moreover, to another pair of bristly ears,

for again the bushes opened, and forth into the patch of clear ground thrust a grand old grey boar— to whom, I believe firmly, his porcine consort had hastily but quite plainly remarked, "My dear! there are hateful men here. Rip them up—if you can."

At all events he did not seem surprised to see us, but champed his lips, grunted in a quick, angry way, and came straight for where we stood.

"*Maro! maro!*" cried Raghu—"shoot, shoot!" —and, truly, it was no time to have in mind the regulations of the Poona Hunt Club. I could just catch the sight of the rifle in the dim evening, as I sank on my knee, and fired quick, to get both bullets in. The first caught him on the right-hand tusk and sent it spinning—itself glancing aside. However, the boar turned its head away a little at the shock, and just slackened a bit in a manner to show his broad neck fair and square, not twelve yards off, so that my second bullet went clean through the cervi- cal vertebræ. At the cost of a venatical impropriety Raghu and I were saved.

XIV

THE WEALTH OF POVERTY

BEN. BOOTHBY.

"HE HAD A GARMENT OF SOME SORT SPREAD OVER A BRIAR BUSH, AND WAS
TARRING IT ASSIDUOUSLY."   P. 267.

XIV

THE WEALTH OF POVERTY

I draw from the portfolio of memory the recollection of a man who, more than any other, taught me
in early days how very slightly human happiness
depends upon material possessions. The tendency of
the present age is, it may be feared, to take the other
view too strongly. If you will listen to the persons
who make most noise on behalf of the working classes,
and do least for them, you would incline to believe
that another penny per hour more, or another hour
of labour per day less, must make all the difference
between misery and felicity. Is it not rather true
that a man's life or a woman's life depends for real
happiness upon the inner nature with which they
are born, or to which they have educated themselves; that in all ranks and under all circumstances
people can train and form their temperaments as
easily as they can make a scarlet-runner climb upon
strings? Everybody has a great deal of realised
wealth to start with; even if there should be no
silver-spoon ready to his mouth. Think only of the
wonderful and beautiful body, with all its inherited
developments of exquisite adaptation to common uses
and daily delights. Why need the poorest girl or boy

envy the millionaire's steam-yacht, or the jewelled opera-glass of the duchess, when they have got their five senses in perfect order, with such machinery as engineers can only marvel at, and possess eyes—be they blue, or grey, or brown, or black—to see with. Over everybody's head is daily built a roof so glorious, so various, so arabesqued with fleecy clouds and filmy mists, that fresco-painted vaults of princely halls are dull matched with it. The fresh air and the sweet smell of flowers, and the taste of white water to the thirsty mouth, and the flavour of a fresh apple or of bread and cheese when you are hungry ; and the soft, accommodating, refreshful sleep when you are tired : and beyond them all the sense—if we will only open heart to it—of the love, and mercy, and final safeguarding of some vast and just Power never to be named, but never to be doubted—all these things are to be had by everybody for nothing or next to nothing. When the charm of a warm and equable climate is added to such splendid common gifts, one sees whole nations —like the Malays, the Hindoos, and others —quite content with life just as it goes, and only doing such light work as suffices to make to-day feed to-morrow. Our English climate is not so indulgent, and consequently there arise here some few artificial but necessary wants which have to be supplied. But the difference between the pleasures of the rich man and of the poor man need not be nearly so great as envious people pretend. "The gods sell everything at a fair price," and the money they take in exchange is not gold and silver, but goodwill, right-

heartedness, honest effort to make the best of all circumstances, and reasonable sweetness of disposition.

The happiest individual I ever knew was the poorest.
His appellation was Draper. That was all there was
of his style and title, for he would have regarded anything additional as superfluity, and nobody indeed
would have ever dreamed of asking such a waif
for his Christian name. A Christian name implies
christening, and parents, and god-parents, and
being born beforehand in a regular manner; whereas
Draper had never, to his knowledge, or that of anybody else, been inside a church or chapel, and had
no more idea of who his father might have been
than a cuckoo has. When I enjoyed the advantage
of his acquaintance, he was a person of middle-age,
square build, supremely perfect health—manifested
by his magnificent appetite, white teeth, ruddy face,
and eyes like grey diamonds—abominably bad
clothes, battered hat, gaping boots, and an eternally
radiant smile, with an ever-ready joke. He was
Shakespeare's Autolycus in rags and tatters, gifted
with the same wit and the same philosophy—being
of a long-settled opinion that

> A merry heart goes all the way;
> Your sad heart tires in a mile-a.

But his rags and tatters were peculiar in this, that
they glistened from a distance like the sides of a
fishing-smack, and for the same reason. Draper was
covered with tar inside and out. He was panoplied
in it. What he liked best in the world was doing

nothing.   In the winter, whenever he could, he did
this in the nice soft straw of somebody's barn ; in
the summer he did it, deep in the foxgloves and
ferns of some coppice bank, where he could lie on
his stomach and watch the little creatures of the
insect world go and come over and under their green
bridges of the grass, and along the shady avenues
that stretch beneath the buttercup leaves and gold
balls of the crow's-foot.   He knew and liked all
woodland things, large and small, as if he had been
a Faun ; and understood the minds and the ways of
weasels and foxes, hares and hedgehogs, field-mice
and beetles, as if he had been himself in turns
dipterous, coleopterous, quadrupedalian.   But though
he agreed with Aristotle that meditation was the
only proper pursuit for a wise man, the need of beer
and tobacco to assist meditation had forced him to a
profession.

" There is lots of things," he once observed to me,
" in the hedges wot's good to smoke, and wot makes
werry nice tea—and I knows where to find wittles
and a drink, where them fools" (pointing to the
world in general) "would starve.   But 'taint ekal to
twist and porter.   That's why I works ! "

What he worked at was tarring the farm-premises
of the yeomen and gentry of that part of Essex.   The
profession had immense advantages.   It was mainly
practised in the early part of the year ; it was very
well paid for, because it was dirty and dangerous ; it
wanted no capital, since the farmers and squires
supplied tar-kettles, brushes, and ladders ; and it

kept its professor in touch with the one commodity which he loved and valued, the scent of which was the breath of life to his nostrils—namely, what he designated "Stockhollum tar." The famous philosopher who wrote a treatise on "The Virtues of Tar-water" would have found in my resinous friend a man after his own heart. One day, wandering with my gun, I came across Draper at the end of a long green lane, which was called the Pikehull, so busily engaged that the spectacle of his unusual animation was astonishing. He had a garment of some sort spread out over a briar-bush in full and fragrant blossom, and he was tarring it assiduously with the long brush used in his avocation. This conversation ensued :

"Why, Draper ! what on earth are you doing ?"

"Mornin', sir ! Lor, sir ! the money that it 'ud save in soapsuds if people was only up to what I'm a-doin'."

"What is it ?"

"Well, dow my bright buttons !" (this was his usual ejaculation in moments of earnestness) "'tis a bad thing for the washerwomen ; and I dessay you'll have shirts enough not to want me to larn it to you ; but 'tis my yearly rig-out that I'm gettin' ready."

"Your yearly rig-out ?"

"Yus. Onst a year I goes to Billericay and I buys a cotton shirt, and I tars him inside and outside like this 'ere. You mustn't wear him before he's dry both sides, and has been well crinkled in wood-smoke ; do, it 'ull never keep good. Arter that's all done I puts him on, and wears him night and day till the year comes round again."

"Draper, you must be as tarry as the side of the barn!"

"There's nothing like it, sir, to keep a man sound. What's good for the buildings is good for the stuff we're made of, inside and out. Look here, sir! you just give me a drop out of your flask, and I'll fill it up with 'Stockhollum,' and drink your werry good health."

He did, too! for there was a broken teacup lying near, which he washed; and after I had poured two fingers-breadth of whisky into it, Draper cheerfully brimmed the liquor up with tar out of his ladle and tossed off the mixture with the utmost apparent gusto. He wiped the brown strings from his lips, and went on:

"Why shouldn't it be good, sir? 'Tis the life out of the green woods; the blood of the trees! You can't have no ache in the innards if you takes a little now and then of real Stockhollum. Not too much, mind yer! Smell to it! What's these yer hedge-roses to the waft of the tar-pot? I was werry nigh going to sea onst, only for the sake of the ropes."

I am afraid he liked the tar, though, all the better for the whisky underneath it. Still, he was a sober man—too fond of the feeling of perfect health to throw that away for the townsman's costly and melancholy pleasure of inebriety. There is an art even in tarring the side of a cowshed or stable, and Draper in his line was an artist to be depended upon.

Working high up upon his ladder, he could make a kettle of tar go farther and cover up more weather-boarding than any ordinary hand, and the farmers were glad to employ him. Most of his spring and summer money thus earned was saved for the winter, when, after wandering about among the works of his brush—which he always regarded with as much pride as a Raphael or Perugino could have felt over any finished canvas—he would retreat to the seaside and hybernate among the fishing-smacks and the tarry cordage, doing a little professional job or two for the fishermen, until spring brought him forth again to buy a new shirt and renovate the farm premises of half the county.

He was a little too omnivorous for civilised society. One day he saw me taking a rabbit-trap from a burrow —I am sorry I ever set one ; I would not do it now ! I drew my hand out quickly with an exclamation of pain, for it was a hedgehog which had got itself caught, not a rabbit, and about a score of sharp needles had been driven into my fingers. He asked for the poor little trapped beast, and when I next passed that way he was enjoying a midday meal of fat bacon, cheese, and the whole bottom of a half-quartern loaf, with what looked like an open melon or a split cocoanut. Examining more closely, I found he had cooked, and was eating with high satisfaction, the prickly prey begged from me.

" There's nuthin' ain't a better flavy, sir," he said, joyously, between two mouthfuls, "than a young hedge-pig. You opens and cleans 'em—did you ever

see the inside of a hedge-pig, sir? 'Tis like a posey
of flowers. Then you rops 'em in a ball of clay and
makes a went-hole and shoves 'em into the middle
of a wood-fire, and when 'tis done you splits it open,
and the pricks and skin comes away just like the
husk of a chestnut; and you eats 'em. Won't you
just try a little bit?"

I said I thought I would not; but I perceived that
Draper could live sumptuously where other people
would go empty. Knowing so completely the habits
of every living thing in the country, this easy-going
philosopher of the tar-bucket would have made a
desperately successful poacher; but two sentiments
held this innate propensity in check, one was his
profound fear of the squires and magistrates, with
whom it was all-important to stand well—and they
could forgive anything except poaching—the other
was his deep and unaffected love of the wild creatures. I found him on one occasion setting the
broken leg of a young thrush with as much tender-
ness and solicitude as if it had been his own child.
He had wound the fluff of some thistledown over the
place, and lightly but securely bound two tiny pieces
of split willow-bark round it, making such a good
operation of it that when he let the bird loose it
chirruped what sounded like thanks, and perched
upon a branch near at hand. "There!" he said,
"that ain't the first job of the sort what Doctor
Draper's done for you and your likes—pooty cree-
turs! Dow my bright buttons, sir! I ain't got no
better friends than the birds and the beasts, nor I

don't want none." Still, I have reason to believe that, now and again, when somebody's wife was ill that had been kind to him, Draper, in the dark, would hang a hare or a couple of rabbits upon the poor woman's door-handle, and when she got up in the morning and went out to fetch sticks for fire, there was breakfast, dinner, and supper all provided, with no card to say that they came from the estates of my illegal friend.

He knew plants and trees and flowers, and their virtues, almost as well as Solomon, in spite of the arch-heresy of preferring the scent of tar to the perfume of a wild rose. An instance of his agricultural acumen comes to mind. There was a field of winter wheat about which we were anxious, as it had been sown with doubtful success and was very late in showing above ground. Out one morning early about the estate, I met Draper at a stile, tarry from head to foot, his stubbly beard and short black hair like tarred oakum, his hands and wrists like tarred tub-staves, his face streaked with tar strings, with a bit of the golden sallow-blossom between his white teeth; and his eyes shining with the delight of being alive on such a morning.

"We shall have to plough this twelve acres up," I said; "the blade won't come."

"Won't it, sir?"

"No. Look for yourself. It is as brown—well, as brown as you are, Draper."

Down he went upon his tarry stomach, put his cheek to the ground, and gazed along the surface for a moment, then, rising to his feet, exclaimed :

"Dow my bright buttons, sir! 'tis five quarters to the acre your guv'nor will reap off that, if he lets it alone."

And, surely enough, when you looked along the level of the soil in this cunning manner, catching all the ridges together, there was a beautiful light green film of young wheat spreading from headland to headland, and the whole field had become changed from brown to emerald.

I am afraid I cannot speak of my bituminous, but ever-cheerful and resourceful acquaintance, as a strictly moral character. He was a philosopher, a naturalist, and a kindly-hearted vagabond; but to one who wears only a single shirt from year's end to year's end, many of our most respected institutions must naturally present themselves in an otherwise than sacred light. He was accompanied occasionally upon his tarring expeditions by a not uncomely female, whom he called sometimes his "wife," albeit it was doubtful if she could have shown any legal claim to that title. A young woman of tastes so unconventional as to put up with the perpetual society of Draper and his tarpot was not likely to have been particular about "lines" or settlements. Yet this Audrey of my Essex Touchstone seemed positively attached to her gay, worthless, easy-hearted associate, and did his biddings as cheerily as he dispensed them. Riding one day far away from their proper beat, and in a district where the couple were not known, I came upon them under a beech-tree in a lane dining luxuriously upon cold pork-chops and sausages.

Questioned about such unaccustomed luxuries, Draper
put that extra twinkle into his grey eyes which always accompanied a confession of wickedness, and
told me how they had come across the country from
union to union to get to the tarring again.

"But skilly every night, and stones to break every
morning," he said, "gives yer appetite for suthin else.
So my missus here ties her shawl in a lump under her
apron, and we goes together to the big house yonder,
and knocks at the kitchen door, me a limpin' on a
stick, and she lookin' heavy and faint; and I ses,
ses I, 'Could you give us a little broken wittles?
the wife's expectin' every minute, and I've turned
my ankle trampin', and 'twould be a good charity.'"

What became of Draper eventually is beyond my
knowledge. The last I heard of him he was in gaol
for poaching, which seemed so unlike his usual
prudence about game that I made inquiries. And
it must be confessed that the true story of this
ultimate transgression was not so very discreditable
to the tarry optimist. He was out on one of his moonlight tramps from farm to farm when he saw an
acquaintance carrying a gun, with a hare and a brace
of pheasants lying beside him. The man had been
poaching, and the keepers being after him, in jump-
ing a gate he had hurt his leg and could go no farther.
"Here, Tar-pot," says the poacher, "take this hare
for your dinner to-morrow. They'll have me soon,
for I can't stand up; and I'm sorry for the sake of
the wife and little ones." "How many chillun ha'
ye got, matie?" "Five, and that's why I was out

to-night. 'Tis too dear to buy the butcher's meat, and they was pinin'!" "Look here," says Draper, "I ain't got nothin' to do till the fore part of March. If they didn't see the shape of ye, gi' me the gun and the birds, and you creep in under them hollies. I'll go up the road and fire the gun, as if I catched her trigger in a thorn runnin' away, and they'll pounce out and be satisfied with Draper. You crawl in, matie! and give my respects to the missus and the kids!"

Which nefarious plot was duly carried out, and Draper—very demure and contrite in the dock for his heinous offence, got six weeks, and an awful warning from the bench. I sent his friend, the real sinner, a little gift to convey to those sadly immoral but generous hands when the imprisonment should be over; and that was the very last I ever knew about the light-hearted tar-man.

STRONGER THAN DEATH

"YOU WOULD NOTICE THAT GRACE FALTERED A LITTLE AS SHE CAME UP THE
PATH, EVEN WITH THE LIGHT WEIGHT OF A BUCKET OF WATER."

P. 281.

XV

STRONGER THAN DEATH

SPRING comes upon the sea with almost as much grace and change and sweetness of season as upon the land. The meadows of the ocean have their times of cold, dark fallow in the winter, of re-awakening in the spring, and of large fruitfulness in the summer, just as the fields ashore have them; but you must know the elements well to observe the various signs which show this. Anybody, of course, can notice the bettering of the weather, and the lifting of the sky, and the new colours of the waves and waters when the last of the east winds has blown itself out and the days begin to be longer than the nights. Anybody can feel and welcome the difference in the breeze which comes over the quiet sea along with the early whisper of May, and those bitter, howling winter gales which chill and kill. But only sea-birds and fish and sailors can tell, by what floats and swims and flies, that the good days are coming upon the water before they come, and when it is the season to look out for this, that, and the other token of the weather which brings the bright side of the fisherman's and mariner's life. There was a village which I used to know well—in the West of England—where you could study all this sea-lore as advantageously perhaps as anywhere in the world, and where the fisher-folk were as fair specimens of the honest, brave, loyal, and industrious "common people" of England as a man would wish to meet and be friends with. It is because I remember along with that village a rather touching story of humble but true love that I draw to-day this particular little picture forth from the portfolio of memory.

I remember it especially by the wonderfully pretty girl who lived with an old aunt and two small sisters in the cottage close under the great cliff which rose to the westward of the hamlet. Everybody must have experienced how often a place will associate itself in the mind with a face, when much more important localities pass clean out of the thoughts for want of such a link of human interest. I don't think anybody with eyes could have forgotten Grace Williams if he had once seen her—she possessed such real distinction of feature, and such natural elegance, without being in the least discontented with her station and her lowly daily duties. In full health, she had a mouth like a rosebud, long black hair, dark shining eyes, and a step along the cliff's edge like the pacing of a hen-peacock, if you have ever noticed how grandly that bird walks. But when I and my wife first saw her near her cottage door she was not quite well. Her comely face was pale, her lips seemed a little thin and colourless, and, stately and symmetrical as her figure showed, you could notice that Grace faltered a little as she came up the path, even with the light weight of a bucket of

water. This was so evident that I remember taking
the pail—with a joke—from her hand, and finishing
the hill-climb for her, while she talked with my
wife; and so we learned that she was indeed somewhat weak in the chest, in spite of all her stateliness
and splendid beauty, and seemed to be threatened
with consumption.

All this did not prevent two of the best-looking
and most prosperous of the young fishermen of the
village from falling over head and ears in love with
her, of which we quickly heard, because everybody
knew it, and nobody better than Grace herself.
They are a simple and manly breed—down on those
shores—neither ashamed of their emotions nor wont
to give them any very sentimental expression. They
love—as they work, and as they fight, and as they
worship God—in quiet earnest, and I expect that
one thing which worried Grace, and helped to pull
her down, for she always showed herself as good
and honest a girl as she looked lovely, was just
the troublesome pleasure of having two such handsome young fellows as John Petherick and William
Clannen in love with her, and not quite knowing
which she liked best, nor how on earth such a resolute rivalry as theirs was going to end. Even
when we grew to know her a great deal better, and
the subject of her lovers was quite a permitted one
in conversation, she never would give any sure clue
to her secret feelings. She always spoke of them
both with womanly respect and modesty. From
the very first close observers thought it was William

who was the favoured swain, but this was a mere
guess, and came out of an incident which happened
one stormy afternoon in the autumn.

The morning had been fine, but at midday a wind
rose up from the south-west suddenly, and rolled a
rough sea along the feet of the cliffs.   Clannen had
gone out after his lobster-pots alone, and whether
one of them had drifted, which he was trying to
recover, or whether, skilful boatman as he was, he
misjudged the force of the incoming surge, he got
his dingey flung upon the rocks and stove in, while
he himself, in scrambling out upon a ledge of the
cliff, sprained his ankle, and by the same fall broke
his right arm.   This was not known until the broken
boat of Clannen was seen driving over the rollers
eastward, at which time the tide was already half-
flood, and the place where poor crippled Will was
perched had become perfectly inaccessible from the
sea.   How they found out that place was all through
Grace, who forgot entirely about her languor, and
went out in the wind and rain with the rest of the
villagers.   It seems a smack, scudding across the
bay, had somehow signalled that there was a man
on the ledge of the cliff; but the difficulty was to
find out where.   The surf and the wind created too
much uproar for human voices to be heard, and the
cliff in many places overhung its base, so that it
would never have been discovered where the unlucky
Will had lodged but for Grace, who hit upon the
idea of throwing great stones wrapped in newspapers
over each possible point, until one thus flung was

answered by one thrown with a splash upon the face of an incoming "smooth," and the anxious village knew just where its man was waiting for help.

At first what was to be done appeared obvious and easy. A light line was lowered over the cliff's brim with a small stone and the body of a child's kite at the extremity; and, sure enough, by walking along the edge slowly and letting the gale blow this inwards, it was presently seized. Then a strong rope was lowered exactly in the same spot, with a length of floating thread at the end, and this also was caught by the invisible Clannen. All these shore-folk can climb like goats, and hang to a rope like spiders, so the folk now quite expected Will to make a bowline in his rope, and signal to be hauled up. Instead of this he jerked hard at the thin cord, which they could now afford to pull up, and when it came in sight there was a bit of paper screwed into its loop, on which was pencilled:

"Broke my arm, and can't stand. Sea over rock in half hour."

Well, that meant sharp work if Clannen was to be saved, and the villagers were puzzled, for it would be probably useless now to lower him even a boatswain's stool. They were eagerly discussing the problem when John Petherick pushed the talkers aside, and, flinging off his sea-jacket and tightening his belt, said, with a hard look at Grace's quiet but pale face:

"Here! cast me over, mate, in a bow-line, and lower a chair along of me. I'll put Bill safe and sound on the grass, or break my own neck."

They offered no objection, because it was touch and go, and people thereabouts are not afraid to die, or to see others die, where they live lives so simple and faithful. So, over the red rim of the sandstone crag went Jack, with a coil of spun yarn in his hand and the second rope; and it was noticed that Grace picked up his pilot coat and carefully folded it over her arm. After he was out of sight it was impossible to hear his voice or to communicate; but as he slung himself across the crumbling brink into the gusty air, he said to the sturdy group holding on to the ropes—

"Haul up when I jerk three times. Hold hard when I jerk once; and if I do it twice send me down another man."

There was a long awful pause, awful because Will might be washed away, or a hundred bad things happen; but the rope presently lost its strain—Jack had reached the ledge. There he found Clannen faint and soaked with the spray, which was now and again running green over his rock, and threatening to wash him off as he clung with one hand to it. He managed, however, to help his rival athwart the boat-swain's stool, and to lash him with the light cord to the rope, after which he gave the three jerks, keeping his own line quiet until the injured man was well aloft. Then he put his leg farther into the bow-line, and shook his own rope thrice, and first Will came to safety, sadly broken and soaked; and after him Jack, pretty nearly drowned with the breakers, which would have washed anybody off the ledge in another ten minutes.

Days passed; poor Will Clannen went into hos-

pital to be patched up for his winter work, and
Petherick in his hours of leisure hung much about
Grace's cottage, and always had at least kind words
and looks from her. But the day's exposure upon
the cliff had done the girl serious harm. There

"THERE HE FOUND CLANNEN FAINT AND SOAKED WITH THE SPRAY, WHICH
WAS NOW AND AGAIN RUNNING GREEN OVER HIS ROCK."

was a foolish doctor living near at hand, who had
frightened her already nervous spirits, telling her
she was in a very bad way indeed in regard of her
lungs, and would hardly live out the winter. Possibly

his unlearned croaking might have come true, for the
cottage she inhabited was in a stuffy nook of the
shore, and she was working too hard, by far, upon
indifferent food, for her aunt and little sisters, besides the pain it gave her gentle heart to see Jack
and Will glaring like lions at each other, whenever
they met on the quay or the sands, all for her sake.
But one day my wife found her at home crying, and
trying to hide away some needlework upon which
she was engaged. It was black stuff that she was
making up into children's dresses, and she had to
piteously confess that it was mourning, and that, as
she felt sure she should die before long—just when
life was so pleasant, and she had the choice of the
two best young men in the place—why, she was getting together something for her aunt and the little
ones to wear after she was gone, that everything
"might be respectable." We were both very much
disgusted and angry when we heard what a melancholy result the doctor's visit and examination had
had upon pretty Grace. What she wanted was merely
change and sunshine, and therefore having made
some very easy and inexpensive arrangements with a
captain whose ship was at Plymouth, we broke into
her cottage one day and rallied her into hope, and
happiness, and excitement, something in this brutal
fashion : " Rubbish, Grace ! The doctor is an ass.
You are not going to die—but to live and grow stout
and strong ; and come back as fresh as a cabbage-
rose, and marry the lad you love, whichever he is,
and put the other one out of his misery."

And then it was unfolded to her rapidly brightening eyes how there was a fruit schooner going inside of a week to the Azores, and how her passage was paid for in it, and a three months' stay ashore in the Sunny Islands all provided for ; and how she would be with nice and kind people all the winter, and must eat her head off, if she could, on the island grapes and pineapples and beef, and how the African mail-steamer would bring her home in the late spring fat as a quail.

All which duly happened, and Grace did, indeed, come back in May as beautiful as any low-born and uneducated angel could look, and as strong and well as a Devon heifer in the clover. Jack and Will had been going on fairly peaceably during her absence, and had even taken spells of friendly work together, though they never talked about Grace, and once or twice punched the heads of village chatterers who ventured to supply this deficiency in daily village gossip. But when Grace Williams came home in company with the May-blossom—which was not one bit sweeter or more fresh—and took her first walk along the cliffs and down upon the sands by the little harbour, the truce was perforce at an end between these two manly young fellows, of whose honest hearts her beauty had made "roast meat." I heard afterwards that something like the following conversation occurred at the boat-building yard by the quay :

"You'll be clean quit of that crack in your arm-bone now, I'm reckoning, Bill."

"Ay, Jack. The doctor at Exeter fished it fine. 'Tis sound as a new spar."

T

" And the leg, Bill ?   Is that in good fettle again ? "

" I don't to-day know so much as that I ever even wrenched it. 'Tis wonderful what them hospital bandages did."

" Well, then, Bill, I want you to do me the biggest kindness a man could ask of another man."

" Look here, Jack, I'll do for you just anything in the world—except one thing. I ain't forgotten the day you come over the clift to fetch me up out of that mess."

" Well, then, now that you're all right and fit again, I want you to fight me to a regular dead finish, and see who is the best man, and the man that loses to clear out of this place, and the man that wins to be free and lonely to ask Grace Williams to be his wife."

Those who heard about this and told us, related that Will hung in the wind a little.

" I know you ain't a coward," Petherick broke out. " Why don't ye answer ? "

" I'm afeard, if we onst begin, I shall kill 'e, Jack ! And then suppose the wrong man won, and Grace wouldn't have him ? "

" If I chance that," answered Petherick, " you can chance it.   Will 'e fight ? "

" Ay, lad ! " was Clannen's reply ; " I owe you too much.   I ain't no right to say no.   I'll fight ! "

Thus it was all privately settled, as afterwards appeared, that the ancient ordeal of combat should decide the possession of the fair ; and these Devon-shire men were so straightforward and ·truthful that I feel sure they would have stuck to the contract.

But while their loving though pugnacious souls proposed, Heaven had otherwise disposed. It was said by the few in the secret that the time and place were fixed for the duel, and that Grace herself had heard something about it, since she was seen speaking to Will Clannen outside her aunt's door, and handing him something in a packet. However this may be, my little story must have, I regret to say, a sombre end, for that Homeric combat—as it must certainly have proved—never came off.

There broke forth a great storm with the early summer, blowing right on to the coast; and in the darkness of one wild night a large barque came ashore on the reef at the outer horn of the bay. We had a lifeboat station, and as soon as daybreak rendered things at all plain she was launched, but in such an unseamanlike hurry that some of the life-belts were left behind. Jack Petherick and Will Clannen were both among the volunteers who manned the boat, which was started with great difficulty, owing to the heavy rollers, but nevertheless reached the vicinity of the wreck, and proceeded to veer down within rescue distance of her distressed company lashed in the mizen rigging. I was not at the village at the time, but was informed that pretty Grace Williams stood in the throng at the launching, and was seen to turn away with tears in her beautiful eyes when Jack Petherick passed by her to jump into his place. During that manœuvre of veering down to the wreck an enormous wave broke upon the lifeboat

and capsized her, flinging all the crew into the
boiling sea. Petherick was a splendid swimmer;
but Clannen, like too many seafaring men, was
utterly ignorant of the art. I don't like to think
of what ensued, and will cut short the close and
careful account which afterwards reached my ears.
In the hard rowing and the shock of the capsize
Clannen's sea-shirt had got torn open, it seems,
and they say there was a long wisp of black-
braided hair, tied with a bit of scarlet ribbon—
the colour Grace always wore—hanging round his
bared neck, in a length of thin marline. Whether
poor Jack's eyes lighted upon this in the confusion
cannot surely be known. Some say they did—
some say he expected to see the lifeboat right
herself directly, and felt himself safe enough in
the water to be, as he always was, generous. At
all events what happened, and what was witnessed
and heard, was this: Clannen was sinking, when
Petherick pushed the oar he was holding under
the drowning man's arms and called out, "Catch
hold, Bill; that fight's off!"

They never clapped eyes on him again till his
poor body was picked up by a trawler westward
of the Start, much disfigured with long soaking
in the sea. The coxswain of the lifeboat thought
he could easily have saved himself. I don't know.
I only know that Grace became Mrs. Clannen, and
that she and Will had a boy named Jack Petherick
Clannen the last time we visited the village, now
years and years ago.

XVI

HOW THE DEAD SAVED THE LIVING

"WHEN THE FOG LIFTS, HE LOOKS AND SEES A LITTLE BIT OF A TWINKLE."

P. 295.

XVI

HOW THE DEAD SAVED THE LIVING

In times that are past I was myself a sea-gleaner occasionally, going out now and then by night as well as by day in those little sailing craft of the Thames and Medway called "borleys;" or, in the winter, on sprat-boats; or putting the trawl down on moonlit evenings or bright cold mornings from some little vessel of my own. At the present season, when the fishing for the lordly salmon is just recommencing, it might seem trivial to talk of such small fry as flat-fish, shrimps, sprats, crabs, and the like. But if you had once known anything about these minor industries of the water, and made any close acquaintance with the honest, hardy men and boys who pursue them; if, above all, you have sailed in their tiny but well-handled craft, the interest in their labours and their lives could never quite depart. Besides, it is more true of them and their ways than of almost any set of toilers by land or sea, that "many a little makes a mickle." Small as their daily catch may be, the dwellers on shore would miss their service very soon and very much if they were not almost always out upon the tide, at the mouths of our rivers, gathering up the "unconsidered trifles of the deep." And it "runs into good money" for them and theirs when the winter, as now, proves an open one, and when the "little fishes" are fairly plentiful. Of late, for instance, there has been an excellent time all round the Kentish and Essex coasts with the sprat, which is not, as was once supposed, the young of the herring, but a separate species, distinguished by its size and serrated ventral edge. True whitebait, also a great resource of the winter river-fishermen, should consist of young sprats and young herrings; for there is no such specialised fish, as naturalists once thought, giving it, indeed, a Latin name "all to itself." The whitebait, as it comes to table, comprises, under its fair mask of fried batter, all sorts of fry, including those of gobies, weevers, sand-eels, plaice, dabs, shrimps, and stickle-backs. Sprats, if they were only more expensive, would be regarded, probably, as the greatest dainty of the deep; more toothsome, as they are far more nourishing, than salmon, sole, whitebait, or than smelts among ourselves, than blue fish and lake-trout in the States, than even the Bombay "duck," or the Japanese *tai*. And when the sprats come, it is "in battalions." The average catches lately made among the forty-five to fifty boats employed from Deal round to Dungeness have been 3000 measures for each boat on each tide, which means £7, 10s. a day per craft, since there is a ready sale, now that factories near at hand have taken to potting and tinning the little fish. When the takes have been paid for, there will also be scores of women kept busy in preparing the sprats, and other hands engaged in soldering up

the tins. At Deal recently the boatmen cleared
£475 among themselves from a catch of three days
only ; and there are three hundred people employed
in one factory at that town, so that the sprat is
becoming locally more and more important.

It was not an unpleasing experience in the crisp
wintry weather of bygone years to sit in the well of
a sprat boat, when the " stow-net " had been shot.
The men fish from November to February, and the
mouth of the Thames is as good a place for the business as any in the world. The stow-net is immensely
long, a full-sized one measuring from fifty to sixty
yards. First there is a great square mouth, 30 ft.
high and 20 ft. wide, called the " quarters ; " then
comes the " enter," a sort of network tunnel 80 ft.
or 90 ft. long and 6 ft. in diameter, followed by
another long tube of 80 ft. or 90 ft., comprising first
the " sleeves " and then the " dock-hose " or " cod,"
where the net fines down into a mere point and the
meshes grow very small. The smack takes up her
position at the beginning of the tide in a spot where
she can see signs of fish, or knows that they will
come ; casts anchor, downs canvas, and puts the
vast net overboard, under the vessel. There is a
line fast to the anchor from the bridle-rope, and net
and ship thus ride by the same tackle, while the
" quarters " can be raised or lowered by means of
upper beam-ropes to the proper elevation, the lower
beam being weighted so as to hang down and keep
the square entrance wide gaping. Into this open
gateway of meshes drives the shoal, and myriads of

the little fish swim, or get thrust deeper and deeper,
along the "enter," till the "cod" begins to stream
out, full and heavy, astern of the smack. As likely
as not the anchor may drag a little with the weight
of the ship, of the close-wove net, and of the gathering fish ; but that matters little. So long as the tide
runs, the stow-net continues to stream, and the sprats
to crowd in, until the first sign comes of slack water,
when the chain is tightened which lies across the
mouth of the net, thus closing it ; the beams are
hauled up under the bolt-sprit, the long brown
tunnel of meshes is drawn on board with the help
of iron hooks until the "cod" is reached, and then
that also is dragged in-board by the tail-rope. This
rope being cast loose, out flashes a living river of
silver, which the master, like a maritime alchemist,
stirs and puddles and measures out, three bushels
at a time, using a wooden implement called the
"mingle." Tons and tons of the tiny silvery prey
may thus be taken in a few hours, and while the
weather is steadfast it is agreeable enough to rock
in the well of the smack, waiting for the slack water,
and well assured by the excited screaming of the
gulls that the sprats are moving, and that the
patience of the hour will be rewarded. With sudden
squalls and a quick-rising sea the stow-net is an
awkward affair to handle, and there are times when
the "cod," with all its water-wealth of glittering
food, must be cut open and emptied to save net and
ship.

In the wide open waters of the Thames and

Medway mouths, where these "little people of the sea," the sprat-smacks and borleys, gather in humble fleets, there shows no such majesty of the element as Victor Hugo has so wonderfully described in his "Travailleurs de la Mer." No wild play of billows occurs among such rocks and caverns and rugged reefs as the great French poet has painted. No iron-bound coasts arise with a fierce line of leaping breakers at their feet. There are no mysterious caverns full of sea secrets, where dead men are lost to sight, and marine monsters lurk. The shores are almost everywhere low-lying saltings and marshes, of immense expanse, of monotonous character, of the most desolate and lonely scenery which could be imagined. Interminable creeks and ditches intersect these salt and sour meadows of the North Sea; their waving growth of weeds and rushes is the breeding places of wild-fowl; their muddy banks are perforated everywhere with the holes of myriads and myriads of crabs, which, along with water-rats, shrimps, and small flat-fish, tenant the melancholy streams. These prodigious wastes of rank sea-grass, samphire, and salted mud—especially where they lie outside the sea-walls—are so solitary that it seems "a land where no man comes, or hath come since the making of the world." Many and many such a tract exists within sixty miles of London town amongst these amphibious wastes, half water and half gull's ground, where a man can be more alone than in the desert of Sahara. He might die there, and remain longer undiscovered

than if his bones had been deposited on a reef of
the Roccas, or a cay of the Bahamas, or a sandbank
of the Pescadores. And they possess their own
dangers, too, these nameless, unvisited, far-extending
saltings of the Kent and Essex and Suffolk coasts—
dangers to landsmen as well as to seamen.

There is a place I remember where a vast, flat,
lonely, outlying island is cut off from the main-
land by a broad strait, miles across, which goes dry
at low tide, but fills up on each flood, and, at spring-
tides especially runs very deep and strong. The
spot is well known, and the track across the sands
is marked with willow-poles planted here and there,
if the winds and waves have not carried them adrift.
The spratters and shrimp-boats sometimes steal up
this passage on the flood, and a barge or two may
blunder through it for a short cut. But ordinarily
the place is as lonely as any sea-front at Cape Horn,
its solitude intensified by the wail of the gulls, the
cry of the curlew and peewit, and the croak of some
crow flying homewards, full of cockles. Woe to the
wild-fowl shooter or belated traveller who comes to
that passage, that dry strait of sand, without knowing its peculiarities! He would think nothing safer
or simpler. There is the wide yellow stretch of
apparently firm crossing; upon it, perhaps, the
track of footmarks or the impression of wheel ruts.
Beyond, a few miles away, rises dimly the green
outline of the Essex farms and woods. The light
is good, the sea is down; why should he not go
over? But he will cross at peril unless he notes

the time of the flood-tide and the direction of the wind, for the speciality of the spot is terrible. It will beguile you to the passage, and then midway, before you can see the far edge of the flood-tide making, or hear the low hissing murmur of it creeping into the creeks, the sands under your feet will suddenly become wet, glistening, sodden; the sea will enter, as it were, from beneath; the ground which was firm becomes shivering and soft; and when the tide makes, it will come sweeping in, breast deep, neck deep; at last, sometimes, and in places overhead, bringing volume enough to drown not only a pedestrian, but even a horse and cart with its driver.

Lying up in that very creek one day on board a small smack, near to a solitary fisher's cottage which stood on the edge of the land-wall, I remember inquiring of our old skipper why he had a lighted candle and an open book rudely carved upon the beam of the half-deck.

"'Tis odd ye should ask that here, sir," he said, taking his black clay-pipe out of his mouth and pointing with the stem of it to the cottage, "for it's all along of that werry house there, and so's this boat all along of it, too!"

"How can that be?" I inquired.

"Well, it's like this!" the grey-headed fisherman answered; "the name of this boat, as ye know, is the *Grateetood*, and that 'ere open book on the beam, why 'tis a Bible; and that there candle figured is a candle what saved a man's life and built the

Grateetood; leastways, she'd never have been launched without it."

And then, in response to my natural curiosity, he narrated, with frequent clouds of retrospective tobacco-smoke, this little marsh-story, here greatly condensed, and freely translated from his Essex dialect :

"'Tis many years ago, now, sir, for I've sailed this little boat off and on for twenty-six seasons. And 'twas a gent that came down on horseback to these parts, making pictures of the sea, and the boats, and the 'mushes,' though what he could find in the mushes to put into colour I can't say. And seems like he wanted to paint the island, or to shoot there, for he went over one day alone, and carried with him on his saddle a fowling-piece, along with his paintbox and his paper. He must have gone over by hisself early, because the flood, I know, made about ten that day. And he must have rode about in the mush and painted picters all that winter's day pretty near, starting to get back again at night. Well, there was a moon, and he'd find the other end of the passage quick enough; and having a strong horse, he'd think it an easy matter, don't ye see, to gallop back across the hard sand to the main; not knowing that the flood was doo at ten, and that the sea comes in, as ye know, underneath, afore it rolls in a-top."

"Hadn't anybody informed the poor man?" I asked.

"He never see nobody to inquire. Do, it 'ud a

been all right. He comes on to the flats, between them willow-sticks, and I dessay he takes it quiet at the beginning, being so sure of hisself and his horse. But by-me-by up drives, all of a sudden, one of our long-shore sea-fogs which blurs out the moon, and before he could get any bearings, being nothin' like half-way over, he misses the sticks, and goes here and there groping for the road."

"What should you have done yourself, then?" said I.

"Me! sir? You wouldn't catch nobody born about these here parts, crossing Foulness Crikk on a winter's night with a rising tide. But was I that gent, I should have got off and hunted for my own foot-marks, and then rid back to the mush as quick as I could. He didn't. He kept a searchin' for the road, till presently he notices that the sands is all alive and soaky, not being aweer before of the deadly natur' of the place. That makes him think he's a-going too fur seaward, so he turns back; but everywhere he finds the sands turning sloppy, and begins, I suppose, to hear the sob of the sea a-comin' in under the fog."

"A horrible position, skipper."

"Couldn't well be worse, sir, for anybody that didn't know the ropes—as they say. Well, he was wastin' the time away, and pretty soon in comes the first water of the flood, and the horse was soon over his fetlocks in it, snorting, poor thing! and scared; and the gent, by this while, more frightened than the beast."

" Well, and then ? "

" Then he goes hither and thither, galloping up and down in the gathering water, that was, by this while, over his nag's knees; the birds screaming about him, the night as thick as wool, the dreadful sea pouring in with more and more vollum, for it was a' easterly wind outside, which allus makes a quick flood. A right bad job 'twas become, if you'll think of the unfortunate gentleman cavortin' about in the swelling tide, not knowing which way to turn his bridle, now and then plunging into a hole, and out again all wet and cold, and the horse screamin' and shudderin'."

" I don't see what chance there was left for the poor fellow."

" There wasn't no chance, sir, only in God A'mighty's mercy, and that's just what happened; for when the horse was beginning to give in, what with terror, and what with cold, and what with tearin' up and down, the easterly breeze comes over the flats and blows the fog away, just like a curtain rollin' up."

" Well, but even then, captain, it was up to the girths with them by this time, and no guide back to the lost road."

" 'Twas so, sir! but, when the fog lifts, he looks and sees, quite away from where he was trying to go, a little bit of a twinkle, might be a mile, or half, or two miles off, he couldn't tell; nor he couldn't tell whether 'twas a boat's light, or a mush-glare, or what it was. But he makes for it, for a last chance, spurring his horse, which catches sight of the gleam, too, and goes headlong through the sand and water, more like a porpoise a-rollin', I allow, than any shore-travellin' beast. And what with shoutin', and spurrin', and beatin' the horse with the brich of his

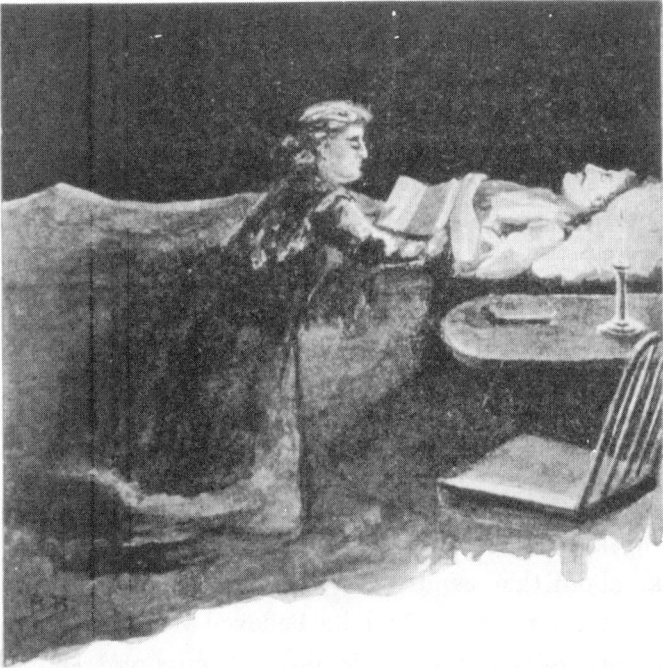

"A WOMAN ON HER KNEES BY HIS SIDE, WITH A BIBLE OPENED ON
THE COVERLID."

gun, he gets him through the raffle of the tide till they comes to a willow-stick, and then another, and the sand begins to shallow under his hoofs and treads harder, and just when both of 'em was pretty nigh

U

done they draws out on to the dry, close under that cottage there, on the wall."

"What did he do?"

"Why, sir; he rides straight up to the light, which he sees now is a candle shining through a winder. And here's where me and the boat comes in, 'cause he opens the door, which was on the latch, and a'most falls into the room, and there he spies a dead man a-lyin' in a cot, and a woman on her knees by his side, with a Bible opened on the coverlid, and she a tryin' to read words of comfort by the glimmer of the candle at the window."

"How strange! how sad! Who was the woman?"

"'Twas my own mother, sir! and that was my dead father what she was a watchin', and we boys was gone away to 'range with the neighbours about the buryin', seeing that he had been drowned in the wreck of his borley and washed ashore."

"I think I can guess the rest, skipper."

"No manner of doubt you can, sir. The dead had saved the living! The gent was very grateful-like about that candle and the reason of it; which had saved his life. And he behaved very handsome to mother—sending her bank-notes enough to build this 'ere wessel and fit her out. 'Only,' ses he, 'mind you cuts a Bible and a lighted candle somewheres or other upon the new boat.' And that's how the *Grateetood* come to have them carvings what you noticed."

Such recollections make one think kindly of the "stow-nets," and the "shove-nets," and all those small folk of the sea, who used to ply in the mouths of Thames and Medway—and still ply, as I suppose. Very skilful in their way, very observant they are, and excellent boatmen in their own waters. Nor is their labour any little matter to the community. Of shrimps alone as much as two thousand gallons will sometimes be sent to London in a day from Leigh in Essex, and the annual take of those humble crustaceans round our coasts is worth at least £120,000. I used to admire—sitting in the shrimp-boat and trawling for *Crandon vulgaris*—a device which only deep study of the waters could have inspired. The difficulty is to catch the shrimps in the fragile net, and not also to catch the sea-slush, broken bottles, culch, and stones and weed which would break it and spoil the take. How would the naturalist ashore manage that? The simple fisherman, by observation, has solved the problem. He has noticed that, on the approach of danger, the shrimp always leaps upward about six inches from the sand where he crawls. Accordingly the shrimper leaves an open space between the lower edge of the net and the little ground beam, and all the shrimps hopping up are caught in the meshes, while the rubbish from the bottom passes harmlessly through the aperture.

XVII

DAYS AT SEA

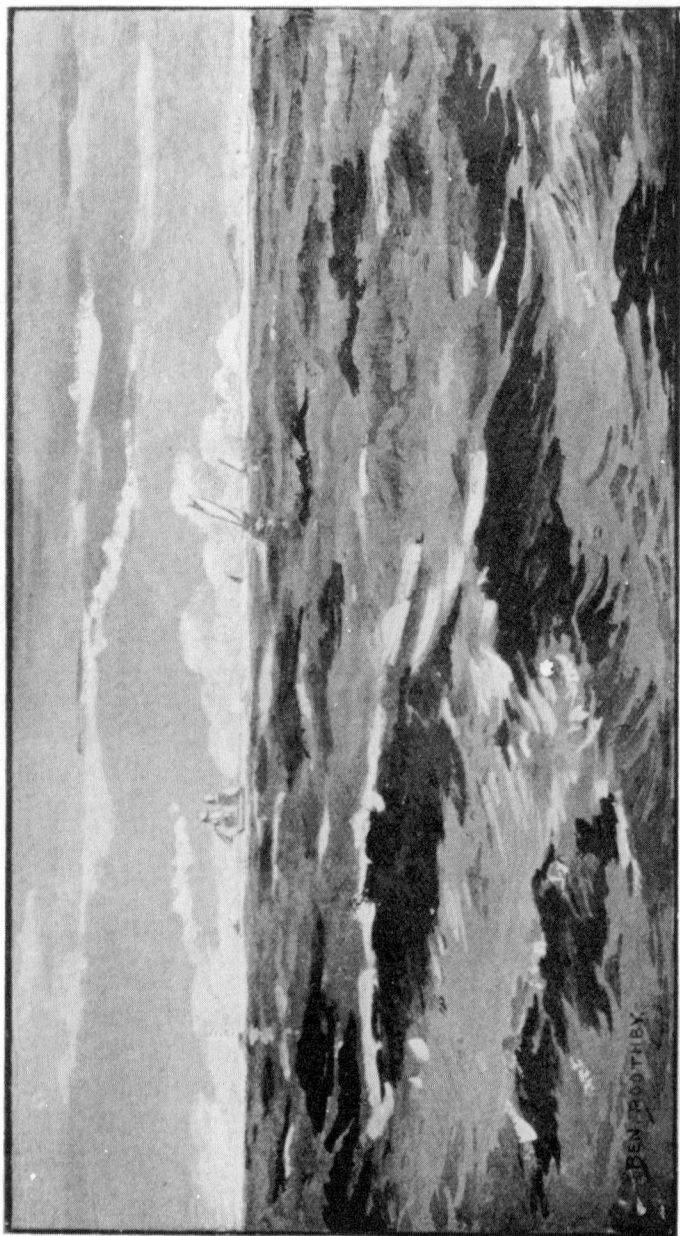

BEN BOOTHBY.

"A DAY OF BLUE AND GOLD, LIGHTING UP AN EXPANSE OF FRESH AND FREE SEA-MEADOWS."

P. 311.

XVII

DAYS AT SEA

IF books, poetry, and journalism had not claimed me
for their own, I should have been a sailor. Born
by the waterside, and accustomed from earliest
times to boats and shipping, I have always loved
the sea and everything connected with it — so
much so, that I can never, even now, keep long
away from the sight and smell of the ocean, and
am always full of secret and indefinable pleasure
when I go on board a vessel for a visit or for a
voyage. As a little lad, I could cut out a boat
from a chunk of deal wood with any of my age,
and rig it too, in a fairly correct manner, either
as a cutter, yawl, or schooner—since types of all
these craft were constantly passing before my eyes.
Above all, her Majesty's Navy filled my thoughts
with wonder, reverence, and loyalty. Living near
two great dockyards, the ships of that navy, then
of the grand old three-decker pattern—some of them
still even paddle-wheels—grew deeply familiar to
me, until I knew their names and looks much
better than I knew those of my cousins and aunts.
I read with eager admiration the stories of all our
sea-fights, from the Armada down to Navarino, of
which latter action an immensely big and, to my

eyes, superb painting was suspended in my father's dining-room, showing the *Asia* line-of-battle ship —Admiral Sir Edward Codrington—passing at the head of the British squadron down the ill-fated Turkish lines in a storm of thunderous artillery flashes and battle-smoke. Above all, I learned to adore the memory of Lord Nelson, whom I still faithfully consider to be the bravest, noblest, gentlest, and most perfect of all our British heroes. And this strong love of the sea, as well as of all connected with it, which has never yet quitted me, was fed by a small event in my boyish days, that came very near to being decisive as to my future career. My father, who was a man of large ideas, as well as of boundless kindness, had observed me very deeply absorbed in the perusal of an old book of travels called "The Adventures of Philip Quarles, Mariner." "If you so much like books of travel and adventure," he said, "to-morrow they shall bring you some." And the very next day his serving-man came into my room with a large washing-basket upon his shoulders full to the edge with huge folios and quartos. These old-fashioned volumes lent a special, almost a majestic, charm to reading. Unlike the many hastily-printed and flimsy productions of to-day, they were massive, large-typed, serious tomes, solemnly dedicated to "the King's most gracious Majesty," or to some imposing personage of the time, and embellished with quaint, elaborate plates, and amazing maps and diagrams. When "John" shot out that

precious cargo upon the carpet, I felt like the
possessor of perfectly unlimited wealth. There
were the two stately quartos of "Captain Cook's
Voyages of Discovery;" there was "The Expedition of La Perouse;" piled up in golden wealth
of joy and novelty before me were the Voyages of
Dampier, of Anson, of Drake and Frobisher, Sir
Walter Raleigh's Expeditions, the "Discovery of
America by Christopher Columbus," and many
others now clean forgotten. Most of them were
too ponderous to handle for such childish strength
as I had. I used to push them along the floor
into a sunny corner, and there lie full length, my
chin upon my hands, devouring the glorious particulars of these ancient seafarers.

Captain James Cook especially became enshrined
in my admiration, as the worthy counterpart of
Nelson. What courage! what resources! what
seamanship! what unfailing humanity and equity in
that noble Yorkshireman, destined to the splendid
duty of opening up half the world to civilisation,
and perishing so sadly at the hands of those
island-people to whom he was so true a friend!
In later years I used often to see one of his
famous ships, the *Endeavour*, lying as a coal-
hulk in the river Thames, and never passed her
without the same profound feeling of reverence
with which the sight of the grand old *Victory*
in Portsmouth Harbour always to this hour fills
me. Day after day I revelled in that rich feast
of ocean adventure, and day after day wished

more and more, for myself also, to sail the sea
and to cast eyes upon those fair and various
lands, those strange peoples, those lovely islands
set like jewels in the silver of the main, and shining
under such glad and warm skies. Especially do I
remember one prodigious volume which described
some old worthy's travels in India, and which
contained a plate that charged my imagination
brim-full of wonder and interest. It represented
a scene upon the Malabar coast, with the sea
gently breaking along a sandy bay, the curve of
which was fringed with cocoanut trees and tropical
vegetation. Monkeys were climbing the stems of
the palms, or perched in their frondage; and
curiously shaped and coloured birds hovered over
the edge of the waters or waded in the lagoons.
It saturated me, that ancient picture, with the
passion and the purpose to see India some day
and to study the trees and flowers and birds and
beasts and inhabitants of such a surprising country.
All which has since duly befallen, for books are
mighty in guiding and controlling us. I recall
one hot, silent, memorable day in the Concan of
India, when we came down from the hills where
we had been shooting, to take passage in a
pattimar for Bombay. We sate under the shade
of some cocoa-palms by the edge of the rippling
Indian Ocean. Where had I seen that beautiful,
wild, quiet scene before? When had I before
visited that sleeping, sunny bay of the Malabar
shore, with its long curving lines of cocoanut

trees fringing the blue water, its milky wavelets
breaking upon the golden sand, washing the shells,
and star-fish, and clumps of bronze seaweed, and
blood-red rocks? What made the spot, upon which
I was certainly now for the first time planting my
delighted feet, so impossibly familiar, so unreason-
ably known? I seemed to recognise every feature
in the landscape and the seascape; the very boats
fishing were such as I had viewed in the very same
places, and the cut of the mat-sails on the trading
barks, and the dress of the sailors and fishermen
bore no new appearance. Puzzled and meditative,
I was wondering if the Hindoo doctrine of former
existences was indeed true, when my Mahratta
shikari called out, " *Bandur lôk! dekkho, Saheb!* "
"Look at the monkeys." Behind us, in a near
clump of cocoa-palms, some of the four-handed
folk were demurely ascending a tree full of nuts,
and two of them were already ensconced in its
crown plucking the green fruit. In a moment I
remembered. It was the veritable scene depicted
in that old book of travels! By accident—if
anything in human life can so be called—my
boy's dream and desire had come precisely true.
There was the place before my eyes over which
I had hung entranced in the nursery; it was the
actual spot realised; if King George's artist had
limned it by my side he could not have hit off that
lovely nook of Malabar with happier precision.

But books hold so much more in them than
geography and maritime adventures, that when I

went wider and deeper into the world of them I
was lost to the sea. To this day I half regret my
early and too eager studiousness. I might have
been captain of an Indiaman or a Cunarder, or
possibly of an ironclad—perhaps even an Admiral!
To this day there seems to me no post so splendid,
so honourable, so utterly satisfying to the heart
of a loyal Englishman, as to walk a quarter-deck,
bearing the Queen's commission, under the glorious
flutter of the White Ensign. But the books—the
marvellous, absorbing books—led me inland farther
and farther away from those early and happy visions
of Anson chasing the galleons, Cook picking up
the jewelled islands, Columbus and Raleigh sailing
to find new worlds, and Nelson's genius making
England great and safe. I read too much. I was
over-successful—I should say to-day sadly successful
—except for the beautiful poetry of Homer and Virgil,
of Shakespeare and Keats and Shelley, of Ariosto
and Tasso, of Calderon and Camoens, of Hafiz and
Sadi, and the dark wisdom of the Sanskrit Upani-
shads and the Mahabharata, which came afterwards,
and are more mighty and delightful than even the
ocean. I gained an important scholarship at my
school, and was, therefore, marked off for Oxford
and a literary life—*sic visum Deis!*

But the salt has always been a little in my blood,
and whenever I could, in a life without much
leisure, I have always gone back to play with the
sea. If I come anywhere near it at any time,
something of the crab in me makes me sidle away

from fashion and land pursuits to the handiest quay
or harbour wall. My one and chief objection to
London—which otherwise is to my mind the dearest
old foggy, muddy, dingy city on the globe, as well
as the biggest and the grandest—consists in the
inconvenient fact that King Lud planted it too far
from any green water. I have generally, however,
managed to own and use a craft of some sort. First
it was the *Star of the Sea*, a little 2½-tonner, which
was, nevertheless, "all boat," and made her way
in her time from the Thames to the Land's End.
Then it was the *Catharine*, of 12 tons, on board of
which, with good old Harry Pocock, the Upnor
fisherman, we took much pains to get drowned,
but unsuccessfully. Then came the *Fannie*, a cutter
of 19 tons, in which, with a friend, Sir Thomas
Miller, a born seaman, albeit a Scotch Baronet, I
learned the East Coast almost as thoroughly as any
collierman ; and afterwards the schooner yacht *Hadassah*, of 120 tons, which used to take us on charming cruises to the Scilly Islands, to Guernsey and
Jersey, and up and down the Channel ; and the yawl
yacht *Harelda* of 80 tons. Yachting is a noble pastime, whether you race or cruise, and all the more so
because it is unconnected with the pain or destruction
of any beautiful and happy living creatures. Avast
heaving, though ! Yes, we used to trawl, it must be
avowed ; and many a time have I myself helped—up
to the knees in slush—to haul the "purse" of the
great ground-net on board, and see it gush forth
upon the planks with an avalanche of soles, skates,

dabs, flounders, tom-cods, lobsters, crabs, oyster-shells, star-fish, broken bottles, dead men's fingers, jelly-fish, seaweed, stones, and oozy mess unspeakable.

It comes as near, perhaps, to faultless physical happiness as earth can bring, to sail, under fair weather and with pleasant company, in such a little ship as the *Hadassah*, and on such brief but sufficient voyages as the Channel in summer-time permits. I hate bad weather at sea. If you meet it, it must be faced; but the sea in her bitter and dangerous moods is horrible, ugly, infamous, treacherous, deadly, detestable. North and south of latitude 32 degrees, the ocean is indeed never to be trusted; inside these parallels alone you almost always get such weather and such waters as the best days of our British summers but partly suggest. Many of those " best days " do I recall with gratitude and lasting pleasure. Sail over-night, for instance, or in the very early morning, from Dartmouth for Guernsey, keeping a sharp look-out in the first twenty miles of open water for the coasting steamers, which will run you down if they can. Then, let the morning break over the Channel, as it often will in July and August, a day of blue and gold, lighting up an expanse of fresh and free sea-meadows, ploughed into shallow furrows of silver and green by the share of a north-easterly breeze, free on your quarter. No land is in sight, but a line of fishing-smacks astern marks the limits of the trawling-water, and the mid-Channel will be diversified with more than one sailing-ship and with steamers trailing their

flags of smoke across the sky. You have break-
fasted with a sailor's appetite, and the easy heave
of the water, running long with the wind over an
ebbing tide, lulls you in your deck-chair into peace
with yourself and all the world. Forget that in
the wild winter-time this very passage of the sea
can be a hell of angry waves and cruel weather,
the tides secretly dragging the ship into peril, the
fierce billows leaping up to wash her seamen to
their watery graves, the clouds and mist blotting
out the sight of land and the pleasant lights of
home from their gaze. To-day it is a heaven of
peace and bright circumstance, the little ship
seeming really to live, with her white wings and
white deck, as the green milky-crested rollers leap
up at her bow, and the sea-lace weaves and unweaves
itself in fathom-breadths on the broken faces of the
waves in her wake. If you will not steer her yourself—and what, after all, is horse-riding or bicycling
to the holding of the tiller of a lively, answerable,
well-trimmed yacht!—repose under the shadow of
the ivory-textured mainsail and read, while the wind
fans you and the waters lull. Read the Odyssey in
the glorious Greek; it is the best book in the world
to take yachting, and suits all the seas. Or, if you
do not read Homer in the only way in which he
should be enjoyed, then don't waste your splendid
hours upon a trashy novel or some scandal-loving
society paper, but open one of the noble sea-poems
in prose of Mr. Clark Russell—of which he has
given so many and such admirable examples to his

time—and, while you hang over his perfect pages of manly adventure and maritime romance, you shall have the great sea interpreted to you by one of the very few who know its mysteries and its majesties; you shall enjoy the subtlest of all intellectual delights —that is to say, the translation of Nature into a living thing by the magic of genius; and you shall be gratefully aware that England, to whom the ocean belongs, has found a Marryat of the Red Ensign in these latter days to keep up in all our hearts the love which we must never lose for the " Great Green Mother."

Somehow or other I have in a desultory and occasional manner managed to sail or steam in almost all the seas north of the Equator. I have crossed the Pacific from continent to continent three times, the Indian Seas many times, the Black Sea, the Baltic Sea, the Ægean, Adriatic, North Sea, China Sea, Bay of Bengal, Atlantic, Bay of Biscay, and every nook and corner of the Mediterranean. One cannot accumulate even such a mere landsman's small experience and not have witnessed some rather bad weather; and, indeed, I myself have witnessed boats washed away and decks swept, bulwarks smashed and davits twisted, ships battened down and canvas torn cracking from its bolt-ropes, and have been even wrecked by the capsizing of my own craft. I have been on board a steamer afire at sea, 900 miles from the nearest land, and stood by while the honest fellows who fought the flames were dragged suffocating from the crackling hold.

So I dread as well as love the wonderful waters, which hold death in a hundred forms, as well as life in its most lovely and perfect combinations and conditions, within those kissing circles of dark blue sea and light blue sky that make the mariner's home. Nevertheless, I have a secret conviction, which I would not like to utter when afloat, that the grandeur and majesty of the ocean are vastly exaggerated. Waves "mountains high" are myths. The sea can, no doubt, swamp the biggest vessel that was ever launched—and will, if you allow it— but the means by which she does this are brutal and clumsy rather than colossal or imposing. I have watched the Bay of Biscay slop itself, green and grey, in a solid mass across the deck of a great liner, but it was, after all, only a "slop," though it lifted boats out of their chocks, and washed the waist clear. There was plenty of misery and mess in it, but, to my thinking, very little sublimity. Similarly, the largest rollers of the Atlantic always appeared to me too ugly, and low, and monotonous for praise or admiration, though one must confess and respect their power of dull mischief. It is the summer sea one loves—the sea in its obedience to man, and not in its rebellion; the Greek sea; the sea as Aphrodite rose from it—joyous, pearly, and benign; the sea such as it sweeps and sparkles through the clusters of the South Pacific, under the palms of Malabar, and along the yellow sands of Ceylon and Singapore; or even sometimes beneath the red hills of the Riviera, and among the island

x

groups of the Levantine Archipelago. Therefore I well know I shall go down to it again and again while I live; and so must every Englishman who has once felt the meaning of the music in the hollow of an ocean-shell, and once taken into his veins the spell and magic of the "cool blue wine of the seas."

XVIII

ORIENTAL STORY-TELLERS

XVIII

ORIENTAL STORY-TELLERS

I SOMETIMES wonder that, among the many new forms of public entertainment in this and other European countries, nobody has thought of introducing from the East the good old profession of story-teller. Of course I do not allude to any branch of the science of saying "the thing which is not." That is practised with quite sufficient frequency and ease in the West as well as the East; and, indeed, the generally prevailing idea that Orientals are a less truthful race than Occidentals might be combated with many remarkable facts to the contrary. The "story-telling" of which I am thinking is that charming ancient art of spoken fiction which has for many centuries, it may be for thousands of years, taken the place of our novel. Not many people in the East can read at all fluently even to-day, and in bygone times the number of literates was naturally fewer, so that the masses were shut off from knowledge of their sacred writings, and from all that wealth of fanciful and fabulous literature which in the shape of manuscript made the mediæval Orient so rich. There were the traditional tales and legends, of course, passed along from tongue to tongue, which everybody knew; but it is only children who like to hear the same stories over and over again, and besides, the glory of a story for Eastern minds is in its detail, which gets rubbed off by the friction of many years and many mouths. Consequently, the professional story-teller of the Eastern World arose, who had read, or had caught from the lips of good readers, the exact form in which the piety or genius of his World had embodied its ideas, traditional, philosophic, historical, or fantastic. In many countries he survives to this day—not only a public delight and pastime, but an educational necessity in his way, serving the purpose of a circulating library, condensed into one energetic and retentive memory. Why should we not profit by the example? A striking story, well narrated, with proper methods, tact, and taste, is a very fascinating form of public pleasure, and in India, Japan, Egypt, and Arabia has become quite an indispensable one. An initial difficulty would occur, no doubt, in the fact that, as everybody on our side of the earth reads, stories perfectly unknown to the audience would be hard to select. Another would arise from the circumstance that the reciters of the East permit themselves a range of subjects and a freedom of language which, while immensely enhancing the piquancy and amusing nature of their entertainments, would be swiftly suppressed by our Lord Chamberlain, and, indeed, forbidden by public propriety. They are very candid in the East, and talk plainly about many simple and natural things which Western prudery never permits to be even mentioned, though in many respects this is a modern squeamishness with us, as anybody may see who studies Chaucer and Shakespeare; and does not necessarily lead to better manners and morals.

We could not publicly put up, of course, even from Chaucer, with certain of the brilliant and witty stories of the Canterbury Tales, and we probably do not possess many, or any, performers of such genius in fiction that—like the *Hanashika* of Japan, or the wandering *Byrajis* of India—they could go on for hours spinning perfectly original tales out of their heads, to an entranced circle of all ages and both sexes. But a qualified hand might provide himself with a rich and varied repertoire, and thereby charm thousands with this neglected yet delightful Art; for who can deny that a fresh and well-told story would be ever so much more attractive than dull recitations and tedious readings, where almost everybody knows what is coming? Music might be pressed very advantageously into the service of the performance, with appropriate costume, and, perhaps, a little suitable scenery. At all events, it is an idea, a suggestion towards that urgent reform— far more desirable than anything connected with parish councils and parish pumps—the increase and amelioration, I mean, of the amusements of the people.

The *Hanashika*, or story-teller of Japan, is a highly popular personage in town and country, who, possessing a good voice and tuneful ear, and being primed full of the legends and records which best suit native taste, gives his primitive, but very alluring, entertainments in one spot after another, as he trudges along the Tokaido, or any other main road of the empire. The general place for the performances is a large upper room over the principal shop of the village street. In front of the entrance will be planted bamboo flagstaffs, with dark-blue banners laced vertically to them, bearing the name of the performer, and perhaps the titles of some of the tales or songs which he proposes to offer. During the day an assistant will perambulate the village beating a drum and blowing a horn, after which he proclaims at every corner the eminent gifts of his *sensei*, and invites the public to be present. At evening you go with the crowd, dropping off shoes or slippers at the foot of the polished ladder leading to the *yose*, as the hall of entertainment is called. You may enter for the modest price of four *sen*, or twopence ; after which, if desirous to be ranked with the "quality," an additional payment of ten *sen*, or fivepence, will give you a right to the very best situation upon the mats, and to a cushion on the floor, as well as a tobacco-box and teapot, with perhaps a fan. The narrator sits cross-legged before a low desk, *tsukue*, holding in his left hand a fan, or bamboo paper-knife, with which he beats energetically upon his desk at the critical passages of his story. The company listen, with the admirable patience and politeness of the race ; and, if at all bored, smoke extra pipes and drink incessant tea. Generally they are very much amused, and that too by the simplest stories, for the reciter intersperses his prose with vivid gestures, snatches of singing, and ejaculations that wake up the sleepiest ; while, if there be many children present, he will perhaps narrate one of the old fairy-tales of Japan, which everybody loves, like this, which Mrs. James so well translated, of the fisher-boy who married the princess.

THE FISHER-BOY URASHIMA.

Long ago there lived, on the coast of the sea of Japan, a young fisherman named Urashima, a kindly lad and clever with his net and line. One day he went out in his boat to fish. But instead of catching any fish, he caught a big tortoise, with a hard shell, a wrinkled ugly face, and a foolish tail. Tortoises always live a thousand years—at least Japanese tortoises do. So Urashima thought to himself : " A fish would do for my dinner just as well as this tortoise; in point of fact, better. Why should I kill the poor thing, and prevent it from enjoying itself for another 999 years ? No, no ! I won't be so cruel." And with these words, he threw the tortoise back into the sea. The next incident that happened was that Urashima went to sleep in his boat, for it was one of those hot summer days when the sea rocks its children to slumber. And, as he slept, there came up from beneath the waves a beautiful girl, who climbed into the boat and said, " I am the daughter of the Sea-God, and I live with my father in the

URASHIMA RELEASES THE TORTOISE.

Dragon Palace beyond the waves. It was not a
tortoise that you caught just now, and so kindly
threw back into the water in-
stead of killing it. It was
myself. My father, the Sea-
God, had sent me to see
whether you were good or
bad in your inmost heart. We

THE TORTOISE REAPPEARS AS THE PRINCESS OF THE SEA.

now know that you are good and kind, and do not
like to do cruel things ; and so I have come to fetch
you. You shall marry me, if you please ; and we

will live happily together for a thousand years in the
Dragon Palace beyond the deep blue sea." So Urashima took one oar, and the Sea-God's daughter
took the other, and they rowed till at last they came
to the Dragon Palace where the Sea-God lived, and
ruled as king over all the dragons and tortoises and

THE PRINCESS AND URASHIMA ROW TO THE FAIRY ISLANDS.

crabs and fishes. The walls of the palace were of
coral, the trees had emeralds for leaves and rubies
for berries, the fishes' scales were of silver, and the
dragons' tails of solid gold. All the most beautiful
glittering things that have ever been seen met together there, and the liveliest imagination will never

picture what this palace looked like. It all belonged
to Urashima. Here they lived very happily for
countless years, wandering about every day among
the beautiful trees with emerald leaves and ruby

THEY ARE RECEIVED BY THE FISH-PEOPLE.

berries. But one morning Urashima said to his
wife, "I am quite happy with you, delightful one!
Still I want to go home and see my father and

mother and brothers and sisters. Permit me to depart for a short time, and, by the truth of my love, I will soon be back again." "I don't like you to go,"

PALACE OF THE SEA-QUEEN.

said she; "I am very much afraid that something dreadful will happen. However if you will go, there is no help for it; only you must take this box, which

will protect you, on condition that you are very careful
not to open it.   When you open it you will never be

SERVANTS OF THE PALACE.

able to come back here."   So Urashima promised to
take great care of the box and not to open it on any
account; and then, getting into his boat, he rowed

URASHIMA AND THE PRINCESS AT HOME.

off, and at last landed on the shore of his own
country.

But much had happened while he had been
away. Whither had his father's cottage gone?
What had become of the village where he used to

THE GIFT OF THE BOX.

live? The mountains indeed were there as before,
but the trees on them had been cut down. The
little brook that ran close by his father's cottage was
still running; but there were no women washing
clothes in it any more. It seemed very strange that

Y

everything should have changed so much in three
short years. Just then two men chanced to pass
along the beach, and Urashima went up to them and
said, "Can you tell me, if you please, to what spot

URASHIMA BACK IN HIS NATIVE VILLAGE.

Urashima's cottage, which used to stand here, has
been moved?" "Urashima?" said they; "why, it
is 400 years ago since he was drowned, out fishing.
His parents, and his brothers, and their great-great-
grandchildren are all dead long ago. It is an old,

very old story. How can you be so foolish as to ask after his cottage? It fell to pieces hundreds of years ago."

Then it suddenly flashed across Urashima's mind that the Sea-God's palace beyond the waves, with its coral walls and its ruby fruits and its dragons with tails of solid gold, must be part of fairyland, and that one day in that land was probably as long as a year in this world, so that his swift years in the Sea-God's palace had really endured for hundreds of years. Of course, there was no use in staying at home, now that all his friends were dead and buried, and even the village had passed away. So Urashima was in a great hurry to get back to his wife, the Dragon Princess, beyond the sea. But which was the way? He could not find it without any one to show it to him. "Perhaps," thought he, "if I open the box which she gave me I shall be able to learn the road." So he disobeyed her orders not to open the box—or, possibly, he forgot them. Anyhow, he opened the box, and out of it came—what?

Here the fan of our story-teller would furiously beat the desk.

Nothing but a white cloud which floated away over the sea! Urashima shouted to the cloud to stop, rushed about and screamed with sorrow; for he remembered now what his wife had told him, and how, after opening the box, he should never be able to go to the Sea-God's palace again. But soon he could neither run nor shout any more. Suddenly his hair grew as white as snow, his face got wrinkled,

and his back bent like that of a very old man. Then
his breath stopped short, and he fell down dead
on the beach! Ah, *Zannen! Zannen!* Woe for
Urashima! He died because he had been foolish
and disobedient. If only he had done as he was
told, he might have lived another thousand years.
If we could only go and see the Dragon Palace
beyond the waves, where the Sea-God lives and rules
as king over the dragons and the tortoises and
the fishes, where the trees have emeralds for leaves
and rubies for berries, where the fishes' tails are of
silver and the dragons' tails all of solid gold—never
would we open that stupid box. No! *Anata-kata!
Ne?*

In Egypt, Persia, Syria, and Arabia the *cafés* are
the chief places to see and hear the professional
story-teller, who is long-winded, noisy, and inde-
corous, but very clever and very various. If he be
a favourite, the evening hour will bring great profit
to the *cafedji,* and many piastres or *krauns* to his
own girdle ; while, when he has finished a thrilling
adventure, or come to a full stop, everybody near at
hand will reach out the mouthpiece of *narghileh* or
kallian to him, that he may draw solace and refreshment from the reposeful herb. At portions of his
legend, too wild for credence, he will piously disarm
scepticism by ejaculating, "And Allah, who is All-
wise, alone knoweth the truth," while sometimes,
when he arrives at a particularly exciting moment of
his plot, and all the customers are hanging upon the
fate of his dark-eyed heroine, he will abruptly break

off with, *Fi' Aman' Illah* ("God have you all in His grace!"), and bow his way out of the coffee-house, sufficiently assured that everybody must come again to-morrow to hear how the story ends.

In Egypt many a tale from the "Thousand and One Nights" is still almost textually reproduced. In Persia the *Mahbûb-u-Kuloob*, or "Heart's Delight," the "Book of Sindibad," the *Shumsah*, and such-like literature, are largely drawn upon; but the professionals have their own repertoire, and often affect a flowery metaphorical style, largely borrowed from the old fantastic Persian romances. There is an admirable translation from the *Shumsah* by Mr. Rehatsek which exemplifies very well this elaborate and artificial manner of the story-teller in Shiraz and Ispahan. It is the opening of the "Tale of the Three Wise Women," who are thus described:—

"Once upon a time there were three whales of the sea of fraud and deceit; three dragons of the force of thunder and the quickness of lightning; three defamers of honour and reputation, namely, three men-deceiving, lascivious women, each of whom had from the chancery of her cunning issued the mandate of turmoil to a hundred cities and countries, and in the arts of fraud they accounted Eblis as an admiring spectator in the theatre of their stratagems. One of them was sitting in the court of justice of the Kazi's embrace; the second was the precious gem of the bazaar-master's diadem of compliance; and the third was the bezel and ornament of the signet-ring of the life and soul of the superintendent of police. They were constantly entrapping the deer of the field of deceit with the net of cunning; and plundered the caravan of heart-tranquillity of strangers and acquaintances by means of the edge of the scimitar of fraud. One day this triplicate of roguery met at the public bath, and, according to their nature, they entered the basin of argument. After a while, when they had brought the pot of concord to boil by the fire of mutual laudation, they tempered the bath of association with the breeze of kindness, and came out. In the dressing-room all three of them happened simultaneously to observe a ring, the gem of which surpassed the imagination of the jeweller of destiny, and the like of which had never been beheld in the storehouse of possibility."

Afterwards the reciter proceeds to tell how the ring was to be the prize of the one among the three wives who should most cleverly deceive her husband—for it is the settled maxim of most of these Oriental excursions of fancy and romance that

> Never wearies death of slaying;
> Nor the seas of drinking rivers; nor the bright-eyed
> of betraying.

The bazaar-master's wife is particularly audacious and successful in her trick upon her lord. There is a household diversion in Persia much resembling our "Philippina," where, if you accept any gift without first pronouncing the safeguarding word, you are made ridiculous and must pay a forfeit. The wife of the bazaar-master invites her would-be lover,

the son of a banker, to put on a woman's veil and
come to a feast at her house. On his arrival, she
takes him into the inner apartment, speaks loving
words to him, and tells him to remain comfortably
there until she shall have returned, bringing with her
requisite refreshments. She then leaves him, and
instructs one of her female attendants to cause it to
arrive to the ears of the bazaar-master that his wife
has brought a strange man to the house. This being
done, she returns to her lover, and is engaged in
talking to him when she hears her husband approaching. The young man is dreadfully alarmed, the lady
opens a chest and says, " Conceal yourself in this box
until I see what will come of this affair." Accordingly she locks up the young man, and then goes to
meet her husband, to whom she pretends to confess
all; and finally presents him with the key of the box,
which the husband accepts from her hand. The lady
hereupon bursts out laughing, and exclaims, " I remember, but you forget. Give me a present." The
husband, disgusted at losing the Persian " Philippina," and thinking it a joke of his wife, throws
back the key of the chest, pays his forfeit, and quits
the house in a huff, leaving the crafty dame at ease
with her lover.

In India it is principally the wandering mendicants
and *joshi* who follow this ancient profession; and
the tales which they find most popular are antique
passages of war and miracle, of wild religious legend
and Aryan chivalry, drawn from such inexhaustible
sources as the Ramâyana and the Mahâbhârata. It

is characteristic of the serious genius and philosophic tastes natural even to the peasantry of India
that all the people of a village—women and men,
girls and boys alike—will sit in hushed and attentive
circles round the half-naked Brahman, hearing him
interpret to them from the old-world Sanskrit text of
those immense and extraordinary poems the majestic,
if often grotesque, fictions of Hindoo fancy. Nala
and Damayanti; the tale of Savitri who begged her
husband's soul back from the God of Death; or of
young Rishyasringha, who had never looked upon a
woman's face; or of the "Great Journey;" or of
the "Entry into Heaven," such things—far too grave
and earnest for Paris, or Shiraz, or Constantinople, or
London—will keep the placid Hindu folks squatted
all night at the *mandala*, insatiable to hear of the
greater and the lesser gods, and of the holy saints,
and of the glorious bygone kings of the land; of the
jewelled snake-people, the magicians, the Asuras,
and the great Bird Garúda, who carries off mountains.
Why should we, of the West, so totally neglect this
branch of the divine art of fiction? There is a whole
wide field of popular pleasure and instruction open
to duly-qualified entertainers who would take up
amongst us the forgotten but fascinating profession
of Story-telling.

XIX

A GENTLE MURDERESS

"MINA-MINA'S KNIFE WAS PLUNGED WITH ALL THE WEIGHT OF HER LIFTED BODY INTO THE SHARK'S SIDE."   P. 347.

XIX

A GENTLE MURDERESS

THIS is only a little story! I picked it up upon the beach of Oahu, among the fishing-huts under Diamond Head; in those beautiful Sandwich Islands, where a set of commercial and political sugar-filibusters have temporarily taken away her crown from the rightful sovereign, Queen Lilioukalani. I shall tell the story imperfectly, knowing so little as I do about the locality and the language, but I asked three or four questions afterwards as to the Hawaiian words and phrases, and what follows is, as far as I can remember, the manner in which it was related.

They are wonderful swimmers in the Sandwich Islands, as in almost all those clusters of the Pacific archipelagoes; and no finer sight can be for such as love healthy manhood than to watch the amphibious people play with the sea. It is as much their home as the land. Fishing is quite as important to them as agriculture, and they all know the ways and the whereabouts of the creatures of the deep and of the reef, as well as those of the birds of the grove and mountain-slope. With nets of the *olona* fibre and sweep-ropes of *ki* leaves, they draw the countless variegated finny tribes into the shallows of the lagoon and out upon the sands, and have a trick—

where it is permitted—of placing under heavy stones beneath the water the bruised roots of a plant—the *auhuhu*—which intoxicates every fish coming within the influence of its juice. Excellent boatmen, in spite of the primitive character of the native canoes, they make adventurous runs from island to island, and are especially skilful in handling a little craft in the midst of surf or great breaking billows. It is a treat to see a Hawaiian canoe coming ashore, with or without the *ama*, an outrigger of light wood which steadies the frail craft. The sea-birds skimming over the rollers do not seem more at home in the middle of the huge Pacific surf than the brown-skinned Kanakas paddling to land from a fishing or sailing excursion in the evening. They understand the tricks and dangers of the coral barrier which they must cross, and take the enormous wave which rolls over it with shouts of excitement and delight. If they are capsized, it is nothing to them so long as no sharks are about. They really make the white and blue breakers their play-fellows in their popular sport of *hee nalu*, or surf-swimming, where a party of these laughing water-babies of all ages, naked except for a wreath of sea-weed, or a wisp of bark-cloth, will go down to the reef's edge at sunset, carrying long light boards of koa-wood, eight feet long and eighteen inches broad, stained black, and highly polished. Clasping these, they swim boldly out to seaward, diving, plank and all, under each incoming roller as they meet it, until they have gone as far out as where the ocean feels the first of the coral bottom, and swells for its outer line of long billow. Then, turning their faces shoreward, they lie down flat upon the plank, balancing themselves upon it and holding it with feet and hands straight along the glassy back of the great roller, which foams, curls, leaps, and thunders under them as they tear along, tossed like bubbles amid the milky spume and the whirling sea-lace, until they come drenched and shining to the shore, or into the placid green water inside the reef. The very babies learn to swim almost before they are able to toddle ; and as for the grown boys and girls of the islands, and its men and women, the waves are as much their playground as the woods and meadows, and there are instances where Hawaiians have been thirty hours in the sea after a capsize, and have yet come safely to land.

But one must be strong, and well, and unencumbered for these long swims, and a sick man cannot sport with the ocean in such a fearless way ; which is why Mina-Mina lost her first-born, and bought with his little life her husband's safety. We passed her, walking with a string of fish, and a tiny child upon her arms, under the palm-trees near Leahi, and my friend—an old resident—gave her good-day in the musical Hawaiian, calling her by the name I have mentioned.

"What a pretty word that is," I said, "to call a woman by ! What does it mean ?"

"Oh," he answered, "that's not her right name, but one which the neighbours have given her ever

since a sad adventure that she met with off Koko
Head, round yonder.   Mi-na-mi-na signifies 'regret
for the memory of anything,' 'sadness,' 'something
precious that is gone,' 'sorry to lose.'   She is a
good and brave girl, and she has got another baby
now to play with, but she can never forget the boy
she was obliged to leave to the sharks in the bad
time."

Of course I asked him for the story, and this is
how he told it :—

One day in the season of the change of weather,
Mina-Mina, with her husband, and their little boy
of about a year-and-a-half old, had gone in a canoe
over to Molokai to fetch ironwood and shells.   The
man was weak and ill with fever, though recovering ;
but the wife, like most of these Hawaiian women,
could handle a paddle with the best, and Mauae,
her young partner, was quite strong enough to take
his part in loading the craft and steering her.   So
they were making the voyage homewards under the
little sail of mat spread on the bamboo mast, with
the red bird painted upon it, and Mina-Mina was
suckling her son of eighteen months forward, while
her husband directed the boat ; and all had gone
safely up to about midway in the broad channel.
Perhaps he was singing her an *ipo*, a love-verse —
for the people are like birds, and are always chirrup-
ing ; or she, perhaps, was cooing a sleep-song to her
small son, in the dove's voice, which the island-
mothers have.   But, all in a moment, one of those
circular gusts that sweep the sea at the change of

weather, came upon them without warning out of
the clear sky and over the smooth surface. He was
languid and slow with his fever; she was engaged
with her child, and had no time to let the sail fall
or to fling overboard the heavy stuff in the bottom
of the canoe. The gust forced the gunwale of it
under, though they both leaned well to windward,
and although Mina-Mina reached over and cut the
halliards with her knife. In a moment the little
craft filled and sank from under them, drawn down
by its load, leaving the three floating on the agitated
sea, with only one paddle, which Mauae held. Mina-
Mina had swung her baby over to her back, and his
little round head, like a cocoanut, peeped well forth
from the water as his mother struck out by the side
of her husband for the shore under Koko Head.

Although this lay fully two leagues away, there
was nothing in the situation greatly to disconcert
an Hawaiian family. If only the young husband
had been in his proper strength, he would have
shifted the baby to his own shoulders, and side by
side, while the sea grew quiet again, they would
have managed to make their long swim to the land,
supposing no shark intercepted them. For any one
less familiar with the open ocean than these islanders
no doubt it would have seemed a dreadful plight.
Even from a boat the wide and naked face of the
sea appears terrible in its spread and flatness. The
long, huge, ponderous swell of it, which you did
not notice from the deck of a ship or steamer, gives
a new and awful impression of its elemental weight

and bulk. In the very quietest weather there is a throb of solid motion in the shining surface, which drops a small boat into vast, shallow valleys, and again lifts it upon the breast of gradual but far-reaching slopes, so that the actual peace of the sleeping element becomes dreadful. But when a swimmer beats the salt sea, far from land or help, his chin upon its shining top, his eyes just level with the long glitter of the sea-floor, the vastness and bareness and deadliness of it become to all but the hardiest absolutely terrible. There is no man who, swimming in the ocean, has not experienced, even when he had safety close at hand, that irresistible horror at the littleness of his powers and at the largeness of the chilly death lapping and washing all around him, before and behind, on the right and the left, as far away on every quarter as to where the sky comes down to the sea. And it is worse when he thinks of the deep abyss of liquid beneath his feeble feet—although, for the matter of that, seven feet of water will choke the life from a wearied swimmer as well as the four thousand fathoms of the mid-Pacific. Actual death by drowning is, probably, like most other forms of dying, not at all painful; but never does death appear more visible and dreadful than when you look along the face of the sea, struggling with its waters for every breath that is drawn and every yard that is won, while the dance of the brine washes over the lips and nostrils, and flings its bitter menace into the blinded eyes.

Mina-Mina soon found that her man could not keep the baby's head and his own at the same time above the water. The little brown imp was, nevertheless, laughing and crowing at the sparkling waves, without any mark of fear or tremble, and when she drew him down beside her in the sea, and let him paddle for a cable's length or so, the tiny castaway swam like a small fish, and all three were making fair progress. In the moment of the capsize they had fallen into the sea, of course fully clothed, but both had since loosened and cast aside in the water their garments of tapa for freer swimming, although Mina-Mina still retained her waist-band, in which she kept her fishing-knife. The ocean was quieting down again after the sudden blast, and it was not difficult to rest sometimes by floating, the wife holding up their small companion. Only this would not do for any long time together, because a current was running before the light trade wind, and they might drift too far to reach the land at last.

Presently Mina-Mina's bright eyes perceive upon the water to the right—on her husband's side—a dark edge, moving slowly, like a blade of black seaweed tilted up.

"Oh! Mokuhalii! (great God of the Fish), help us now," she cried. "*He kōkua!* help! here is *he mano*, the shark."

"Your *aumakua* * is the great fish," said Mauae.

---

* Tutelar ancestor. The natives still believe that the spirits of their relations enter special animals, which become the *totem* accordingly of particular families.

"He will not hurt *you*, wife, but he will take me or the little one."

Being of the Fish-God's line, she was indeed *tabu* to sharks, and they to her, and to injure the tyrant of the deep was forbidden to her, for there is plenty of ancient belief still among the islanders, in spite of missionaries. But now she was thinking only of her husband and her baby, and superstition fled to the winds for the dear sake of those she loved. Of all examples of similar religious courage in Hawaiian women, none is better known than that of Kapiolani, the daughter of the chief of Hilo, who broke the spell of Pelë, the Guardian of the great Volcano, eating the sacred berries of the dreaded goddess, and flinging stones into the seething fiery crater of Mauna Loa, thereby converting the people from their antique fears. But "that is another story."

"Beat hard upon the water, *He Luna!* Master! Beat when he comes near, and keep him a little off. I will kill my *aumakua!* Otherwise will he eat my precious son."

At any other moment these words would have seemed too impious to hear or pronounce. Now, however, the enfeebled and weary husband could only sign silent assent, and put his elbow under the child's arm, while Mina-Mina drew her knife from her belt and held it in her pearl-like teeth, silently paddling to meet the shark. There is a spot in these murderous brutes well known to the islanders, where the stroke of a long blade driven hard into the white belly will find the swim-bladder; and when that is pricked the shark sinks or becomes disabled. The cruel fish had seen or divined the baby as a dainty prey, though ordinarily this Hawaiian species is too well fed or too particular to care much for brown meat. As he came within twice his own length of the father and child, he turned slowly over and slipped below the surface, the pale-coloured underside gleaming up through the green water; and just when you could discern the horse-shoe-shaped mouth opening to show the sharp-notched jaws and red palate of the man-eater, Mina-Mina's knife was plunged with all the weight of her lifted body, into the shark's side, whereupon the savage creature bounded half its length into the air, and then, with a furious threshing of its tail, vanished into the depths, leaving streaks of oily scarlet blood upon the foam which its leap had caused.

"Give me the child," she said; but before placing him on her back again, for the baby had grown somewhat wearied and chilled, she rubbed her nose hard against the little nose, after the fashion of Hawaiian kissing, and "*Aloha ino*, oh, my darling," she cried, "*Hiwa-hiwa*, my sweet little black pig! my life is nothing to give for thee."

The land—which meant rest; which meant safety, rescue, comfort, life—had come nigher by this time, and there would not be more than a mile and a half, or three-quarters to traverse. Mina-Mina, with the long black hair knotted on her head, still full of soaked hibiscus flowers, was swimming bravely, keep-

ing the boy's tiny hands upon her shoulders ; and the
sea was still and the current safely passed, when her
ear missed the regular beat of Mauae's arms behind
her. She turned her head over her shoulder, and
saw that he was treading the water in the manner
of a strong swimmer exhausted, his chin thrown
back, his mouth open.

"My king! *he alii moe*," she cried, "come on!
Yet a little more, and we shall touch the coral ledges
with our toes."

"*Olua!*" he answered, "go forward, you two.   I
must die! The fever has taken all the manhood
from my muscles. *Mai huli oe*. Do not turn round
again. Good-bye! I must go down into the night
of the sea."

"No! father of my son ! no," Mina-Mina passion-
ately exclaimed. "The land is so close, I can see
the doors of the huts. The reef is so near, I can see
the seaweed waving on the outside shelves of the
reef. Oh, a little farther, and we shall all be saved !"

The poor fellow struck out courageously again ;
but as she watched—herself gallantly breasting the
sea, which broke gently on either side of her
bosoms as from the bows of some dark ship—she
saw his hands fall down, and the sea-water spill
from the top of a wavelet into his mouth. Her
Mauae was spent ; he could never traverse by his
own strength the distance still to be dealt with.
These island women are placid and slow on shore,
but in moments of crisis quick to act as a sea-bird is
to decide upon its course of flight.

"Fall on your back, friend, fall, *Makamaka!*" she said, "I will give you some rest," and then she executed a wonderful piece of water-learning, fanning the sea beside him, so that in each stroke her returning arm gave him a sufficient support, while she kept herself and the baby still steadily moving in the right direction. But she was too much accustomed to the water not to know that her man was beyond hope if he should be left to himself. Hastily her fond heart made up its purpose. She could not keep them both above the waves; the effort she was making must soon come to an end. She must accordingly choose between the life of the father of her child, and the life of the son of her husband. A Hawaiian woman of her character would never hesitate. Mina-Mina did not hesitate.

"Swim now by yourself for a little, Mauae!" she moaned, with water in her black eyes, which was not from the sea. "I can help one of the two to land, but I cannot help both. My son—*Kahaha!* thou must die for him that gave thee beginning."

"Ah, wife! wife! no!" cries the Hawaiian, striking out anew; "let *he kama* live—let him come to be a man, and keep you when you are old. I must go. It is I will die. I cannot swim one canoe's length farther."

At this moment the baby, from its mother's back, chuckled out, from fun or habit, the word of the little Sandwich Island children when they go to their mats for sleep at night.

"Listen," said Mina-Mina, "he knows it is all

right. He says farewell to you. Oh! my *manu*, my
bird, you will take so long to drown, you are so
hearty. You will struggle, and cry for me, and call
the sharks to you before you are dead. And there
is no time left. Good-bye! rub my nose hard with
your little nose. *Kuh honi ala aloha;* Oh, my last
sweet loving kiss to you! Good-bye!'"

With that she buried the knife-blade in her boy's
heart, and let him slide dead into the sea. Two
thin lines of blood from his little sinking body
trailed backward to the spot where Mauae was just
sinking, and a large blot of bright crimson darkened
the green water where he disappeared. The father
saw, comprehended, but was too far spent to speak.

Almost gone herself with grief and physical
strain, she drew his hands over her shoulders, and
setting her chin hard for the shore, flung out her
strong shapely arms in splendid strokes, supporting
her helpless lord; and gradually neared the coral
reef. Where it opened into the lagoon a couple of
fishermen were drawing their nets inside. They
heard in the evening stillness the beat of her hands,
started up, and saw Mina-Mina on the point of
giving in within a stone's throw of the ledge, quite
exhausted. The two Hawaiians dashed into the sea
and dragged the pair safely to land, where both lay
for a time speechless. When they recovered power
to speak and move, the fishermen were astonished
to see the husband kiss the wet feet of his wife, and
say, very softly, "For my life I am your debtor and
my son's."

Afterwards, when all understood well what had happened in the water, they called her Mina-Mina, and praised her exceedingly; and she has—as you saw—by this time another little baby-boy. But there is never out of her look a wistfulness, such as you may have noticed in passing her, and she will go down of evenings to the sea-edge at Koko Point, or Waikiki, and say things to herself. We think she perhaps says, "Darling! *he hiwa-hiwa!* oh, my little black pig that I had to cast away! If only I could have died for thee!"

XX

TENT LIFE

BEN BOUGHEY.

"WHILE THE EVENING FELL."

P. 363.

XX

TENT LIFE

CRUISING this week about the pleasant waters of the Solent, on board my yawl the *Harelda*, we landed one afternoon for a ramble on shore hard by Calshot Castle. Everybody who knows the locality at all will identify the little edifice, half fortress, half dwelling-house, standing on the spit of marsh to the westward of the entrance of Southampton Water. For the homeward-bound traveller from the Cape of Good Hope or the West Indies it is, after the Needles, the first sure landmark which tells him that he has really reached England; and now that the great Atlantic liners which we used to call the *City of Paris* and the *City of New York* come and go this way from and to America, Calshot Castle must become to many visitors a very familiar and almost famous object. As a fort it is nought. Solidly built, indeed, of a circular shape in well-laid masonry, with neatly-riveted loop-holes and cannon-ports, a symmetrical ditch, and a half-moon glacis, over which frown numerous embrasures, the little for- talice looks very business-like, no doubt, and might have been useful in the days when it was constructed. But to-day it does not boast a single gun; the draw- bridge, which anybody can cross, is immovable, the *enceinte* was full, at the time we saw it, of children's garments hung out to dry, and the only symbol of that warlike service from which it seems definitely to have retired, was the white ensign floating peacefully from its sunlit walls. If an enemy came by this road, something else besides Calshot Castle would have to stop his insulting career. A shell from any one of the huge modern guns which ships of war now carry would knock the shapely little building into "a cocked hat," although it occupies a spot which might very well be formidably fortified, and which would then command two extremely important waters, the West Solent and the channel leading up to the populous and wealthy port of Southampton. The site itself seems, however, in summer weather, too delicious for thoughts of belligerence. If there be such a magnate as the Governor of Calshot Castle, and he does not often reside there, he must be a personage singularly devoid of taste, or else too busy to "take the goods the gods provide him." Seascape and landscape show themselves alike delightful, as you stand upon the gently sloping mound of shingle and sea-shells upon which the small stronghold is planted, and look north, south, east, and west.

A broad avenue of silvery water leads between green banks inwards to Southampton, where masts and towers and spires may be just discerned. All along the left side stretches the verdant embroidery of the New Forest, vandyked here and there with parks and pastures, or indented with narrow creeks.

On the right hand, across the water, Hamble River steals into the sea, with its sleepy little maritime village, living principally upon a trade in crabs and lobsters, brought thither from all sorts of distant places for transmission to London. They are kept until wanted in huge floating cages, the big crabs being then packed alive in hampers after a fashion very neglectful of their private feelings. A mile or two above Hamble the red façade of Netley Hospital faces the water, embowered in woods, a goodly place for the military invalid, and one where many a gallant victim of war and hard service has placidly breathed his last. Turning southwards, the Solent's broad and beautiful expanse stretches far upon either hand, shining westwardly to Yarmouth and Lymington, and eastwardly to Ryde and Stokes Bay; while immediately opposite lies the yachting metropolis of the kingdom, Cowes, and the adjacent towers soar of Osborne and Norris Castle. Cowes, as we stood on Calshot Spit, was a perfect forest of masts, rising from a fleet of yachts of all sizes and rigs, from half-raters to the splendid schooners and steamers, and, amidst them, the majestic *Hohenzollern* lay moored like a white wall under the lawns of the Medina. The sky overhead was cloudless, but cloudlets of white smoke were lazily drifting with the light south-westerly air as we gazed, by reason of the Royal salute that was being fired from the guardship to welcome the Kaiser back to his yacht after the Portsmouth visit. Turning to walk along the sea-face which runs westwards towards Lymington, we traversed as lonely a bit of fore-

shore as could well be wished for. The people of the
Castle and the Coastguard cottages adjoining pursue
an exiguous agriculture with potatoes and cabbages,
which realise perpetually the fate of the seed that
fell upon stony ground. Deriving their sustenance
from sand and pebbles, only the hardiest plant here
and there pushes a leaf or two ; but the blackberries
like the sort of place that it is, and the wild roses
also, and the golden-rods and sloe bushes. More
beautiful than any flowers could be are the branches
of the last-named, full of their small acrid thickly-
clustered plums, bearing a lovely purple bloom ; and
though the wild roses are over, and the blackberries
at present merely green and red, they make with the
unripe cranberries exquisite clusters. On the rim of
the sands, where the wiry grass marks the limit of the
land, sea-thistles rear their handsome branches, with
thorny and corrugated leaves like metal-work wrought
in copper and aluminium, and with blue prickly
flowers. The yellow sea-poppies speck the shingle
with gold, and there pushes to the sun, in places,
through the sandy turf, tufts of a little wort bearing a
delicate pink flower, as pretty as a jewel ; while, for
further colour and beauty, there are cuckoo-pints,
orange antirrhinum, the meadow-sweet, the scabious,
and purple heather. About the wild blossoms hover
and flit light-winged butterflies—the chalk-white, the
painted lady, and the meadow-blue. It is a free,
open, and quiet pleasaunce of Nature, well beloved
by the rabbit, the snake, and the water-rat, whose
paths are countless in the weed-spread ditches.

Yes; it would be good to be made Governor of
Calshot Castle just for a week or two about the date
of Cowes Regatta!

At the far edge of the expanse of this sandy flat—
before reaching Count Batthyany's woods—we came
upon an encampment numbering some six or eight
tents, with a large marquee, and it is these that have
set me writing. A blue ensign floated from a small
staff in front of one of the tents, which bore a placard
inscribed "The Rectory." Other tents displayed
other fanciful appellations—" St. Augustine's Villa,"
" St. Anselm's Priory," and such like, while the
juxtaposition of a Bible, a coffee-pot, a surplice, and
an empty bottle of Bass carried out the odd admix-
ture of clerical and gipsy elements pervading the
"pitch." Nobody was to be seen about except a
sailor lad, who had charge of the camp, and he soon
explained to us that what we witnessed was the
temporary home of some forty young men from an
Association in the inland country, whose clergyman
brought them year by year down to this spot, to get
eight or ten days of pure air and exercise. They
were all away at church at the moment, for the day
was Sunday, and their idle bicycles, cricket-bats,
walking-sticks, and heavy boots were lying in or
about the tents. Yet you could see at a glance
how jolly they had been during the past week, and
would be until the outing was over; and the idea
was borne in upon us all how much wiser and
happier such a plan was than to be mewed up
in plundering and unwholesome seaside lodgings.

Pitched in this delicious nook of shore and sea, upon a sandy table-land, where they could do no sort of harm to any rights of property—and yet where they had the sea and the sky and the wild heath to themselves, as if they owned them all—I thought they set a good example to town-folk, especially young folk, planning a holiday at this season of the year, since there are thousands of places round our coasts where such encampments might properly and harmlessly be erected, and such bell-tents as this party possessed are very cheap to buy or hire, being apparently cast-off military stores.

Nobody knows, who has not tried it, how pleasant and healthy it is to live under canvas. Of course one wants settled weather for the perfection of such *al fresco* life, but the English summer is not always rainy, and you may be as dry in a tent as in a house if the canvas be good and well set up, and if you dig a trench in the proper fashion round the flies. That little group of healthy gipsy homes upon the Calshot Spit set me thinking of the happy days I have myself passed in India under canvas. There the art of tent-life is carried to its utmost limits of comfort and delightfulness, and I should be inclined to say—taking all in all— that the very pleasantest and most delicious way of life in the whole world is that of the Indian official who in the "cold weather" goes "into the districts" for two or three months of existence under canvas in the lovely and ever-diversified jungles of Goozerat, or the Deccan, or the Central Provinces. Ah! the glorious and joyous

days and nights that I myself remember in beautiful
and wonderful India! Ah! the rides and expeditions in that fair and warm Poona country, amid
the hills of Sivaji and the temples of Mahadeo, in
years when I could talk Murathi like a *gaum-
wallah*, and lived week after week under my
bichoba! It is something, however, to have had
such experience even once in a life!

The way is this. The tents made for such use in
India are of cotton, and very strong and durable—
put together after many patterns, of which what
we used to style the "Cottage" was, perhaps, most
commodious. They were largely manufactured at
Jubbulpoor by convict Thugs, and we would buy or
hire a double set of these, including a sort of "lean-
to" for the servants, with "bath tents," and, of course,
the necessary cattle and ox-carts—or sometimes
camels—to carry them and the kit. Then, on an
appointed day, when all had been organised down to
the smallest *gindi* by the proper servants, the first
set of tents was sent forward two marches, the second
set one march, and in the cool of the Indian afternoon we galloped our horses out to the nearest
stopping-stage. Under some splendid mango grove
or tamarind tree, near to a tank or running stream,
and within sight of some picturesque Deccan village,
we found our white jungle homes pitched and awaiting us. Good it was to dismount in the shade from
our sweating Arabs, to shake off the heavy riding
boots, to find the "tub" ready, nicely softened with
a *chatty* of hot water, and then to sit down to a well-

2 A

spread board in the wilderness, while the evening fell,

And all the Indian sky grew purple peace.

Then, after tobacco and chat, what faultless sleep we had upon the camp "charpoys," nowise disturbed by the familiar yells of the inevitable jackals and the hootings of the small Deccan owl, *goobud*, who hated to have his sylvan solitudes invaded! Inside the clean, cool, pretty tent, with its Persian carpets and light furniture of camp utensils, guns, rifles, and saddles, the glimmering *butti* shed a faint light, enough to show if thief or snake entered; scorpions and centipedes you could not always keep at a distance. Outside the canvas the sounds of the night, other than those mentioned, would be the bells tinkling round the necks of the feeding cattle, the horses stamping at their heel-ropes, the soft chatter of the servants and coolies round the fires, and from the village hard by the rhythmical beat of the tom-toms and the barking of the pariah dogs. In the morning we were up before the dawn, while the "wolf's tail," as they call the first gleam of grey light, was still long in the sky; and there was the hot coffee and the bit of toast or biscuit before we mounted for the jungle ride, not forgetting gun and rifle. The glorious mornings that they were—the superb sunrises, when the *dam-i-sabh*, the "breath of morning," moved across the plain, and woke up Asia! We would see the jackals and wild boar stealing guiltily home from their nocturnal trespass; the monkeys

going through their forest toilet with a mutual scratch
or two, and a cuff all round from the elders for the
youngsters; the golden coats of the black buck
shining amidst the *bajri* and *jowari*, and the clamo-
rous, variegated grouse flying in wedges across the
pale, warm sky to drink.   And arriving, after three
or four hours' ride through the ever-interesting jungle,
with its endless variety of animal and floral life, we
would find our second set of white woodland homes
awaiting us, pitched in some spot as charming as
that of the night before, with bath and breakfast
ready.   There would we pass the bright and hot
Indian day, doing what duty—educational or ad-
ministrative—we had in the neighbourhood; while
last night's set of tents and kit crept across the
country past our new stage, and forward to the next,
so as to be pitched in time for our arrival after the
evening ride.   Sometimes it would be cool enough
to stroll out, before the start, along the banks of
some lovely river, or among the quail and snipe in
the green rice-grounds; sometimes only the vultures
and crows could abide the full glare of that mid-day
sun, and we were fain to wait until the shadows grew
long.   Hereafter I may, perhaps, recall to memory
some of the curious civil and criminal cases that
I have heard adjudged round the " *kanauts* " of
these Indian tents; some of the odd interviews
with rajahs and dusky magnates which befell there;
some of the deeper mysteries and marvels of that
wild and silent jungle of Asia.   They were all
brought back to me by the tents upon Calshot

Spit, and I am the more inclined to say, the more
I think about it, that half enough use is not made
by English tourists and holiday-seekers of the delights, the comforts, and the pleasures afforded by
life under canvas.

THE END

DATE DUE

DI